ALF
ALPHABET

Shirley Hughes

Mini Treasures
RED FOX

A

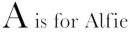

A is for Alfie

a

and his little sister Annie Rose.

B b

B is for bedtime and blanket.

C c

C is for Chessie, Alfie's black and white cat.

D

D is for drawing. Alfie is doing
a picture of Annie Rose.

d

D is also for door. (Be careful not to slam it!)

E

E is for elephant. Alfie's elephant
  is nearly as old as Alfie. He sleeps
  in Alfie's bed every night.

e

E is also for eating. Annie Rose
sometimes needs a bit of help.

F   f

F is for friends. Alfie's best friend
   is Bernard.

G
g

G is for Grandma. She can dance
and sing and tell stories.

H h

H is for hat. This one's a bit too large for Alfie.

I   i

I is for insects who live in the
earth and in the grass and
under stones.

J j

J is for jumping, which is fun
especially when there are
bubbles about.

K k

K is for kitten. This one is called Boots. He loves jumping too.

L   l

L is for lamb, Annie Rose's
favourite toy.

M m

M is for moon. A silver light,
always changing shape.
Magic moon.

N   n

N is for neighbours. The MacNally
family, who live across the street
from Alfie, are very good
neighbours indeed.

O   O

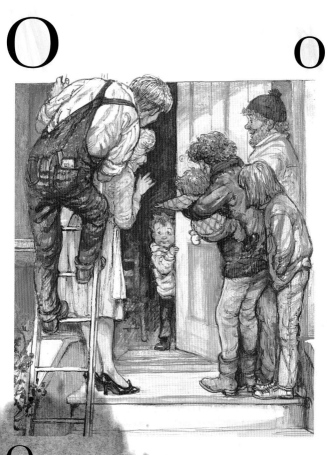

O is for "Open the door, Alfie".

P

P is for park –

p

and puddles!

Q q

Q is for questions. Alfie is very good at asking them. Luckily his friend Maureen is good at answers.

R r

R is for reading. Maureen always reads Alfie a story when she comes to baby-sit.

S

S is for seaside,

S

swimming

and sandcastles.

T t

T is for tent, teatime and teddies.

U u

U is for umbrella, which makes a good tent too, even when it's not raining.

V

v

V is for visit, like when Grandma
arrives in her little red car.

W   W

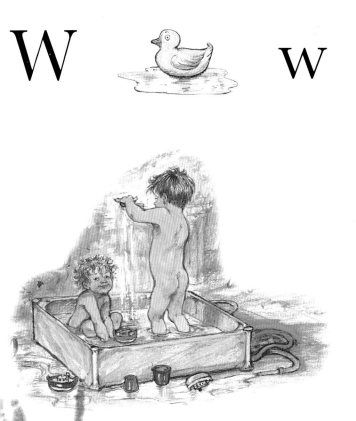

W is for water (better out of doors than in!)

X x

X is for Alfie's xylophone. Each note has its own letter and makes a different sound when he hits it.

Y   y

Y is for yawning. Time for bed.

Z

Z

Z is for zips.

And this is the end
of
Alfie's Alphabet.

Andie Brock started inventing imaginary friends at around the age of four, and is still doing it today—only now the sparkly fairies have made way for spirited heroines and sexy heroes. Thankfully she now has some real friends, as well as a husband and three children—plus a grumpy but lovable cat. Andie lives in Bristol, and when she's not actually writing she might well be plotting her next passionate romance story.

USA TODAY bestseller **Lucy Monroe** lives and writes in the gorgeous Pacific Northwest. While she loves her home, she delights in experiencing different cultures and places on her travels, which she happily shares with her readers through her books. A lifelong devotee of the romance genre, Lucy can't imagine a more fulfilling career than writing the stories in her head for her readers to enjoy.

Also by Andie Brock

The Shock Cassano Baby
Bound by His Desert Diamond
The Greek's Pleasurable Revenge
Vieri's Convenient Vows
Kidnapped for Her Secret Son
Reunited by the Greek's Vows

Also by Lucy Monroe

Kostas's Convenient Bride
The Spaniard's Pleasurable Vengeance
After the Billionaire's Wedding Vows...

Ruthless Russians miniseries

An Heiress for His Empire
A Virgin for His Prize

Discover more at millsandboon.co.uk.

FROM EXPOSÉ
TO EXPECTING

ANDIE BROCK

QUEEN BY ROYAL
APPOINTMENT

LUCY MONROE

MILLS & BOON

First Published in Great Britain 2021
by Mills & Boon, an imprint of HarperCollins*Publishers* Ltd,
1 London Bridge Street, London, SE1 9GF

www.harpercollins.co.uk

HarperCollins*Publishers*
1st Floor, Watermarque Building,
Ringsend Road, Dublin 4, Ireland

From Exposé to Expecting © 2021 Andrea Brock

Queen by Royal Appointment © 2021 Lucy Monroe

ISBN: 978-0-263-28248-1

05/21

MIX
Paper from
responsible sources
FSC® C007454

This book is produced from independently certified FSC™ paper
to ensure responsible forest management.
For more information visit www.harpercollins.co.uk/green.

Printed and bound in Spain
by CPI, Barcelona

FROM EXPOSÉ
TO EXPECTING

ANDIE BROCK

MILLS & BOON

For anyone who has bought my books,
read my books, or supported my writing career in any way.
It is much appreciated.

CHAPTER ONE

THE ENORMOUS BUNCH of flowers wobbled through the air. Without thinking, Emma stepped forward, her arms outstretched, ready to catch it. Her fingers managed to grab hold of the twisted stems, but the weight took her by surprise and she had to clasp the bouquet to her chest to stop it from toppling forward. Only then did she wonder what on earth she thought she was doing.

For a moment she stood there, feeling silly, the crushed blooms held tightly, hopefully, like she was expecting some sort of reward. A future husband possibly. Ha!

But no one was looking at her. All eyes had turned to the woman who had thrown them. On the other side of the security barriers a beautiful female with tumbling dark hair was having a full-on argument with the security guards.

'Do you have any idea who I am?' Her voice echoed around the atrium. 'My name is Vogue Monroe and I've a good mind to have you both sacked.' She positively shimmered with rage, glaring at the guards with flashing eyes and a heaving chest.

Vogue Monroe. Emma had guessed right. Hollywood actress and latest in a long line of stunning women to be romantically linked with Leonardo Ravenino. She edged closer for a better look.

'I'm sorry, miss, it doesn't matter who you are, you are not coming in without an appointment.'

'Fine. Whatever.' Vogue held up her hands, nails like talons. 'But you can give him a message from me.' She tossed her head, dark curls rippling down her back. 'You can tell Leonardo Ravenino that he is nothing but a…a selfish, arrogant, egotistical bastard.' She paused for dramatic effect. 'You can tell him that I actually feel sorry for him. Because he is emotionally sterile, incapable of forming a real relationship with anyone because the only person he loves is himself!'

It was an award-winning performance—Emma had to give her that. And she had certainly got everyone's attention, as a quick glance at the row of receptionists along one wall revealed. They retained a professional air, but their hands on their keyboards had stilled.

'And you can tell him…' Her piercing gaze now fell on Emma, her green eyes flicking from the bouquet still held in Emma's arms to Emma's startled face. 'You can tell him *exactly* what he can do with his flowers.'

Well! Emma stood rooted to the spot. If only she worked for one of the tabloids this would be pure gold.

But Emma Quinn didn't work for the tabloids. She was junior features reporter for the *Paladin* newspaper. A serious, well-respected publication with a politically and socially well-informed readership. She was here to do an interview with Leonard Ravenino on renewable energy. Except he was already over two hours late. If Ms Monroe did but know it, even if she had managed to gain entry to Raven Enterprises, her ex-lover was not around to feel the weight of her wrath.

She watched as, with a final flourish, the actress exited the building, long legs folding themselves into a chauffeur-driven car waiting outside, tinted windows hiding her from view as the car pulled into the traffic.

Drama over, Emma turned back. Two hours of waiting meant she was familiar with every inch of Raven Enterprises' gleaming reception area. A sleek white desk ran along one side, where four receptionists, all dressed in black, quietly turned back to their work. One of whom, Nathalie, had been kindly trying to update Emma on Signor Ravenino's likely time of arrival. Even if she hadn't known herself.

But Emma would wait as long as it took. She was not going to let this opportunity slip through her fingers. Securing an interview with Leonardo Ravenino was the biggest coup of her journalistic career so far. The enigmatic Italian businessman gave very few interviews— in fact, he had a reputation for mistrusting the press. Emma had had the feeling, when her editor had set her the task, that he hadn't really thought she stood a cat in hell's chance—a bit like sending the new kid out for a tin of striped paint. But somehow, against the odds, she had done it. And she was *not* going to mess this up.

She had done her research, reading everything she could about this handsome billionaire. Far more than the interview called for, in fact. But she had found herself fascinated by the man. Fabulously wealthy but notoriously private, he had a penchant for dating high-profile women but loathed the tabloid press.

Even so, there was no shortage of pictures of him, a different actress or socialite on his arm every time, a minor royal draped around his six-foot-four frame as they left a nightclub, or a fashion model lounging on the deck of his yacht, all tiny bikini and golden tan, caught by the powerful zoom lenses of the paparazzi.

Enigmatic was a word the tabloids bandied about a lot, so were *inscrutable*, *mysterious*. Charming when he chose to be but taciturn in equal measure. Rude even, especially when confronted with a microphone or a sea of camera flashes.

His background was puzzling too. It hadn't taken long for Emma to discover that he had been next in line to inherit the title of Conte di Ravenino, head of the Italian principality whose name he bore, which had been in his family since the sixteenth century. But for some reason he had turned his back on the place and walked away, the title going to his younger brother. Try as she might, Emma couldn't find out why.

'Would you like me to take that from you?' Indicating the heavy bouquet in her arms, Nathalie beckoned Emma forward. The two women exchanged a glance.

'All part of the job?' Emma raised her brows enquiringly. 'Spurned lovers turning up, chucking flowers around?'

Nathalie laughed. 'Well, let's just say there's never a dull moment when Signor Ravenino is in town.'

'He has quite a reputation, I gather?' Emma perched herself on the edge of the desk.

'He is a force to be reckoned with, that's true,' Nathalie agreed. 'You'll see what I mean when you meet him.'

'If I ever get to meet him.' She pulled a face.

'I'm really sorry you have had to wait so long.'

'It's not your fault.' Emma hesitated. Maybe she could make use of all this hanging around by gleaning some more information about her subject. Purely in the interests of background research, of course. 'So, do you have to do a lot of this, apologising to people Signor Ravenino has kept waiting, making excuses, re-arranging schedules?'

Nathalie considered. 'He doesn't spend a lot of time in the UK office. But when he is here it's fair to say we earn our money.'

'He is a good employer?'

'Yes. As long as you don't mind working long hours. And having a positive attitude to some of his more challenging requests. You learn to expect the unexpected with Signor Ravenino.'

'What sort of challenges?'

'Oh, you know, arranging a private viewing at the Natural History Museum at a moment's notice. Flying a top chef to serve dinner on a remote Scottish island. He once bought every painting in an exhibition then wanted them hung in twelve different locations. That meant four different countries, two different continents! One of them is over there.' She pointed to a huge abstract canvas dominating the far wall.

'So, what Leonardo wants, Leonardo gets?'

'Something like that. But Mia, that's his PA here in the UK, is the one who has to deal with the more personal issues. The fallout from his complicated love life.'

'Would you say that Leonardo Ravenino treats women badly?'

'Not exactly.' Nathalie frowned. 'It's more that no woman ever manages to get him to behave the way they want him to behave. They all think they will be the one to tame him, to get him down the aisle, but they end up disappointed, just like all the others.' She glanced at the forsaken flowers on the chair beside her. 'Mia has the florist on speed dial.'

Emma followed her gaze. Clearly an exotic bouquet had done nothing to pacify the recipient in this instance. But this was all interesting stuff. She wanted to hear more. 'I'm guessing you must pick up a lot of stories working here.'

'Oh, yes.' Nathalie hesitated, suddenly wary. 'Though you're a reporter, aren't you? I probably shouldn't be sharing them with you.'

'Off the record. I promise.' Emma gave an encouraging smile. 'The piece I'm writing is about ocean thermal energy. Very dry. Well, very wet, but you know what I mean.'

Nathalie laughed. 'Okay.' She gave a quick glance to her side, lowering her voice. 'But you didn't hear this from me.'

Emma mimed her lips being zipped.

'Well…' Nathalie leaned forward conspiratorially. 'There was this one time…'

It was another hour before Leonardo Ravenino finally appeared. Emma had almost given up when a sleek black limo pulled up outside and in a flurry of movement a group of people entered. Moving forward like a swarm, Emma could just make out Leonardo in the centre, tall and dark, his shoulders back, his head held high, issuing orders to his minions as he marched through the echoing space.

She leapt to her feet, joining the edge of the throng, hurrying along beside them, her futile attempt at waving her notebook in the air going unnoticed. They were heading towards the elevator. If she wasn't careful, he was going to have disappeared before she had even had the chance to call out his name. The elevator doors opened and moving as one mass the group entered. No! Something told Emma that this was her one and only chance. If she let him get away now, she might as well kiss her interview goodbye.

The doors were almost closed when she stuck out her leg, jamming her foot between them. Immediately they opened again to reveal the group collectively staring at her, suddenly silent.

'Hi.' Emma gave a nervous cough. 'My name is Emma Quinn, from the *Paladin* newspaper.'

'Remove your foot from the elevator, young lady.' A heavily muscled man stepped forward, blocking her view.

'Yes, yes, of course.' Emma faltered. 'But I have an appointment with Signor Ravenino.' She fumbled in her jacket for her phone. 'Here, look.' She brought the screen to life with a shaking hand. 'This is the email confirmation. I've been waiting for ages.'

'Remove your foot from the elevator.' The guy didn't look remotely interested in her message.

'Yes, but—'

'I'll deal with this, Harry.'

The deep velvet tone, the faint Italian accent, there was no mistaking whose voice it was. Suddenly Leonardo Ravenino was standing before her, all sleek tailored suit, white shirt, perfectly knotted tie. Close up he was every bit as handsome as Emma had been led to believe, but it wasn't his beauty that took her by surprise, more the overpowering sense of *him*.

Nostrils slightly flared, thick, dark brows pulled together over narrowing eyes, his mouth tightly closed, there was an invincibility about him, as if nothing could touch him. Only his shadowed jawline gave any sign that it had been a long day, the close-cut stubble giving him a slightly feral, dangerous edge.

His gaze held hers steadily, dark and all-seeing. He gave a dismissive flick of his hand to the silent group still waiting in the elevator behind him, indicating they should go on without him.

'Ms Quinn, did you say?' His frown deepened as if he was trying to place her. Now that his full attention was trained on her he was even more formidable.

'Yes.' Emma swallowed. 'From the *Paladin*. We had an appointment for an interview.'

His puzzled expression was not encouraging.

'To discuss Raven Enterprises' investment in renewable energy?' Emma tried again. 'It was supposed to be at three o'clock.'

'Then please accept my apologies.'

'That's okay.' It wasn't actually. He had clearly forgotten all about her. Weren't people like him supposed to have a team of secretaries and PAs reminding him of his appointments? Why hadn't that Mia done her job? But he was here now, that was all that mattered. 'Perhaps we can do the interview now?'

'*Mi dispiace…* I am sorry, you misunderstand me. The interview will no longer be possible.' His lips set firmly.

'No!' In a rush of panic Emma grabbed hold of his arm, a gesture that was met with a small, pointed glance. She quickly removed it. 'I mean, it was all agreed.'

'Well, now it's unagreed.' For a moment it looked as though he was going to brush at his sleeve where her hand had been, but he resisted the temptation. 'I do hope you haven't been too inconvenienced.'

'No! I mean, yes, I have! We have to do this interview. You promised.' It wasn't the most grown up of replies, but panic was setting in fast.

'Time has unfortunately made it impossible.'

No, you are the one who has made it impossible. Emma swallowed down her rising anger. *And what's more, you don't even care.* He might be saying the right words, but his eyes held no hint of apology—more a sort of distracted indifference.

She bit down hard on her lip to stop herself from saying what she really thought. There was nothing to be gained by doing that.

'It needn't take long,' she implored. 'An hour, less even.'

'I'm sorry…'

'Well, later this evening perhaps.'

'If you will excuse me…'

'No!' As he started to move away, Emma reached out to grab his arm again, not caring any more what he thought.

'Signor Ravenino.' She tried to steady herself. 'I appreciate how busy you are, but the fact is I was promised an interview with you, I have been waiting for over three hours, and quite frankly I think it is incumbent on you to honour that arrangement.'

She released his arm, tucking her hair behind her ears, waiting.

At least she had got his attention back. She watched, barely breathing, as his leisurely gaze took her in. Slowly he crossed his arms over his chest, all studied nonchalance. Finally, a hint of a smile curved the corner of his finely drawn lips, like a cat playing with a mouse. 'Do you now?'

'Yes, yes, I do.' Emma felt a flush creeping up her neck. 'I think you owe it to me to give me at least an hour of your valuable time.'

He pushed back a starched white cuff to check the flashy timepiece on his wrist. Maybe there was a glimmer of hope.

'I can fit in with whatever you suggest.' Emma rushed to blow on the embers. 'I'm prepared to be flexible.'

One dark eyebrow rose. Emma felt her flush creep higher, but she stood her ground, refusing to acknowledge the way his tone had changed from one of irritation to something more like mild flirtation. Her stomach, however, was doing traitorous little leaps of interest.

'Very well.' He paused, giving her that look again. Assessing, stern but seriously hot. 'My nightclub, this evening.'

His nightclub? Taken by surprise, Emma tried to collect herself.

'To do the interview?'

'*Sì*, to do the interview.' He angled his head slightly, like he was dealing with someone who was a bit slow. Or, worse, someone who had jumped to the wrong conclusion. An awful thought that made Emma cringe. She countered it by putting on her most businesslike voice.

'That would be acceptable.'

'*Bene.*' Leo made a small adjustment to his stance. He had a way of owning every movement, as if it was his alone.

'Shall we say eleven p.m.?'

Eleven o'clock? She was normally tucked up in bed

long before that, reading a good biography or maybe a historical novel. Certainly not prancing about in night-clubs.

'Isn't that a little late?'

Leonardo's response was a take-it-or-leave-it shrug.

'Fine. Eleven o'clock. Thank you.' Why was she thanking him? *He* was the one who had let *her* down. Because he held all the cards, that's why.

'*Bene.*' Leonardo repeated the word. 'You know my nightclub?'

'Yes.' Emma nodded. Of course she did. Hobo was one of the most famous clubs in London, much loved by the glitterati. Rumour had it that Leonardo had won it in a bet, though whether that was true or not Emma had no idea. Like so much about this man, it was shrouded in mystery.

'Then I will see you there. Don't be late.'

Her be late! The cheek of it! With his back turned he left Emma searching for a suitably tart retort, though nothing too contentious, of course. But the glance over his shoulder stole her thoughts. And her breath. His eyes twinkled with mischief. Devilment. He was teasing her. And it felt as if the ground had just shifted beneath her feet.

CHAPTER TWO

EMMA GLANCED AROUND HER. She felt completely out of place in this exclusive nightclub, even though she had been personally escorted to an empty upper seating area, well away from the dance floor and the thump of the bass that held the gyrating bodies in its thrall.

This area was all about comfort, padded red leather seating arranged around low tables, subdued lighting and carefully chosen artwork. More paintings from the exhibition Nathalie had mentioned, perhaps? A handsome waiter had taken her drinks order, the sparkling water arriving on a silver salver and placed before her with a theatrical flourish more suited to the finest champagne.

Emma took another sip. It was foolish of her to have arrived so early but the burning desire to get this interview in the bag had seen her head across town a good hour before she'd needed to. Faced with two liveried doormen, she had anticipated having to explain who she was, but one mention of her name had seen her politely ushered inside.

She stood up, moving to stand by the railing that overlooked the dance floor below. She had a good view from up here, but the dim lighting made it impossible to pick out any faces. Just a writhing sea of bodies, arms raised in the air, heads swaying, long hair tossed about. It looked fun, Emma had to admit. But not the sort of fun she would ever be part of.

Clubbing was not something she had ever done. Her life since she'd been in London had been all about getting some sort of education, finding a job and earning a living. There had been no time for frivolities such as this, even if she'd been able to afford them. Which she couldn't. In fact, this was the first time she had even so much as set foot in a nightclub. Not that she would be telling Leonardo Ravenino that.

'*Buonasera.*' The rich velvet voice came from right behind her, spinning Emma around. Standing very close, Leonardo leaned forward to greet her, kissing both cheeks, the Italian way. 'I hope I haven't kept you waiting?'

'No, not at all.' Not this time, anyway. Emma collected herself. 'I've been watching the people on the dance floor.'

'Ah, yes.' He came and stood beside her, strong hands curling around the railing. 'Quite mesmerising, isn't it?'

Emma sneaked a look at his profile. All fluid grace and hard masculine lines beneath expensive Italian tailoring, it wasn't difficult to see why women fell at his feet. There was a dark, edgy energy about him, an inherent sexiness, that was very hard to ignore.

'Is it true that you won this nightclub in a bet?' She hadn't meant to plunge right in, or even ask this question at all, but somehow it had slipped out without warning.

Her companion turned his head, a hint of warning

in the dark grey eyes. Had she overstepped the mark already? There was a moment's pause before he spoke again.

'I see the interview has started already, Ms Quinn.'

Emma silently rebuked herself. She should have been more subtle. But something about this man was jumbling her carefully planned questions. 'I just noted that it's a divergence from your other businesses.' She hurried to try and make amends. 'And wondered if hospitality was something you intend to invest more in in the future?'

An infinitesimal raising of one eyebrow told her he knew she was bluffing.

'No, I have no plans to go into hospitality. And for your information, Hobo was payment for a debt. Nothing more. You shouldn't believe everything you read in the tabloids.' His stare was one of rebuke. 'You of all people should know that.'

'Yes, of course.' Emma adjusted the cuffs of her jacket in a serious newspaper reporter kind of way.

'Shall we sit down?'

She let out a relieved breath, only to have it stolen again when Leonardo slipped a guiding arm around her waist to move her back towards the seats. A bottle of champagne had mysteriously appeared on a low table. Filling two glasses, Leo held one out to Emma, waiting as she sat down.

'Oh, no, thanks. I think I'll just stick to water.'

'That's very professional of you.' Leo seated himself opposite her. 'If a little disappointing.'

'Disappointing?'

'*Sì*. You see, I was hoping you would join me in a small celebration.'

'What are we celebrating?'

'A successful day.' He smiled, his lips tightly closed, accompanied by a self-deprecating shrug that didn't fool Emma for one moment. She suspected that all his days were successful. That he made quite sure of it. Nevertheless, she accepted the glass and took a sip. It was delicious. Cold bubbles slid down her throat like silk.

Trying hard to ignore his long stare, she reached for her bag to pull out her trusty notepad and pen, and then, after a moment's hesitation, her cellphone.

'Is it okay if I record our conversation?'

'I don't see why not.' Leo crossed his legs, leaning back against the seat. Outwardly he seemed relaxed, but Emma had to be on her guard. She must not mess this up. Setting her phone on the table between them, she pressed record.

'So, Raven Enterprises invests in a number of different renewable energy companies. Would you say that was something you were particularly interested in?'

'The future of our planet is something we should all be interested in.' The reply came back slick and fast.

'Indeed.' Emma began to scribble down notes. A recording was great, but she liked to have everything down on paper too. Belt and braces. 'Raven Enterprises is something of a pioneer in the way it invests in start-up companies, rather than more established enterprises. Why is that?'

'I like to be in on something at the start. It's easier to control that way.' His tone was pleasant, easy. But control was clearly something this guy was all about. It was written in his every feature, every movement.

'And which sources of renewable energy do you think have the most potential for the future?'

'Biological proteins are interesting.' He paused and Emma felt the weight of his stare on her bent head. 'Tell me, Ms Quinn, do you always dress so conservatively?'

Her head shot up; her eyes trapped by his.

It was true that her outfit, navy skirt and fitted jacket, cream blouse, navy court shoes, did look rather out of place here. Briefly she had wondered if she should have chosen some sort of evening wear in view of the location and the time of day. But the fact was she didn't have any, or even enough time for a quick trawl of the local charity shop in search of a lucky find.

'This is my work outfit, Signor Ravenino. And, please, call me Emma.'

'Then you must call me Leo. So, do you never mix business with pleasure, Emma?'

Emma frowned. 'I take pleasure in my work if that's what you mean.'

This was certainly true. Working for the *Paladin* was not so much a pleasure as the realisation of her goal. And vindication, too, that all those awful jobs, living in dank little rooms, eating nothing but beans on toast, studying late into the night until her eyes hurt and her head throbbed had all been worth it. Because each of those things had taken her another step away from the chaos of her family background towards a shiny new future that was just within her grasp.

'Not exactly what I meant, no.' Leo leaned forward to top up her glass again. Emma was surprised to see it was almost empty. 'I just wondered if beneath that stern exterior there is a party girl waiting to get out.'

'No, there isn't.' She returned to her notepad. 'Could you elaborate on the role of biological proteins?'

'Do you like to dance, Emma?'

'No!' She straightened her notepad. This interview was not going the way it was meant to. 'I… I don't know how to dance.'

'Sure you do.' The gaze he aimed at her was like a full-on assault. Bold, roving, cocksure. Which no doubt he was. 'Everybody does. You just relax and let the music move you.' Suddenly on his feet, his hand stretched out towards her.

Emma stared at it in horror. Surely he wasn't expecting her to dance here, now? But the impatient little shake of his hand suggested he was.

'I don't think—' But even as she said the words she found herself rising, taking the outstretched hand, feeling it closing around hers.

The music was little more than a dull thud from up here, a pounding, incessant throb, like a heartbeat. Her own heart sounded almost as loud to her as Leo moved her closer, one hand resting on her shoulder, the other lightly pressed into the small of her back. It was a respectful hold, guiding rather than intimate, but that didn't stop Emma's panic. He was so close she could hear his every breath, feel the heat from his body. And he smelled divine. Relaxed muscles moved effortlessly, taking her with him, small movements drawing her closer still until she had no choice but to tentatively snake her arms around his waist to sway with him.

'Now, where were we?'

He was speaking over the top of her head, and it took Emma's addled brain a moment to work out that he was talking about continuing the interview. This was crazy, he was crazy. *Expect the unexpected*, wasn't that what Nathalie had said? And one thing was for sure, she had never expected to conduct the interview like this. If anything, she had worried he might be rather closed, hard to talk to. Instead he was all relaxed charm, answering politely, though admittedly giving little away. She took a moment to breathe. At least focussing on her questions would take her mind off her rioting senses.

Pulling back a little, she prepared herself to address the wall of his chest. 'Does Raven Enterprises intend to extend its investment to other potential energy sources?' Somehow she managed to drag the question up from somewhere.

'I'm always open to new ideas.' His body rocked gently to one side. 'You have to look at the scientific evidence and decide which one to back. A bit like horse racing.'

'Would you say you were a gambling man?'

'There is a certain thrill in taking a chance.' She could hear the confidence in his voice. 'And satisfaction when it pays off.'

'And when it doesn't?'

'Then you move on, Ms Quinn. Life is too short to agonise over failures.' His hand fell from her shoulder. 'More champagne?'

'No!' She moderated her voice. 'No, thank you. But I would like to sit down now.'

'Of course.' Leo gave a small accepting shrug.

Suddenly the air seemed terribly hot. Taking off her jacket, Emma laid it neatly on the seat beside her, undoing the top button of her blouse. That was better. Marginally. She reached for her notepad again, determined to ignore the way Leonardo was watching her every move. She crossed her legs, cleared her throat, pen ready.

Leo surveyed the *Paladin*'s junior reporter through

lowered lashes. She was an interesting subject. Despite losing the jacket, she managed to look more prim than ever, her defences pulled firmly around her. If his suggestion of a dance had been to make her feel less ill at ease, it had clearly failed. But despite her conservative clothes and haughty manner there was something inherently sexy about her—the pout of her lips, her habit of nipping the bottom one with small white teeth when she was thinking. The way she looked up at him through that fringe…

She had a refreshing lack of conceit, as if she paid no heed to her natural beauty. And she was bright too. Leo ran his hand across his chin. No, the dance hadn't been about settling her nerves. It had been about him. He just couldn't help himself.

Today had been manic but successful. His favourite sort of day. Deliberately packing everything into the shortest possible time frame was the way he liked to work. He thrived on the pressure and seeing how other people coped with it. It sorted out the weak from the strong. And sometimes, like today, working at speed meant closing a deal before a rival company got a look in. Which was always satisfying.

He'd forgotten all about this interview. If his secretary hadn't been so busy no doubt she would have cancelled it. If Ms Quinn hadn't been so persuasive when he had come upon her in the foyer of Raven Enterprises, he would have dismissed her. He had only agreed to do it in the first place to try and silence a few board members who were starting to make noises about the lack of positive publicity. Too many photos of him coming out of nightclubs were not good for the confidence of investors, apparently.

Tempted though he was to tell them his private life was none of their business, Leo knew that where money and leadership was concerned, no one, no matter how powerful, was totally immune. So when an email from the *Paladin* happened to arrive straight after another tedious board meeting, he had agreed to the interview. An article about Raven Enterprises' investment in renewable energies. What could be more positive than that?

And Ms Emma Quinn was certainly very thorough. The questions had been coming at him hard and fast for some time now.

'Clearly you are interested in the future of our planet and yet you own a private jet, you fly all over the world. Does that not bother your conscience?'

She briskly flipped over the page of her notebook, tucked her hair behind one ear, her pen held in position. Like he wasn't going to notice the barb held in her question.

'You are assuming I have a conscience, Ms Quinn.'

The pen stopped scratching across the paper, but she didn't look up. Instead a stillness came over her, as if she was holding herself in check.

Leo did the same. He should fight the desire to play cat and mouse.

'International travel is a necessary evil in the world of business,' he continued. 'A private jet saves time, it's as simple as that.'

'And the flashy cars, the luxury yacht?' Now she came back at him, going for the jugular this time. He couldn't resist a counterattack.

'It's true, fast cars are a weakness of mine.' He gave her a small but deadly smile. 'I never said I was perfect.'

He watched with satisfaction as those full lips pursed, the effort of not saying what she wanted to say pinched there, written right across her face. He was enjoying this.

'I have disappointed you, Ms Quinn?'

'No.' The reply was too quick, too vehement. 'Why would I be disappointed when I never thought you were perfect in the first place?'

Ha—good reply! The more this woman refused to be lured by him, the more interested he became. He leaned back in his seat, crossing one leg over the other at the knee. 'I can see I need to be careful not to underestimate you, Ms Quinn.'

'Are you in the habit of underestimating women?' Quick as a flash she struck back. Clever.

'No, I do not underestimate women. I very much admire them.'

'And they you, it seems.'

Leo gave a self-deprecating shrug.

'Would you say you were an honourable man, Signor Ravenino?' Her eyebrows disappeared under her fringe.

'I would.'

'Only I happened to be waiting in the reception of Raven Enterprises this afternoon when Vogue Monroe showed up.'

Ah, so this was where she was going. Leo sat forward again. He had been right to caution himself for underestimating her. Despite her innocent looks, she was a journalist after all, and a sharp one.

'That was…unfortunate.' The goading look in Emma's eyes made him elaborate, even though he knew he shouldn't. 'But women I date know the rules. If they choose to ignore them, that's up to them.'

'So you make all the rules?'

'Yes.' He sat back. 'Do you have a problem with that?'

'It's not my job to have an opinion of you. Merely to ascertain the facts.'

But her opinion was there all right, held in the wide, accusatory gaze. Well, so be it. It didn't matter what she thought of him. But it did matter what she put in this article she was writing.

'Your job, as I understood it, was to find out about Raven Enterprises' investment in renewable energy. I wasn't aware it extended to an examination of my morals.'

'It doesn't.' Flustered, she hurried to put him straight. To emphasise the point, she laid her notepad and pen down on the table.

'As long as we are both clear on this matter. I should hate there to be any misunderstanding about what I agreed to in terms of the content of the interview.'

'No, there's no misunderstanding.'

'Bene.' He gave her a polite smile. 'Then perhaps our interview is concluded?'

'Yes, of course. And thank you.'

He rose with her, watching as she put on her jacket, fastening the one button across her waist.

'How will you get home?'

'Oh, I'll get the night tube.'

'It's too late to be using public transport. My driver will take you home. In fact…' he warmed to his theme '…why don't I drive you myself? In one of my *flashy* cars.'

His pointed use of her phrase was acknowledged with an upward glance.

'No, really, that won't be necessary.'

'I insist. I like driving round big cities at night. It would be my pleasure.'

His arm went loosely around her waist to guide her forward before she could argue any more. For some reason he wasn't quite ready to bid farewell to this woman yet.

CHAPTER THREE

As the car cruised along the banks of the Thames, Leo stole a glance at his passenger. The postcode he'd entered into the satnav indicated an area way out to the north, somewhere he had never ventured.

His knowledge of London was pretty much limited to the City, the West End and the affluent areas where the privileged few lived in beautiful Georgian terraces or penthouse apartments. He owned neither, preferring to stay in a hotel when he visited the city. It made life less complicated. He had quite enough complications as it was.

His new life, the one he had carved out for himself when the old one had so spectacularly imploded, was crazy busy. His focus had been all consuming, his determination to create a multi-billion-dollar business empire in the shortest time possible driving him ruthlessly on. And he had succeeded. In three short years Raven Enterprises had become hugely successful, and Leo Ravenino one of the most highly respected businessmen in the world.

Described as the man with the Midas touch, his uncanny ability to seek out start-up companies and then have the courage to back them when more experienced traders considered them far too speculative had earned him the reputation of a reckless trailblazer. Leo himself put his success down to hard graft and meticulous research. Though even he had to admit luck had played its part, particularly when his frequent trips to the casinos failed to put a dent in his fortune.

But quite frankly he was due some luck.

'So, are you a Londoner, Emma?' He rested his hands on the wheel, enjoying the smooth feel of the leather, the soft purr of the engine.

'No.' She had a low voice, smooth, sexy. 'But I've been living here for eight years.'

'Where are you from originally?'

'Um…the West Country.' Deliberately vague. Something about her reticence made him want to dig deeper.

'So you came to London to find fame and fortune?'

'Not exactly.' She gave a short laugh. 'More to start a new life.'

Interesting. Leo kept his eyes on the road ahead, waiting for her to elaborate, but she remained stubbornly silent.

'Did you always want a career in journalism?'

'I like writing, particularly research-based information. I thought about doing a history degree to start with, then decided I'd stand a better chance of getting a good job if I went in for journalism.'

'Even so, I imagine it's a competitive world, isn't it?' Tough too. She looked too innocent to be competing with the hardnosed hacks he'd come across. But he'd already caught a glimpse of steel behind the wide blue eyes. He already knew she was clever.

'Yes, it is.'

'So you have done well to secure a position at the *Paladin*?'

'Yes.' He briefly sensed her pride before she checked herself. 'Though I have to confess this is the first solo interview I've done. Up until now I've been mostly shadowing the features editor, checking facts, writing up his pieces for him.'

'Which explains why you were so determined it shouldn't be cancelled.'

'Yes.' He finally heard her smile. 'There was no way I could go back to Don saying I'd failed.'

'Then I'm sorry I made it difficult for you.'

'That's okay.' She turned to him. 'We got there in the end.'

Leo stopped the car at a red light. It was a warm night so he lowered the window, resting his arm on the sill as he gazed at the near empty streets. A small group of people was clustered around a kebab van on the corner.

'Are you hungry, by any chance?' He turned back to his companion.

'No!' That startled negative again, just when she had been starting to thaw.

'Do you mind if I get one?'

Pulling the car over, he sauntered across to join the short queue. Looking back, he could see Emma's outline in the passenger seat, just make out that she had pulled down the visor to check her reflection in the mirror. So not totally without vanity. And not totally impervious to him. The thought pleased him and as he gave his order to the proprietor, a large gentleman wielding a lethal-looking serrated blade, he decided Ms Emma

Quinn was his challenge. He would find a way to break through that prim exterior even if it took all night. It was a surprisingly tempting thought.

Emma had no idea how she had ended up sitting on a bench on the bank of the Thames at two o'clock in the morning with a handsome Italian billionaire by her side, but somehow she had.

The kebabs had been eaten watching the wide, dark river snake its way past. Despite her saying no, Leo had come back with two polystyrene boxes, handing her one in such a way it would have been churlish to refuse. And all pretence of not being hungry had vanished with the first bite. She was starving.

Conversation between them picked up between mouthfuls, being outside, cocooned in the dim light, doing something as ordinary as eating a kebab breaking down the barriers between them until Emma felt herself start to relax. More than that, she felt happy. Leo, too, appeared to be at ease. Not the practised, urbane charm he had shown her in the club, but a more casual, laidback style that only made him all the more attractive.

Asking about her job he appeared to be genuinely interested in her replies, following up with inciteful comments, anecdotes of his own. Conversation had flowed easily, from her favourite places in London to whether she liked chilli sauce. Musings about how deep the Thames was, where pigeons went to sleep. Safe, silly things.

Leo was clever, quick-witted, good company. He made her laugh. And he also made her tingle with desire. All over. Everywhere. From the top of her scalp to the tips of her toes. Like she had been electrified. Like he only had to touch her and a bolt of light would fizz between them. Somehow his inherent sexiness had infiltrated her veins like a silent assassin.

'It's a clear night tonight.' Running his arm along the back of the bench behind her, Leo tipped his head back to look at the sky. An hour had passed and still neither of them had made any attempt to move.

'Yes.' Emma copied him, her head thrown back. 'I love looking up at the stars. As a child I tried to learn the different constellations.'

'Then here is your challenge, Ms Quinn.' He moved closer. 'What can you see up there?'

'Well, there's a lot of light pollution...'

'No excuses.'

'Okay!' Emma laughed. 'Well, there's the Big Dipper, right overhead. Though technically it's not a constellation, just part of Ursa Major, the Great Bear. If you follow the handle towards the southwest, the next star you meet is Arcturus.'

'Fascinating.'

'And beyond that Corona Borealis.'

'Did anyone ever tell you that you have a beautiful neck?'

'N-no.' Emma stopped breathing, her head still thrown back, her heart racing.

'And I should very much like to kiss it.' So close now, his breath felt like the flutter of a bird's wing against her skin.

There was a second's stillness and then his lips were at the base of her throat, hot and damp, gentle yet firm. Emma's eyes closed, pinpricks of desire shooting through her body, all over, everywhere. Slowly, almost imperceptibly his mouth moved up her neck, goosebumps trailing in its wake, the brush of his hair another, exquisite torture. At the base of her ear he stopped, pulling back, waiting. Emma opened her eyes. The stars were still above her. Very slowly she raised her head. Their eyes met. Leo's dark head moved closer. And then his mouth was on hers.

Sensations detonated in her head, elation flooding every part of her body. Tingling, clenching, twitching feelings, assaulting her nerve endings, affecting all of her. *So this was what a kiss could be like.* Something extraordinary. Something that made you feel things you'd never felt before, leaving you reaching for an unknown that you couldn't quite grasp, yearning for something you had never even known existed until that moment, but which now seemed vitally important. Hanging on to the yearning sensation, refusing to let it slip away, because that, too, was beautiful in its own right. Affecting, astonishing.

On a shared gasp of breath, they pulled apart, just enough to find each other's eyes. Leo's fingers gently threaded through her hair, cradling her head, the swelling silence holding them still but offering no answers. A swallow moved the column of his throat and for a moment it looked as if he was going to speak. But instead he angled his head until his lips were on hers again.

An explosion ripped through Emma once more, her neural pathways ready for him this time, like following the flattened track through a field of corn. Her arms went around his neck, registering the heat of him, the form of his shoulders, broad and strong, the powerful, sleeping strength. Beneath closed lids she let herself drift without thinking, take without question, give without shyness. She let herself go.

Leo's arms strayed to her waist, and then they were both standing, the kiss still hard and hungry, Leo leaning in to her until she could feel all of him beneath his clothes, hard planes, jutting bones, warm skin stretched over bunched muscles. And the unmistakable swell of arousal pressing against her stomach. Emma edged closer, seeking more, her hands shaking until she linked them behind Leo's head, pressing as tightly as she could to make them stop, to prevent her whole body from convulsing. Even if that felt like heaven too.

'Emma?' Her name on his lips was both a question and a promise. A search for truth wrapped in a quiet dare.

He waited, but when met only with Emma's thrumming silence he continued anyway. 'My hotel is not far from here.'

Emma swallowed, the frantic pulse of her blood acknowledging exactly what he was saying, the pound of her heart repeating it over and over. Dragging her eyes away from Leo's black gaze, she took a step back until Leo's arms dropped down by his sides. She looked down at herself, expecting to be somehow changed, altered by what had just happened. By the tumult still coursing through her. But, no, she looked exactly the same, the plain navy suit still stopping demurely at her knee, the jacket buttoned at the waist giving no sign of the tumult beneath—breasts swollen with heat, skin pulled tight, nipples hardened peaks. No visible sign of the pulsing ache that was gripping her core.

She turned her head, making herself focus on the wide pavement in front of them, the ornate streetlights, and beyond that the river, quiet and dark.

Leo Ravenino was dangerous—she knew that.

His reputation went before him, she had seen the evidence for herself. Vogue Monroe's outburst in the foyer of Raven Enterprises a classic example of a woman scorned. The stories Nathalie had told her only confirming everything she'd thought she knew. In affairs of the heart, Leo Ravenino was a dark and lethal force.

But forewarned was forearmed. Emma tried to order her thoughts. She knew exactly what Leo was offering. She also knew with every sensible, practical bone in her body that she should turn him down. And before that kiss she would have done. No question. Even though Leo's seduction had been in the air all evening, it had been sufficiently subtle, casual for Emma to ignore. She had just assumed he was programmed to do it; part of who he was.

And equally she was programmed to repel such advances. Not for nothing had she earned the nickname *Ice Quinn* by the teenage boys who had found their advances swiftly rebuffed when she'd been younger. A moniker that had lodged in her brain all this time.

But she didn't feel like an ice queen now. She felt heat in every part of her body, every cell jumping with excitement. She felt a recklessness urging her on, ordering her to take this chance. Sucking in her kiss-swollen lips, she waited for sanity to kick in, for her rational voice to finally pipe up and tell her to primly decline Leo's offer and ask to be driven home. It was what she would have sworn her reply would be if you had asked her at the start of the evening. And yet…still that voice didn't come. Instead there was another one clamouring for her to take this opportunity, to step out of her straitjacket and live life for the moment for once.

Watching those dancers in the nightclub, their bodies so fluid and loose, so uninhibited, had made her see how tightly she was strung. Back then, held in Leo's arms, she had been rigid with tension. But not now. Suddenly one night of reckless indulgence seemed overwhelmingly tempting. One night when she threw off the shackles of responsibility and stopped being so damned sensible, just living for the moment, impossible to resist. One night when she let herself go to see what would happen.

Leo was waiting for her answer, the patient silence belied by his heated stare. Eyes that shone as black as night. Under the streetlight his short, dark hair gleamed richly, shadowed hollows shaping his face. The air was thick with the pull of his magnetism, but he made no move to touch her again, to influence her decision with another bruising kiss. Instead an old-fashioned courtesy prevailed, a quiet respectfulness she hadn't expected of him. Sure, there was an arrogance in the way he held himself, an inbuilt confidence, but it was clear that the decision was hers and hers alone.

And Emma knew she had already made it. She swallowed hard, flashing Leo a smile that arrowed straight to his groin. 'Let's go.'

Finally letting the air out of his lungs, Leo felt for Emma's hand, holding it tightly in his, as if to bind her to him. Waiting for her to make her decision had tested him to breaking point. With rampant impatience firing every cell of his body, he'd had to harness all his self-control not to make the decision for her, in the form of another blazing kiss. But somehow he had managed to restrain himself and now the wait was over. Almost.

They were only ten minutes from his hotel. He could last that long. He took in a breath that did nothing to calm his libido, both fascinated and shocked by the extraordinary effect she was having on him. What had started as a mild attraction had rapidly morphed into a desperate need. He wanted Emma more than he had wanted any woman in a very long time.

With unseemly haste he led them back to his car. Ten minutes, he told himself. That's all. Opening the door for Emma, he waited, expecting her to slide inside, but instead she turned to face him, tilting her face up to his, her expression hard to read in the low light. Solemn, thoughtful, but still as sexy as hell. She had changed her mind, was that it? Leo braced himself for the crushing news that he would be taking her home, chastely dropping her at her door.

But instead her arms wound around his neck, lowering his head until it met hers. A fresh bolt of arousal jerked through him as she started to kiss him, tentative at first, but then long and deep, full of hunger. Dio, *what was she trying to do to him?* His hands felt for the button of her jacket, sliding beneath to the silky shirt, over the gorgeous swell of her breasts, nipples tightening beneath his touch. He wanted more. So much more. He longed to feel those curves beneath his fingertips, to make her tremble beneath his caress. But not here, like this.

Urgency fuelling every movement, he got them both in the car, the roar of the engine echoing the roar in his blood as he navigated the empty roads back to his hotel in a silence that thrummed with need. Chucking the car keys to the doorman, he hurried Emma inside, their footsteps echoing across the marble lobby, their lips meeting as the elevator doors slid closed, still locked when they opened again.

Clasped in each other's arms, they half stumbled in the direction of the bedroom, tripping over each other, laughing at their eagerness, the madness of what they were doing, the heat of their breath flushing their faces, the hammering of their hearts loud enough to feel. But no words. Words were superfluous.

Arriving at his bed in a tangle of twisted clothes and eager limbs, Leo took a moment to stare down at Emma. So beautiful. How had he not noticed it right from the start? Wide eyes, full lips, her shoulder-length brown hair spread out on the pillow. The jacket already gone, now he undid the buttons of her blouse as slowly as his desire would let him, moving the fabric to expose her bra, the swell of her breasts. His breath was as hot as fire as his tongue found the valley of her cleavage, dipping down as low as he could reach. Her soft moan drove him on, matched by a groan of his own as she reached behind to undo her bra, shrugging it off along with her blouse.

Leaving her just long enough to rip off his clothes, Leo reached for a condom packet, impatiently ripping it open with his teeth. By the time he was back, Emma was naked, her arms above her head, stretching her breasts, her legs together, writhing gently as they twisted around one another.

Leo had never seen such a beautiful sight. His urge to take her more extreme, more mind-numbingly vital than anything he had ever felt before.

Gazing into the shadows of Leo's face, Emma tried to capture the moment, knowing she was about to be changed for ever. Dilated pupils, a jaw set hard with concentration, mouth pulled tight now, like he was teetering on the edge. Like he meant to own all of her. *She had done this to him.*

Winding her arms around his neck, she threaded her fingers in his hair, pulling him down to kiss her again. His mouth came down on hers, feverish and crushing, mind numbing. *This was it.* She arched up to meet him, her breath stolen as Leo lowered himself down, skin on skin, the jut of his hips hard against her own, the solid weight of his erection pressing against the sweet, damp fire of her core.

'Cosi bella.' He rasped the words as he nudged himself against the aching folds, a throbbing shudder of pleasure pulsing through her. 'So beautiful.'

Then he was inside her, thrusting hard and deep, the cry she let out making him hesitate until she wrapped her legs around his back, urging him on as she started to convulse ecstatically around the length of him.

And all rational thought was instantly obliterated.

CHAPTER FOUR

THERE WAS SOMETHING about her head on the pillow, the untidy curtain of hair, a solemnity held in her features, even in sleep. Leo allowed himself to stare, just for a few moments. But not with pleasure. And certainly not with any sense of satisfaction. Far from it. His overriding emotion was guilt.

He watched as her eyes fluttered beneath closed lids so delicate he could make out the tiny blue veins. Her mouth twitched. The mouth that had felt so good beneath his own, that he had encouraged to explore his body, to touch and taste, leaving him shuddering with pleasure beneath its featherlike stroke. But not there... at least he had held back from that, even though she had wanted to. At least he didn't have that first on his conscience.

Who was he kidding? His conscience had no place to hide. In the cold light of this grey London morning he had to face the facts. *Emma had been a virgin.* He had taken something from her that she could never get back. He hadn't known, not until the last moment, but even then it wouldn't have been too late. He could have stopped. He *should* have stopped. Despite Emma urging him on, he should have found the willpower to pull back, to say no, to wrench himself from temptation. *Such temptation.*

But instead he had greedily taken her soft assurances at face value, firmly ignored the voice in his head telling him this was wrong. And not just once. But repeatedly. All night long, in fact. Her generous, giving body obsessing him in a way he had never experienced before. And the more she gave the more he took. After all, there was no going back now, so what difference would it make? What was done was done.

But now he saw that twisted logic for what it was. The selfish and greedy actions of a man who thought of no one but himself. The man he had become. Somewhere along the line his power and success had taken him down a path to a place he no longer liked, turned him into a man he no longer respected. Dating a succession of beautiful high-profile women, just because he could, no longer felt like any sort of achievement, just fatuous vanity.

As Emma stirred beneath his scrutiny, Leo felt his lip curl in self-disgust. This rare woman deserved someone so much better than him. Taking one last look, he turned away, walked quietly through the suite of rooms, picking up his belongings as he went. This he could do for her. Get out of her life before he messed it up any further. A clean break. She deserved nothing less.

'These came for you.' Don, the features editor, appeared from behind an enormous bunch of flowers. 'Seems like you made quite an impression on someone.'

By 'someone' it was clear he knew perfectly well who. A blush staining her cheeks, Emma took them from him, laying them down heavily on top of the papers on her cluttered desk.

'No need to look like that.' Don gave a short laugh. 'How you choose to do your research is up to you. But I'll be expecting a great article.' His wink as he turned to go only mortified Emma still further. 'End of the day, okay?'

Emma cleared her throat. 'Yes, sure.'

She made herself look at the flowers, her stomach twisting. *It was exactly the same bunch he had sent Vogue Monroe.* The innocent bouquet stared back at her like an insult. So, this was how little last night had meant to him. How little she had meant. Despite the sick feeling in her gut, she still found her fingers parting the blooms, looking for a note, looking for some confirmation, no matter how small, that she had got it wrong. That the closeness they had shared had been special. Not just for her but for him too.

But there was nothing. *He has the florist on speed dial.* Nathalie's comment came back to haunt her. No doubt the work of seconds, she had been dealt with, dismissed, forgotten.

Not that she was surprised. Waking up alone in Leo's hotel suite had sent a very clear message. Realising he had gone without even saying goodbye had hurt. A lot. But what had she expected? Sweet nothings and clasped hands over a leisurely breakfast? Promises that they should keep in touch, that he would look her up next time he was in London? That wasn't Leo Ravenino's style, and Emma knew it.

But that hadn't prevented the hollowness inside, an emptiness that had only seemed to expand as she had hurried home, showering and dressing, the same as she did every day. Taking the underground into work, nodding good morning to her colleagues as usual, sitting at her desk, preparing to start work.

Reading through her interview notes, it felt like they had been written an age ago, by someone else entirely. But the recording on her phone remained unplayed. Emma wasn't ready to hear his voice again. It was too personal, too *him*. If she was going to hold it together today, she had to blot out everything that had happened last night and concentrate firmly on the article she had to write.

And up until now she had succeeded. It had been a struggle but keeping her head down and all her focus on work, she had managed to get the first five hundred words done. Concise, informative, impartial, a quick readthrough confirmed she had done a good job. And she still had plenty of time to finish it. But the arrival of the wretched flowers had derailed her. The fragile hold on her concentration gone, the enormity of what she had done last night reared up, filling her mind. Stealing the words she wanted to write.

It wasn't like she regretted it exactly. How could she regret something so amazing, so *altering*? It was more that she felt cut adrift, like she didn't know who she was any more. Yesterday she would have sworn she would never get involved with a man like Leonardo Ravenino, that the idea of going back to his hotel and spending the night with him was inconceivable. And yet she had. Willingly. Urgently. Giving herself freely, taking greedily.

She felt somehow duped by her own self. And she felt annoyed that she had succumbed to Leo's practised seduction the same way so many other women had in the past, and no doubt would in the future. She had imagined herself cleverer than that, sharper. Now she knew she wasn't. As the pretty blooms by her side made all too clear.

She picked up the bouquet, steadying the weight with her hand. She would just get rid of them, that was the answer. Emma looked around her. They were too big to dump straight in the bin and offering them to someone else would only provoke questions and she couldn't bear that. So instead she shoved them under her desk as best she could, deciding she would deal with them later. Drawing in her chair, she turned to her article again.

But it was no good, the right words refused to come. Instead of his business affairs all she could think of was Leo the lover. Fevered thoughts tumbled over each other, fighting for centre stage. The stories in the tabloid press, the things she had heard from Nathalie, the look on Vogue Monroe's face… What was it she had called him? *A selfish, arrogant, egotistical bastard.* And this was the man she had chosen to lose her virginity to. The first man she had ever wanted. Well, more fool her.

She had never viewed her virginity as some sort of prize, more a sort of mothballed corner, one she wasn't sure she would ever expose to the light. The succession of men coming and going in her mother's life, and hers, too, by default, had firmly put her off casual relationships. The last one, in particular, had put her off both sex and men in general. The trauma of that incident had definitely left its mark.

So when no one she ever met even tempted her to change her mind, Emma had decided maybe that was it. She really was the Ice Quinn. She was too cold or too scarred or somehow wired the wrong way to ever want to have sex. Celibacy was fine. From what she could see of other people's messed-up relationships, she was better off staying single anyway.

But meeting Leo altered everything. She had been completely swamped by the power of the attraction. Drowned by it. Drugged by it. It didn't justify what she had done, or make her action remotely more sensible or acceptable, but it was the best explanation she could come up with.

Emma stared at her computer screen, her hand on the mouse opening up a blank page almost before she realised it. The written word had always been her refuge. Part of a chaotic and largely dysfunctional family, her way of coping had been to take herself off, to write down her worries and fears, her frustrations and anxieties, commit them to pages in a notebook in all their funny, febrile or furious glory, depending on what was inside her head at the time. And then she would destroy them. Because just the act of writing the words made her feel better, it released the pressure in her head.

Tentatively, her fingers touched the keyboard. Maybe this would be a way to vent her feelings, to take away the drilling in her head, the annoying ache inside. For her eyes only, she could write a no-holds-barred exposé of the life and loves of Leo Ravenino. Get it all out. Then maybe she would be able to concentrate on the piece she was supposed to be writing.

Inside the world of Leo Ravenino: the life and loves of a billionaire Latin playboy!

The headline wrote itself. And before long her fingers were flying over the keyboard.

* * *

Che diamine! What the hell…?

Leo stared at the article in horror. No, it couldn't have been written by her. It wasn't possible. But there was the byline, clearly written beneath the offending title: *by Emma Quinn.*

He threw the newspaper down in disgust, anger coursing through him, rushing through his veins as he thought back to the interview, to what had happened afterwards. To the woman he had thought she was.

Snatching the paper back up, he scanned the article again, the words jumping out at him like knives. Details of his private life laid out for all to see. Personal, intimate things, painting him like a heartless philanderer, some kind of lascivious monster. The sort of man no woman was safe to be around.

> *Breaking the heart of a British socialite after she had told her family they would shortly be wed.*
> *Abandoning an Italian heiress on his yacht in the South of France when she refused to accept that their relationship was over.*
> *Expecting his staff to deal with hysterical ex-lovers turning up at his offices.*

Leo's hands curled into fists. How dared she…? And not content with raking over his private life, exposing his misdemeanours for all to see, there were the comments about his background. Questions posed about the principality of Ravenino, the ending of his engagement, the reason for his rapid departure.

Was his ex-fiancé yet another victim of this cold-hearted lover?

Or perhaps the responsibility of running a principality was just too arduous a life for this Latin playboy?

Leo dragged in a breath of fire that scorched right through his lungs. How the hell could he have got this woman so wrong? He, who prided himself on his intuition, his ability to read people so well, had been totally fooled by this Emma Quinn. Totally fooled by her guileless 'innocence'. To think he had actually felt guilty for the way he had treated her! Agonised over taking her virginity. Now he saw her for what she was. A ruthless opportunist who had been prepared to trade her virginity for a scoop. For the sake of a tawdry newspaper article.

Well, she would soon realise her mistake. No one double-crossed Leonardo Ravenino and got away with it. Reaching for his phone, he quickly found the number he was looking for and pressed dial. Emma Quinn's precious career at the *Paladin* was just about to come to an end. He would make sure of it.

'Well, this is one hell of a mess.' Don raked a hand through his hair, his eyes, when they finally met hers, heavy with defeat. 'I hold myself partly responsible for not checking the article, but ultimately it's you he wants gone.'

'Gone?' Emma repeated the word faintly.

'Yep. He was quite explicit. Either you quit, forthwith, or he's going to sue the *Paladin*. And, quite frankly, we wouldn't have a leg to stand on. Not when we are faced with this…' He gestured to the newspaper spread out on the desk before him, folded back to the features page, where Emma's article stared back at them in all its black and white horror. A wave of sickness passed over her again.

Writing in the heat of the moment, with a churn of emotions going round in her head, she had not held back. She had poured everything into it, adopting classic tabloid language to spell out a torrid mix of truths and rumour about Leo Ravenino's many love affairs, his callous treatment of the women, his lack of morals, his egotism, the ruthless streak behind the urbane charm, on and on. For good measure she had even chucked in some speculation about his past, pointedly wondering what exactly had happened to make him leave Ravenino in such a hurry, why the title had never been passed down to him.

It was an explosive bomb of a piece, the fragments flying far and wide. *But it was never meant to be published.*

Emma slumped in the chair opposite Don, her elbows on her knees, her head in her hands. Like some sort of dreadful nightmare, she kept hoping she would wake up. That Don hadn't hurried over to her desk the day before, saying he had just heard they needed the piece on Ravenino right away. That she hadn't rushed to finish it in a terrible panic, her head still all over the place, lack of sleep mushing her brain. That she hadn't clicked 'send' without checking what she was doing…

She had only found out she'd filed the wrong article this morning. Hauled into the office at first light, she had been met by Don's horrified face holding the newspaper before him like a weapon of mass destruction. Which it was really. The destruction of her career.

'Is there nothing we can do? I can do?' She raised her head, searching for a flicker of hope. But Don's bleak expression made it clear there was no hope to be had.

'I'm sorry, lass.' He reached for her hand. 'You're a good writer and we'll make a journalist out of you yet. But there is no going back from a mistake like this. Ravenino wants your blood and the *Paladin* is going to make sure he gets it.'

CHAPTER FIVE

Two months later

SHIELDING HER EYES from the sun, Emma gazed up at the headquarters of Raven Enterprises. Located in the heart of Milan's business district, it was the tallest, most imposing building of all, a gleaming metal tower of postmodernist construction. She returned her gaze to the pavement, focussing on steadying the thump of her heart.

She hadn't made an appointment, knowing full well that any request to see Leo would have been denied without a detailed explanation. And that explanation needed to be made face to face. But now she risked being refused entry. Parallels with Vogue Monroe in London flashed through her mind. At the time she had felt sorry for Vogue, but she had only lost her boyfriend, her pride, maybe a little bit of her heart. In comparison, Emma had lost everything.

But luck, if you could call it that, was with her today. The revolving doors turned, and two men stood on the pavement, speaking in rapid Italian, shaking hands.

Emma's stomach swooped.

'*Guardero le figure e ti farò sapere. Ti prego di tenere questo tra noi.*'

There was an exchange of farewells before the taller man turned back. And suddenly his slate-grey eyes were on hers. Shock flitted across his face, his jaw visibly hardening, his senses on high alert.

'Ms Quinn.'

Nothing more, just that. Her name on his lips like a curse. His gaze aimed like a weapon.

'Leo.' Emma tried to match his tone. She had prepared hard for this moment. She wasn't here to try and justify herself, to make friends, even if that were possible, which she knew it wasn't. She was here to say what needed to be said and then leave. She had to be calm and logical. Keep her emotions at bay.

Who was she kidding? There was nothing calm or logical about the visceral impact of seeing him again. It was hot and hard and terrifyingly real. Just one glance at him had seen her emotions detonate like a bomb inside her. She mentally amended her objectives: she needed to keep her emotions hidden.

'There is something I have to speak to you about.' She choked out the words on a dry breath.

Leo closed the space between them with a couple of lethal strides, his eyes never leaving her face.

'Something so important that it brings you to Milan?' Suspicion furrowed his brow, narrowed his eyes.

'Yes.'

A fleeting look of unease crossed his face before it was banished by command. 'Very well.'

Taking her elbow, he turned Emma around, issuing rapid instructions to a receptionist as he marched them through the foyer towards an elevator. As they were whisked noiselessly skyward, he made no attempt

to speak to her, the silence an almost palpable indictment in itself.

'Follow me.'

He led her down a wide corridor, touching his finger
to a keypad to usher her into a huge glass office with
windows on all sides, a panoramic view of Milan in
every direction. Following Leo towards his desk, Emma
concentrated on putting one foot in front of the other,
looking neither left nor right. She was feeling queasy
enough already, without vertigo kicking in. Pulling out
a seat for her, Leo moved to the other side of the desk.

'Go ahead.' Wasting no time, he fixed her with sharp
grey eyes. With his elbows resting on the desk, his fingers, Emma noticed, had threaded together to make a
fist. 'Say whatever it is you have to say.'

Emma swallowed hard. His tone was harsh, his cold
demeanour not making this any easier. But, then, what
did she expect?

'I'm sorry...' she hesitated. 'About the article I
wrote.'

She hadn't meant to start with this, or maybe even
mention it at all. It felt as if years had passed since her
stupid mistake, rather than a couple of months. Events
since had overtaken it, overtaken her, skewing time. But
faced with Leo again, his blatant hostility, she knew she
should apologise. And she had to do it now, before the
maelstrom of what was to come took away this chance.

'You have come all this way to tell me that?' Distaste coloured his words. 'Because, if so, you have had
a wasted journey. I neither need nor want your apology.'

'But you are going to hear it anyway.' Her voice was
low but determined. Leo might not want to hear what

she had to say but she was still going to say it. Even if it was just to salve her own conscience.

'I made a mistake, Leo. That article was never meant to be published.'

'No?' Sarcasm scored his voice. 'So how come it ended up splashed all over the newspaper?'

'Because I filed the wrong copy.'

'You lied to me, Ms Quinn. You lied about the subject of our interview. All along you intended to produce that grubby little exposé.'

'No, it wasn't like that, truly.' Emma sat forward. 'I wrote that piece solely for myself. I was trying to make sense of what had happened…between us… I was confused and muddled… No one was meant to see it.'

'You expect me to believe that?'

'It's the truth, Leo.' She lowered her voice.

A bruised silence stretched between them. Emma looked down at her clasped hands.

'Well, either way, a vicious concoction of half-truths and fictitious garbage was written by you and printed in a national newspaper for the world to see.'

Emma winced. It was true, she couldn't deny it.

'The *Paladin* did issue an apology.' It was a feeble defence as his dismissive huff made clear.

'I just hope you felt better after you had got that off your chest.'

'Of course I didn't feel better.' Heat bloomed on her skin. 'I felt terrible. I lost my job. You made sure of that.'

'And are you surprised?'

No, she hadn't been surprised, not really. She had made a dreadful blunder.

'You are lucky I didn't personally sue you for slander.'

But she didn't feel lucky. Not at all. At the time losing her job had felt like the biggest calamity that could ever befall her. Now she knew it was just the start of her troubles.

A couple of seconds passed. Leo picked up a pen, tapping it on the desk.

'If that is all you came to say, I believe our business is concluded.'

'No.' Emma's stomach tightened. If only it were that straightforward. 'That is not all I came to say. There is another matter we need to discuss.'

'Go on.'

The weight of his gaze felt heavy enough to flatten her, every nerve-filled second dragging longer than the last. She took a brave breath.

'I am pregnant.' The words felt like boulders in her mouth, too big, too unruly. 'I am going to have a baby.'

Like a predator surprised by his prey, Leo remained perfectly still, his entire focus trained on her. Light played over the dark sheen of his hair, emphasising the stark angles of his face. His silence was total, torturous.

'I thought you should know.'

He rose from his chair suddenly, sending it flying behind him. Turning his back to her, he moved towards the window, feet planted apart, his broad shoulders set in a menacing line, silence following in his wake. 'And you are telling me this because…?' Addressing the view, his voice rang with measured authority.

'Because you are the father, of course.'

That silence again, before he slowly turned. His gaze, when it met hers, fierce enough to leave marks. Emma refused to blink, refused to swallow. She was not going to be cowed.

'And why should I believe you? After all...' his voice dropped to an almost conversational burr '...you have done nothing but lie to me since the moment we met.'

'I made a mistake and I have apologised for it.' Emma felt her nails dig into her palms. 'But, trust me, on this matter there is no mistake. You are the father.'

'And how can you be so sure?'

Deep breaths, Emma, deep breaths.

'Because I have never slept with anyone else.' She spoke slowly, deliberately, scratching around for every bit of control she possessed. 'You are the only person I have ever had sex with.'

Leo forced his lungs to start working, his mind scrabbling to take in this shocking news. *Pregnant.* Was that possible? He had used a condom every time they had made love, hadn't he? *Every time?* Now his tortured mind tried to recall, he couldn't be one hundred per cent sure. How many times had he taken her that night? His desire refusing to be sated, sleep evading him in favour of nestling up against her soft curves, sliding his hands between her thighs, pressing the hard length of him against her back, hooking his leg over her hip. And every time she had responded he had experienced the same surge of exhilaration, the thrill of possessing her anew never diminishing. Something about the sweetly naive way she had given herself to him had called to his most basic instincts. If he'd had a cave, he would have slung her over his shoulder and carried her off there, made her his and his alone.

But he didn't have a cave, just a ridiculously huge penthouse hotel suite. And in the morning, when he had realised his mistake, berating himself for taking advantage of such an innocent, he had left. For her own good. The flowers had been an ill-judged after-thought when the memory of her had plagued him throughout the day.

The irony was that while he was being racked with guilt, agonising over his behaviour, even whether or not he should have sent her flowers, Emma Quinn had been doing a hatchet job on him. Writing a vicious exposé that the most seasoned tabloid hack would have been proud of. Maybe she *had* submitted that article by mistake. He didn't care. None of that mattered any more. Except he now had an insight into exactly what she thought of him. Which could prove useful for future negotiations.

Seeing her standing there outside Raven Enterprises, all wide eyes beneath that brown fringe, had sent a bolt of shock right through him. Like he had conjured her up just by thinking about her. Because he *had* thought about her, way too much. Not only that, but his usual appetite for female company had deserted him. He had told himself it was all about pride. Being duped by Emma Quinn had made him question his judgement. It was no wonder he was in no rush to date again. No wonder he couldn't get the woman out of his mind.

And now here she was, back again. Ready to rock the very foundations of his carefully constructed world. Not with some stupid article, that seemed insignificant now. But with a pregnancy. A baby. His child.

If it was true. Leo sat down again. He needed to think this through calmly. Who was to say she was really pregnant? He already knew he couldn't trust her. This might be some scam to try and get money out of him. And even if she was, the baby wasn't necessarily his. Denial started to force its way to the surface. She could have hooked up with anyone in the past few weeks, found she was pregnant, then decided to say it was his because of his wealth. He had no idea what she was capable of. After all, he barely knew her, as he had discovered to his cost.

And hadn't he himself been the victim of just such heinous subterfuge? His own mother had concealed from her husband the true paternity of her elder son, to further her own ends. Leo had no intention of being taken in by Emma Quinn the way Alberto had been tricked by his mother.

Fixing her with a punishing stare, he hardened his voice.

'You will forgive me if I need further proof.' She didn't look as if she would forgive him. She looked like she wanted to hit him over the head with something hard and sharp. 'How do I know you are pregnant? You might be making the whole thing up.'

There was a brief, angry silence. 'And why on earth would I do that?'

Leo had to admit she did look genuinely nonplussed, as if she had no idea what he was talking about. With flushed cheeks and too-bright eyes, her hair falling over her shoulders, he was forced to remember how attractive she was. But then if you were trying to trick a man into raising a kid that wasn't his, you would make the effort to look appealing. Except she didn't appear to have made any effort. Wearing skinny jeans and a baggy check shirt, well-worn sneakers on her feet, she gave the appearance of someone who had thrown on the first things she could find. So why was he so drawn to her?

He shrugged, affecting an insouciance he was far from feeling. 'You wouldn't be the first gold-digger out to trap a wealthy man.'

Her look was one of utter disgust, but there was hurt there, too, like she had been verbally slapped. Well, so be it. He knew he sounded cruel, but the brute in him had taken over. If she was messing with him, she needed to be put straight.

'For your information...' she dealt him a vicious stare '... I have no desire to trap any man, least of all an arrogant, narcissistic one like you.'

On her feet now, she picked up her canvas holdall and slung it over the crook of her arm, snatching up her handbag.

'I came here to tell you that you are going to be a father, because, like I said, I thought you had a right to know. If I'd had any idea you would react in such an insulting, barbaric manner, I wouldn't have bothered. But at least I can go back to London with a clear conscience, knowing I have done my duty. And when my child is old enough to ask about his father, I will be sure to tell him, or her, that he was such a paranoid egotist he refused to believe in their existence. Goodbye, Leo. Have a nice life.'

She swung violently around, her bag catching on the arm of her chair, sending it toppling sideways. She hesitated, looking as if she was about to pick it up, then changed her mind and headed towards the door.

'*Aspetta!* Wait!' Leo was behind her in a couple of seconds, his hand on her arm. He could feel the resistance there, but eventually she turned to face him again. And the brute in him started to subside. Because the colour had dramatically drained from her face, her eyes wild. 'Come and sit down. We need to discuss this rationally.'

'If by rationally you mean you insulting me by telling me I am either lying about you being the father or that I have made the whole thing up, then I won't bother, thank you very much.'

'You need to calm yourself.' So did he, come to that. Leo pulled in a breath. 'Getting hysterical is not going to help the situation.'

'And neither is you behaving like a barbarian.' Emma glared at him, making his jaw clench. His composure was wearing dangerously thin.

Picking up her chair, he lowered her into it again, then went back to his position on the other side of the desk. He looked at down at his hands, clasped tight, the knuckles pulled white. This was one hell of a mess. How could he have been so stupidly, recklessly careless?

'Assuming everything you say is correct...' he saw her start to speak but cut her off with a raised hand '... we need to find a way to proceed.' Somehow, he had to minimise the damage. He just didn't know how yet.

Think, Leo. Think.

'You have been to see a doctor?'

She nodded stiffly. 'She confirmed that I was eight weeks pregnant. Nearly nine now. I am booked in for a scan at twelve weeks.'

'Very well.' His decisiveness returned in a crazy rush. 'You will have the scan here in Milan. I will find the best obstetrician.'

She was looking at him with a mixture of surprise and alarm, but he didn't have the capacity to work out what either emotion meant or how he should read them.

It made no difference anyway. They would be playing by his rules.

'In the meantime, you will move into my villa.'

Emma raised her chin, all pulled-tight defiance. 'Actually, I plan to return to London, tonight if possible.'

'No, Emma. That won't be happening.' The calm in his voice was getting harder and harder to find.

'You don't get to tell me what to do, Leo. I came here to tell you that I am pregnant, not to have you take over my life.'

'The fact that you are pregnant means inevitably our lives are going to change.'

'Yes, but—'

'No buts.'

He heard her sigh. Caught the flicker of unease behind the hard blue stare she wanted him to see.

'Leo...' She tried again. 'I think you have misunderstood my motives. I'm not looking for any sort of commitment from you. I'm not asking for anything. Rest assured...' she folded her arms across her chest '... I am quite prepared to raise the child alone if necessary.'

Leo felt his temper inching up by steady degrees. Emma Quinn had a lot to learn about him.

'And you misunderstand me if you think I would ever consider the idea of allowing my child to be raised anywhere other than with me.'

My child. Leo furrowed his brow. Where had that come from? Five minutes ago he had been prepared to deny its very existence, now he wouldn't countenance the idea of it being raised anywhere other than here, with him.

'So you accept the baby is yours?' Her words, deliberately aimed, were nevertheless spoken gently, inching their way towards a conscience he didn't want them to find.

Leo frowned deeply. '*Sì*, yes, I do.'

Roughly raking a hand through his hair, he let out a breath. Deep down he knew the child was his. He had known right from the start.

His initial stunned disbelief had quickly given way to stark acceptance. And with that had come the compulsion to take control of the situation—right away. Because Leo Ravenino had a reputation for thinking on his feet, making quick decisions and acting upon them. It had stood him in good stead in the world of business. It was his only option now. He had to bring some order to this chaos.

There was a moment of stillness, time holding its breath. It was Emma who eventually broke it.

'We don't need to make any decisions yet.' Her tone was more conciliatory now. 'The baby won't be born for another seven months after all. I can always come back in a few months, or you could come to London?'

'No. You will stay here, in Italy.' He was not going to be beaten on this one. He wasn't sure himself why he was so certain she shouldn't leave the country, only that the more she pushed against it, the more he was determined that she stay in Italy. Close by, where he could keep an eye on her. Before the board got wind of this fiasco and tried to use it against him. Or this woman went to the press. Or disappeared. Or all of these things. Like a spreading stain, he had to contain this situation as fast as he could.

From nowhere, a thought rushed into his head. As obvious as it was startling, it crowded his mind. Leo tried to let it settle, to test how it felt. Tried to work out if he had found the answer or totally lost the plot. Yes, it was the right decision. He allowed his gaze to travel over Emma's heated face, his conviction solidifying. This was the only course of action. *Marriage.* And the sooner the better.

A small chink of light glimmered through the black clouds. By marrying Emma he could keep a close eye on her, make sure there were no more unfortunate disclosures to the press, intentionally or otherwise. And there was another advantage. It would silence his critics on the board. That wretched article in the *Paladin* hadn't gone unnoticed. Comments had been made; whispers heard from behind closed doors. Raven Enterprises was riding high, but confidence in any company could crash as fast as it rose. One wrong deal, one more scandal could see the board members and shareholders start to turn, investors get nervous. News that he had fathered a child would not be well received. But if he were to get married, that was different. Settling down, starting a family, that was exactly what they wanted to hear.

Decision made; Leo just had to work out when to drop his bombshell. And despite everything, a little frisson of satisfaction went through him. Emma Quinn didn't know it yet, but she was about to be made an offer she couldn't refuse.

CHAPTER SIX

EMMA STARED OUT of the window as Villa Magenta finally came into view, the lush green parkland doing nothing to ease the tension gripping her body. Sure, it was beautiful, the golden turreted edifice standing proud against a deep blue sky as her chauffeured car swept her up the long driveway. A fairy-tale castle, which was very fitting, as none of this felt real.

Cutting short their meeting, Leo had announced in that high-handed, autocratic manner of his that Luigi, his driver, would be taking her to his villa in the country. They had matters to discuss, he had informed her. He would join her there later that evening. Too weary to argue with him any more, Emma had accepted his order. He was right, they did have things to discuss. Perhaps it would be better to spend a few days here to get things settled before she made her escape back to London.

The woman waiting on the steps introduced herself as Maria, Signor Ravenino's housekeeper. Removing Emma's tatty old bag from Luigi's hand, she showed her into a grand salon, all sky-high ceilings and modern chandeliers, and seated her on a designer leather sofa. Their eyes met as Emma thanked her for the proffered glass of water and Emma couldn't help but wonder what

this neat Italian woman must think of her, turning up
like this out of the blue, dressed in her scruffy jeans
and baggy shirt, hair all over the place and wearing not
a scrap of make-up. No doubt she was very different
from Leo's usual female guests. But Maria was giving
nothing away. She was way too professional for that.

Villa Magenta was every bit as beautiful as Emma
had imagined. She had read about the sumptuous villa,
recently purchased by Leo and completely restored at
enormous expense. She had even seen aerial photos. But
never had she imagined herself being here, especially
under these circumstances—pregnant with the Italian
magnate's child. Surreal didn't begin to describe it.

As she wandered from room to room, waiting for
Leo to arrive, Emma tried to order her thoughts, bring
some clarity to the mad situation she found herself in.

Her decision to come to Italy to tell Leo she was
pregnant had not been a difficult one. Every man had
the right to know he was going to be a father and every
child the right to know his father had at least been informed. Morally it was a no-brainer. And that was how
Emma had dealt with it. She had simply come here to
state the facts, expecting nothing in return. Because life
had taught her that expectation only led to disappointment. The only person she could rely on was herself.

Her own mother had shunned commitment in any
form, preferring instead to not tie herself to any one
man. Scarred by Emma's father, who had deserted
them when Emma had been just a toddler, moving to
Ireland and severing all contact, Mary Behenna had
decided never to rely on one man for her happiness,
instead choosing a succession of casual relationships.
And Emma had hated it. Hated the insecurity of having

a parade of different men walking in and out of their lives. Hated one man in particular. One thing was for sure, no way was she ever going to subject her own child to such an upbringing. She was determined that her son or daughter would have the stability that she had craved so badly. She just didn't know yet how to achieve it.

By seven p.m. she had driven herself half-crazy trying to figure out the best way forward, what to say to Leo when he finally deigned to show up. When there was still no sign of him by eight o'clock her anxiety had ratcheted up another notch, joined by simmering indignation. Maria had bustled in with a supper tray for her, but Emma had no appetite. Enquiring what time Signor Ravenino was expected home had produced no results, Maria looking slightly nonplussed that Emma thought she might be privy to such information.

Eventually, she decided to go outside and take a walk around the grounds. It was still light, and a beautiful evening. But she had only descended the first few steps when she realised she wasn't alone. Looking over her shoulder, she spotted Luigi lurking behind her.

'*Buonasera...*' Emma spoke uncertainly.

'*Buonasera,*' Luigi replied politely.

She went down the rest of the steps, heading towards the corner of the villa, when she heard the crunch of gravel behind her. Luigi was following her! By the time she had reached the formal gardens he was just a few steps behind. Quickening her pace, Emma darted behind a perfectly sculpted yew hedge, reappearing by a classical fountain, only to find Luigi had beaten her to it. This was getting ridiculous!

She was about to stomp over to him, make it clear that his presence wasn't wanted, that it was downright creepy, when it suddenly occurred to her. Luigi wasn't pursuing her out of some dodgy interest of his own. He was obeying orders. Leo's orders. He had been told to watch over her, make sure she didn't escape. How insulting was that? No, worse than insulting—it was criminal. She was effectively being imprisoned. Well, they would see about that.

Silently seething, Emma turned on her heel, marching back towards the villa and stomping in through the open front door. And straight into a solid wall of tailored suit. Winded, she pulled back, but not before Leo's hands had closed over her shoulders.

'I need to speak to you.' She shrugged off his hands, furious with the way her heart had done a traitorous little leap of welcome. 'Right away.'

'And I you.' Coolly shrugging off his jacket, he handed it to a waiting Maria, issuing some instructions to her in Italian before picking up the leather attaché case at his feet. 'If you would like to come into the salon.'

His arm snaked around Emma's waist to propel her forward and immediately the kiss of his heat through her clothes set her senses on fire. She tried to move away, but Leo stayed infuriatingly close, only letting go once they were in the salon, when he shut the door behind them, put down the attaché case, and crossed to the sideboard.

'Can I fix you a drink?' He spoke over his shoulder.

'No, thank you.' Emma took several steadying breaths while he had his back to her. 'Well, maybe some water.'

She watched in silence as Leo clinked ice into two glasses, filling one with water and the other one with a generous measure of whisky. He came towards her again, handing her a glass.

'Please, sit down.' He gestured to the sofa; his manner polite, relaxed. Not the same man she had left in Milan a few hours before.

Emma reluctantly did as she was told, then wished she hadn't as Leo remained standing before her, assuming a position of power.

'Maria said you hardly touched the meal she brought.' So they had been talking about her behind her back. She started to seethe again.

'I wasn't hungry, okay? And while we are on the subject of your staff…'

'They haven't been treating you well?' The tone of his voice suggested he would be prepared to fire them on the spot. But, then, he was good at that.

'No, it's not that. But what is the meaning of having Luigi follow me around?'

'I gave him instructions to keep an eye on you, that's true.' Leo seated himself on the sofa opposite Emma, placing his glass on the table next to him. 'Is that a problem?'

'Yes, it is!' she fired back. 'I tried to go for a walk around the grounds and he was tracking me like a bloodhound.'

Slowly, deliberately, Leo lifted his glass to take another sip of whisky.

'Under the circumstances, I thought it only prudent to keep track of your whereabouts.'

'Why, what did you think I was going to do?' Heat stained her cheeks. 'Run off with the family silver?'

'There is no family silver.' With tightly reined composure, Leo leaned back in his seat. 'However, you are in possession of something much more valuable. My child, my blood, my future.'

A shiver of awareness prickled over Emma's skin, the words resonating inside her. Sober. Portentous. There was no escaping how real this was—and how deep in she was.

'You seem to forget that I came here of my own volition.' Swallowing the tightness in her throat, she fought to stand her ground. 'I chose to tell you about the baby, when I could easily have kept quiet about the whole thing.'

'And you expect me to be grateful for that?' His words were chilling.

'No, not grateful exactly.' She looked down. 'But I didn't expect to be treated with such suspicion.'

'You have already betrayed my trust once, Emma. Therefore, I will treat you accordingly.'

Emma bit down hard on her lip. Leo had the infuriating capacity to twist her in knots every way she turned. 'I explained about that.'

His dismissive shrug said it all. But seemingly bored with tormenting her, he rose to pour himself another drink. Turning back, he trained his level gaze on her face.

'I have given some thought to the situation and come to a conclusion.'

Had he, now? But something about his fixed stare silenced Emma's rebellion.

'I have decided that we will get married.'

Leo watched Emma's mouth fall open in astonishment, not without some gratification. 'Married?'

'*Sì*, straight away. There is nothing to be gained by

waiting.' He pushed on, watching her reaction intently. It felt good to be in control again.

Panic joined her astonishment. 'No... I mean...we can't.'

'We can and we will.'

Her hands separated a length of hair, pulling it over one shoulder, twisting it round and around. 'I think you must still be in shock, Leo.'

Ha! The only one in shock was her. 'I can assure you I am perfectly rational.' He offered her a raised brow of sincerity. 'Marriage is the only solution.'

Her mouth twitched, then pursed. He could almost see her mind whirring as she formed her next objection.

'Why would you consider such a drastic step before the baby is even born?'

Leo hesitated. 'Because no child of mine will be born out of wedlock.' Despite his caution, the growled words rose from somewhere deep inside him. From a dark place where the wounds of his own illegitimacy still lingered. Still festered. And Emma had noticed. There was a quizzical look in those blue eyes. Leo reined himself back in.

'But this is the twenty-first century.' She continued to watch him closely. 'Nobody worries about a child being born out of wedlock these days.'

'*I* do.' Still too vehement, he could see Emma trying to figure him out, to get inside his head. Well that wasn't going to happen. 'Practical decisions need to be made. It is vitally important to have everything on a legal footing from the start. I have seen too many deals go wrong through lack of forward planning.'

'But this isn't a business deal, Leo.' Her soft mouth pouted. 'This is a baby!'

'All the more reason then.' He shot her a punishing stare, designed to silence her objections, to quash the curiosity in her eyes. And when that didn't work, he took a firmer stance. 'We are getting married, Emma, and that's an end to it.'

Emma watched as Leo picked up his briefcase, clicking it open to remove a sheaf of papers. For one crazy minute she thought it was a marriage licence, that Leo had somehow contrived to forgo any sort of ceremony and have her bound to him with nothing more than a signature. But it was a different contract he had in his hand. A pre-nup.

'I have had the details drawn up. It is all quite straightforward, but if you want my lawyers to go over anything with you, it can be arranged.'

'I have no interest in your vast fortune, Leo.' Emma tried for a scornful huff but beneath the derision lay hollow despondency. How could he know her so little as to think she would care about his money?

'*Bene*. Then there should be no problem.' He closed the space between them with a couple of strides, the papers in his hand, coming to sit beside her. So close she could feel the warmth from his thigh setting her senses alight, making it hard to breathe. 'I will leave these for you to read through. My lawyer will be here to witness our signatures in the morning.'

This was the way Leo operated. Ordered, fast paced, everything done to his precise instructions. Work, leisure, lovers. Only this afternoon Emma had brought chaos to his door. Now that chaos had been controlled, dealt with. She and the baby were just another business contract to be signed and sealed in the fastest possible time. A deal to be sewn up.

'I suggest the wedding takes place next week. Shall we say Tuesday?'

Very deliberately, he directed the full, lethal force of his gaze on her. As if he could impose his will through the power of his eyes alone. Maybe he could. Emma could think of a hundred reasons not to marry this man. A thousand. And yet...

Her heart gave a feeble stutter as she took in the hard perfection of his face, the strong, clean lines drawn tight, the granite set of his jaw. Despite the studied calm, she could sense the pressure he was under, see it in his eyes. The need to get this problem sorted. To fix it. Now. They were both fire-fighting the same blaze— just from different angles.

Duty, propriety and a fierce need to take control lay behind Leo's decision to marry. But first he had to future-proof himself against this woman who had the potential to wreck his life even more than she already had. Hence the pre-nup.

Whereas for Emma it was about protecting herself, her heart, her very sanity. She knew how badly this could end. Not because of any financial repercussions— his billions were quite safe. But because there was no escaping the way he made her feel. Somewhere deep down, somewhere she had no control over. Stirring up wild, reckless emotions that could only bring trouble. That could so easily tear her apart. The same emotions that had got her into this mess. There was no lawyer in the land that could draw up a contract to protect her from that.

'I don't remember agreeing to marry you at all, let alone on which day of the week.' She tilted her chin in rebellion, but turmoil swirled inside. Defiance was the only protection she had against this formidable man.

'But you will.' A command wrapped in silk. That cast-iron assurance that he could make her do whatever he wanted. That his will would be obeyed.

'Well, just supposing I did agree...' Emma felt like she was slowly slipping underwater, with nothing and no one to save her. 'What sort of marriage would it be? Just a legal document, or would you expect us to be a couple in...in the true sense of the word?'

She regretted her line of questioning before the words had even left her mouth. For Leo had gone frighteningly still, his dark stare, when Emma finally forced herself to find it, holding all the dangers she was trying so hard to avoid.

'That depends.' The thick swathe of his lashes lowered drowsily, but there was nothing sleepy about the challenge in his narrowed gaze.

'On what?' She rasped the question from a throat that was bone dry.

'On how we get on.' He lifted her hand from where it lay clenched in her lap, slowly unfurling her fingers one by one until they were both left staring at her open palm as if it could tell the future.

Emma snatched back her hand before every suppressed desire that Leo had to be deliberately stoking broke cover and betrayed her. The idea of permanently tying herself to Leo made her feel cut adrift from a reality that had already been dangerously shaky. Her stomach was twisting in all sorts of ways she couldn't begin to address. A complicated mix of emotions too tightly knotted to unpick. But she had to be practical now. She had to try and think with her head.

Agreeing to marry Leo *did* make sense, so was there any point in making a battle out of it? For one, she would never win. Leo Ravenino was a skilled negotiator, a ruthless businessman, someone who always got what he wanted in both his public and personal life. She had no chance against such a man.

But, more important, what would she be battling against? As she stared into Leo's flint-grey eyes, fighting with everything she had to ward off their hypnotic spell, she had to admit that the security he was offering was tempting.

Emma was used to fighting her own battles. She felt like she'd been doing it her whole life. She had been telling the truth when she'd informed Leo she would be prepared to raise their child alone. But that didn't mean she wasn't scared. She would love it with all her heart, she had no doubt about that, but was love enough?

It wasn't like she could go to her mother for guidance. Their views on parenting were polar opposites— Emma had no intention of subjecting her child to the sort of upbringing she had had. Far from being someone to turn to, her troubled relationship with her mother only added to her worries. What if there was something wrong in her genetic make-up, meaning that the child failed to bond with her, the way she had failed to bond with her own mother? Or that she passed on the insecurities that had so disturbed her own childhood, that still lurked dark and silent in her soul. The responsibility of raising a child was immense. Supposing she wasn't up to it?

And even if these fears were unfounded, there was the financial situation. Since losing her job she hadn't been able to find any work with real security, just picking up whatever she could to keep the money coming in. The gig economy may have kept the wolf from the door, but it was still there, crouching on the garden path, ready to pounce at any moment. She lived in a dingy room in a shared house, she had no help and very little money. Whichever way you looked at it, it wasn't a great way to welcome a baby into this world.

Then there was the other big one. Emma believed every child deserved two parents. Despite her mother refusing to ever discuss her father, let alone allowing her to try and contact him, it still hadn't stopped a young Emma from fantasising about finding him one day, establishing a relationship with him, maybe even going to live with him. A fantasy she had still nurtured as she had hurriedly packed her bags to leave home that fateful day. Only to have her mother cruelly dash her dreams. *'And don't go thinking you can run back to your daddy, because you can't. He's dead.'* Emma could still remember the look of triumph on her mother's face.

The wave of grief for the man she had never known had hit her hard, her sorrow far deeper and more painful than logic demanded. After all, he had abandoned her. Struggling to process the rest of her mother's gloating rage, she just about managed to glean a few details, that he had been killed in a riding accident two years previously. That the world was better off without him.

Her regret at never knowing her father still ran dark and deep. Given the choice, she knew she would never want to subject her own child to such a fate. And Leo was giving her that choice. He may have wreaked havoc in her life, turned it upside down and shaken it so hard she barely knew which way was up, but he was facing up to his responsibilities. He would always be there for their child; Emma had no doubt about that. He could give them both the security that had been painfully lacking in her own childhood. Be the second parent she so wanted their son or daughter to have. He was offering to marry her—no, not offering, insisting. But who was she to challenge that? Deep down, she, too, would like their child to be born in wedlock, in a way that neither she nor any of her siblings had been.

But the payoff for this security would be surrendering her independence, at least in the short term. Emma was under no illusions about that. Leo would expect them to live where he dictated they live, lead the life that he decided they would lead. No doubt it would be a life more comfortable, more extravagant than anything she had ever imagined. But Emma had never craved wealth. She did, however, have to accept that wealth brought opportunities. Maybe in time, when things had calmed down, she could use those opportunities to her advantage. Pick up her career again or go back to studying. Somehow she would find her independence again, she just needed to be clever about it.

Far more worrying was the way Leo affected her, deep down. Could she marry a man who squeezed her skin tight over her bones with nothing more than a glance from those grey eyes? Whose hard-edged words and ruthless determination left her feeling hollowed out, empty, as if she had lost something she hadn't even known she'd had?

Leo Ravenino was the epitome of the alpha male. A powerful, hugely successful man at the top of his game. A man who made all the decisions, called all the shots. Power was in his genes, in the set of his shoulders, the length of his stride. It was the blood in his veins, hard-wired in his brain. It made him who he was. To try and fight this control would be futile, like attempting to hold back the tide.

But for all his high-handed autocracy Emma was forced to admit that Leo's proposition was an honourable one. Should she just accept it? Did she have any choice?

'So, are we in agreement?' Leo broke the silence, his hands resting in his lap, his eyes never leaving her face, as if he had been tracking her thoughts. 'The wedding will go ahead on Tuesday?'

'Very well.' Emma took in the biggest, bravest breath of her life. 'I agree. It will.'

CHAPTER SEVEN

MORE DEEP BREATHS were needed today.

Morning had dawned clear and bright, like every other morning since Emma had been here at Villa Magenta. Outside, the parkland sparkled in the low sunshine, long shadows dramatically striping the grass, holding on to the dew, as the birds hopped around looking for their breakfast.

But the shutters to Emma's room were firmly closed. Her bed was empty, there was no sign of life. Until you went into the bathroom...

Pushing herself back on her heels, her fingers still gripping the cold porcelain of the toilet bowl, Emma felt her stomach churn again. Morning sickness. This was horrible. She concentrated on taking some restorative breaths, wondering how long it was going to last. Wondering why it had had to kick in today of all days—the day of her wedding.

Didn't she have enough to cope with already?

Mercifully, the ceremony was going to be very low key. Informing her that he had booked a register office in Milan for eleven thirty on the morning of the seventh, just five days after Emma had arrived in Milan, Leo had brusquely enquired whether she wanted any of her family to attend, and gave a nod of approval when she had declined.

Presumably he wanted to get this over with with the minimum of fuss as much as she did. Emma had never been one to fantasise about having a big white wedding, never given it much thought. But now she wondered what it would be like to be marrying through choice, not circumstance, to be embarking upon a loving relationship with someone you looked forward to spending the rest of your life with. To feel the swell of love in your heart, instead of this dull, hollow ache.

But she had to face facts. This was a marriage of convenience, even if nothing about it felt remotely convenient right now. She was tying herself to a ruthless businessman purely to secure the future of their unborn child. Marrying a man who, had she not been pregnant, she would never have seen again. And as for embarking on a loving relationship, looking forward to spending the rest of their lives together, neither of those things was remotely feasible. This was simply a practical solution to a difficult problem. A means to an end, a sensible, pragmatic approach to... Oh, God... Emma hung her head over the toilet bowl. She was going to be sick again...

The register office loomed into view, Leo parking his red sports car in one of the allotted bays with typical Latin flair. Coming around to open the door for her, Emma carefully stepped out, fighting to control her breathing, the thud of her heart...*the instinct to pick up her skirt and run as fast as she could in the opposite direction.*

Smoothing her hands over her dress, she concentrated on arranging it just so, the cream silk fabric suddenly completely absorbing, anything to distract herself from what she was about to do. Chosen from a selection that had mysteriously appeared the day before for her perusal, the style was a simple sleeveless shift, no frills or flounces but beautifully cut so that it fitted her perfectly. All that was left was to paste on what she hoped passed for a semblance of a smile. At least she had stopped feeling sick.

The ceremony was over in a matter of minutes. Stepping out into the bright sunshine, Emma no longer bore the name Quinn, the surname of a man she had never known, but Ravenino, the surname of a man she barely knew. There was an irony there, if Emma had the capacity to dwell on it. Which she didn't, because she was way too busy trying to control the jumping nerves, the surge of adrenaline threatening to take her legs from under her.

For a moment they stood silently facing each other, caught in the enormity of what they had just done. Shading her eyes, Emma tipped back her head to look at the man who was now her husband. Standing tall and proud, immaculately dressed in a dark suit and a grey tie, he was every woman's fantasy of the perfect groom. Hot, hard male perfection. But with his eyes hidden behind designer sunglasses, she wasn't able to read his expression, only his unnatural stillness betraying any sense of unease.

She realised she had no idea what he was thinking, what life held in store for her and her unborn child. Twisting the new gold ring on her finger, she found herself wondering, yet again, just how she was going to cope with a life so changed, with a man she knew so little of yet who still managed to affect her so deeply.

'I should get back to the office.' Leo's attention was drawn to his car, where a couple of teenaged boys were peering inside enviously. 'Do you have any plans for the afternoon?'

'No, not really.' Emma swallowed. What plans would she have, other than trying to figure out how she was going to live the rest of her life?

'Well, you have a car at your disposal.' Leo indicated the sleek black limo that Emma now saw had pulled up alongside the kerb. 'Luigi will take you anywhere you want to go.'

'And has he been instructed to make sure I don't escape, like before?' She raised her chin.

'No.' His lethal focus was back on her, steel in his voice. Emma blinked, her startled face reflected in the lenses of his glasses. 'We are married now, legally bound, the documents all signed. I no longer need to keep track of you. Should there be any transgressions, it would be a matter for the lawyers.'

Well, that made her feel *so* much better. 'There won't be any transgressions,' Emma huffed quickly. 'Not on my part at least.'

She hoped she sounded authoritative but, truth be told, she had no idea what she'd signed. When the lawyer had arrived to witness their signatures on the prenup, she had almost snatched the pen out of his hand in her hurry to sign her name at the bottom of the pages. Done to show Leo that she had zero interest in his billions, her hurry had also stopped her from thinking too deeply about what she was doing. Which had been pretty much the only way to stop her hand from shaking.

'Neither will there be any transgressions on my part.' Raising his sunglasses, Leo pushed them up onto his head, ruffling his hair in a way that made Emma want to reach out, delve her fingers through the silky dark waves, feel them brush against the sensitive skin of her palms.

'Well, that's good.' She lowered her eyes to try and escape the persistent, unwanted tug of desire. 'I'm glad we've got that sorted.'

'*Sì.*' There was a second's silence before Emma felt the stroke of a finger against her cheek, so light as to almost not be there but enough to draw her gaze upwards, to set her senses on fire.

'I hope you don't find the prospect of being married to me too alarming, Emma.' His finger traced down to her chin, his eyes solemn, questioning.

'No.' With the trail of his touch doing terrible things to her insides she hotly denied everything she felt. 'Why would I?'

'Why indeed?' The words were softly spoken, his eyes darkening.

Emma stayed very still. Alarm was only one of many emotions Leo could stir so easily in her. The mere touch of his finger was triggering the slow stealth of pleasure. A part of her wanted Leo to lean in and kiss her so badly her whole body ached for it. Another part wanted to bury herself in a deep black hole to protect her from all the ways he could make her feel. Did he know the effect he had on her? It was impossible to tell.

She pulled in a breath to calm her nerves. Whatever else, she had to try and keep her wayward feelings to herself. To let Leo see how he affected her, deep down in that intensely private place, would only give him more power. Strengthen a hold on her that was already far too tight.

'I'm fine.' She moved a step away to release herself from the torture of his touch. Her voice sounded hollow, even to her own ears. 'You don't need to worry about me.'

'Bene.' Replacing his sunglasses, Leo returned to the brisk businesslike persona that Emma felt far more comfortable with. *'A proposito*, I have booked a table for tonight. I thought we should do something to mark the occasion of our marriage. I trust you are okay with that?'

'Yes, of course.' Emma nodded with far more enthusiasm than she felt. 'That would be nice.'

Nice? She screwed up her face. It was hardly a ringing endorsement and judging by the way Leo's mouth had tightened, he'd noticed it too. But, then, he noticed everything.

'In the meantime, I suggest you go shopping for something to wear. Whatever you want. Luigi will drive you.'

Emma hesitated. Shopping wasn't really her thing, but on the other hand she had brought so few clothes with her she badly needed a new wardrobe. Maybe if she bought a few practical outfits, and something posher for occasions like this dinner, which she was already dreading, that would be a sensible idea. Of course, it wouldn't be long before she'd be needing maternity clothes, but Emma decided she'd cross that bridge when she came to it. There was only so much upheaval a girl could take at one time.

'Thank you.' She politely accepted Leo's offer. 'I'll do that.'

'*Prego.*' Stepping closer, Leo brushed her cheek with his lips, just once, just enough to send her senses reeling again. 'I will see you later.'

Emma stared in amazement at the items that had been delivered to the villa. Had she really bought all this? Spread out in her dressing room, the sleek carrier bags bearing famous names that Emma had only read about in magazines stared defiantly back at her. Boxes tied with satin ribbons invited her to step closer for a better look.

No, this was ridiculous. She had gone mad. She would send them back. But as she lifted the first dress from its scented tissue paper, holding it against her body, she was seduced all over again. The cobalt blue fabric was so beautiful, the cut of the dress so clever, holding her in in all the right places. Buying the matching shoes and bag had seemed eminently sensible at the time. As had purchasing those perfectly fitting jeans in four different colours, not to mention the silk shirts, the soft leather jacket, the floaty summer skirt. And the lingerie… Slowly lifting the lid on one of the pale pink boxes, Emma broke the seal on the black tissue paper, her heart beating faster as she withdrew the bra and matching panties. They were so stunning they were like a work of art. She ran her fingers over the sheer fabric, imagining wearing them, imagining Leo looking at her wearing them… Enough! Hastily replacing them in the box, she slammed the lid back down. Whatever was she thinking?

But the shopping trip had been Leo's idea, not hers. Maybe she needed to consider what *he* had been thinking. Was he trying to turn her into one of the women he normally dated? Sophisticated, refined. It was a depressing thought. Because Emma was neither of those things and never would be. She now bore the name Ravenino and lived in a stunning home fit for a princess. She would wear these beautiful clothes if that was what her husband wanted. But inside she was still Emma Quinn—still trying to find her place in the world.

Walking over to the window, Emma gazed out at the lush rolling green parkland. All her life she had felt like the outsider, even within her own family. Much as she loved her younger siblings, they were a very different breed. A tightly knit pack, they appeared unfazed by the fact they had different fathers, embracing the chaos of their lifestyle with a carefree enthusiasm solemn Emma had never felt, not even when she was a child. They were also adored by their mother. Something Emma had never been.

Leaving home, she had concentrated all her efforts on her journalism career, securing the job on the *Paladin* her proudest achievement, even if it had been short-lived. But if she was being totally honest, she had never really fitted in there either. Certainly not with the old-timers and their extended lunches and waistlines to match, or even the bright young things, discussing their social lives at high volume, meeting for drinks after work.

Now she had a new life to get her head around, a new role as wife and mother. Truth be told, she felt woefully ill-equipped for either, but that didn't mean she couldn't do it. With a surge of optimism Emma squinted against the evening horizon. Fancy clothes might not turn her into a Hollywood star, but she was strong and she was brave. And she had integrity. Her commitment to Leo might have been squeezed out of her, more coercion than seduction, but now she was married she was determined to make the best of it.

Not that it had got off to a very promising start… Since being at Villa Magenta, Leo had treated her with a polite but cool reserve. All traces of the man who had made her blush that first evening about the way their marriage might play out banished behind a granite façade. That was when she actually saw him at all. Spending his days in his office in Milan, when he finally returned to the villa their exchanges were brief, their evening meals taken separately.

And as for their bedrooms… Villa Magenta was huge and Emma's quarters were situated way across the other side of the building from Leo's. Almost like it had been done deliberately. If Emma had nurtured any foolish hope that this week she and Leo would start to get to know one another, maybe settle her nerves and silence some of the nagging doubts, it had been severely dashed. Leo clearly had no interest in any such thing. Standing in front of the officiant that morning, the tall, dark Italian beside her had been as much a stranger as ever. The enormity of what she was about to do more bewildering than ever.

But the deed was done. They were now married, legally man and wife, and Emma was going to hang on to her optimism and make this work. After all, tonight was their wedding night and, despite everything, she couldn't hold back a feral sort of thrill. Despite the aching uncertainty, her imagination kept leaping ahead, her memory rushing to recall the one night they had shared, where every erotic detail was meticulously stored.

Seeing Leo again, being in his presence, had brought

it all vividly back to life. The sound of his voice, the way he shrugged his shoulders, narrowed his eyes, used his hands to express himself all setting her pulse racing, her muscles clenching in memory. So far she had done her very best to hide her reaction from him. Maybe tonight she could stop pretending.

Heading towards the bathroom, Emma stripped off her clothes and stepped under the shower, the pounding hot water starting to ease the tension gripping her neck and shoulders. Reaching for the shower gel, she began to rhythmically soap her body, closing her eyes to inhale the delicious scent. Slowly, insidiously, a shudder of desire started to creep over her, stealthily making its way to her core. Snapping open her eyes, she turned off the water and wrapped herself in a white towel.

She didn't know what this evening would bring. She had no idea what was going on inside her husband's closed, calculating mind. But maybe she would wear that gorgeous underwear after all. Twisting a towel around her hair, she rubbed at the condensation on the mirror to find her wide-eyed reflection. Surely there could be no harm in that?

Leo watched through narrowed eyes as his wife made her way towards him. *His wife*. Words he had never thought he would use since leaving Ravenino. A situation he had never imagined finding himself in. His hands, held in his lap, flexed.

She looked different. Stunning, in fact. But the smile on her face was faint as she followed the maître d', the admiring glances of the male diners going unnoticed. Not by Leo, though. With a surge of possessiveness he rose, greeting her firmly with an outstretched arm, kissing her on both cheeks. She pulled away quickly.

'*Buonasera.*' He collected himself, drawing back her chair for her, signalling to the maître d' with a curt nod that his job was done.

'*Buonasera.*' She sat down. 'Not late, am I?'

She wasn't late. Unlike some of his previous dates, who seemed to think it added to their allure to arrive 'fashionably late', when all it did was irritate the hell out of him. From their brief acquaintance, he was relieved to find there were several things he liked about Emma. She had an inner strength that he respected. No tantrums, no dramas. A level of detachment in the way she held her head high, tipped chin that might even be called a challenge. Which was an interesting prospect. It had to be said: despite the turbulence of the last few days, she had conducted herself with the utmost decorum.

But right now decorum was the last thing on his mind—far from it. He allowed himself another glance as she opened her napkin, placing it on her lap, his eyes drawn to the creamy skin of her upper chest, the finely shaped collar bones. Unadorned. There was beauty enough as it was, but Leo found himself wondering what necklace he might buy for her, already imagining sweeping her hair to one side to fasten the clasp, lowering his head to plant a kiss on her skin.

This past week had been a lesson in self-control for him. A test to see how he felt about the startling new future he had embarked upon, to give himself time to figure out ways he was going to deal with it. And first on the list had been no sex. Keeping his distance would give him the chance to work things through in his head. Being seduced by her wide eyes and soft curves would not.

But tonight he found his resolve being severely tested.

In a gesture more hesitant than flirtatious, Emma touched her hair, which fell loose over her shoulders, meeting his gaze from beneath that fringe. Free from make-up, apart from a slash of red on her lips, she looked incredibly sexy.

Leo took a breath, reaching for his glass of water. No, he didn't want decorum tonight. He wanted wild, unfettered, hot, passionate, *dirty* sex. And he wanted it with the woman chewing her lip in front of him now. *Whoa*. He hurriedly took a sip of water then braced himself to face her again, feigning nonchalance. '*Sei molto carina*, you look lovely, by the way.'

'Thank you.' She gave an embarrassed laugh, a blush creeping up her neck, staining her cheeks until she had to reach for the menu to fan herself. 'Sorry.' She offered a rueful smile. 'It's the hormones, I expect.'

Was it? Or did she just not know how to accept a compliment? Did she really not realise how beautiful she was?

'The same hormones that made you so ill this morning?' Leo felt for safer ground.

Emma shot him a look as she laid down the menu. 'You know about that?'

'Yes.' He returned her stare. 'Maria told me you only wanted dry crackers for breakfast.'

'Is this how it's going to be?' Her shoulders stiffened. 'Are all my meals going to be policed by you?'

'I need to be aware if there are any problems.'

'It's not a problem, Leo, at least not for you. Morning sickness is perfectly normal at this stage of the pregnancy.'

Leo shrugged. He already knew that. In the short time since he had found out he was to be a father he had made it his business to learn everything he could about the various stages of pregnancy. Not that he had told Emma that.

'Are you hungry now?'

'Yes.' She seemed surprised at herself. 'I am.'

'*Bene*. Do you want me to translate the menu for you?'

'Yes, please.' Her shoulders dropped a little at last. 'In fact…' she peered at him from around the menu '… perhaps you should choose for me, as you know this restaurant, I mean.'

'*Certo.*' Leo suppressed a small smile at her solemn expression. 'As long as I'm not going to be accused of policing what you eat?'

'You have my permission.' She matched his teasing tone. 'This time.'

Emma ate her meal enthusiastically, which Leo noted with pleasure. She denied wanting a dessert, but he ordered her one anyway, watching with satisfaction as she spooned creamy gelato into her mouth, polished off the last biscotti.

They kept the conversation light, polite, both of them feeling their way, being careful not to trample on the new shoots of their relationship. But Emma had the sort of face that spelled out her emotions even when she didn't want it to, and more than once Leo caught a glimpse of wariness behind the composed façade.

'How's your water?' He posed the question lightly.

Emma laughed. 'Good. I can definitely taste the slopes of Mount Fuji.'

She had stuck to water all evening, her face a picture when the sommelier had presented her with a menu to choose from. Picking one at random, she had waited until his back was turned before self-consciously informing Leo that the water she normally drank came out of a tap.

He sat back in his chair, waiting for Emma to pick up the conversation again, watching her from beneath weighted eyelids. The hum in his blood had not left him all evening, the dark need to take his wife to his bed pressing down on him more forcefully than ever. But he would not give in to it. Yet.

He straightened his spine, resting his elbows on the table. He knew so little of the woman before him with the flushed cheeks and bright eyes. In his hurry to take control of the present he had scarcely given a thought to her past, her background. Now he found he wanted to know more. He wanted to know everything.

'Tell me about your family.' He steepled his fingers, resting his chin on the tips.

Emma's head came up, the flash in her eyes betraying her unease. 'There's not much to tell really.'

Instinctively Leo knew that wasn't true. He let his silence speak for him.

'It's just my mum and my siblings. My father left when I was a baby. I never knew him.'

Well, that made two of them.

'Siblings?'

'I'm the oldest of five. But we have different fathers.'

Interesting.

'And where do they live?'

'At the moment Somerset. But they move around, living in various communes in the south-west of England.'

'An unusual lifestyle?'

'Yes, well, alternative is the word my mother would use.' Her eyebrows went up. 'As a child I never went to school, never had a haircut, never wore shoes in the summer. It's the same for my brothers and sisters.'

'But you turned your back on that way of life?'

'Yes.' She traced a biscotti crumb around the tablecloth with her finger. 'Somehow I didn't really fit in. I was always the one begging to be sent to school. Can you believe that!' She pulled a face. 'I used to go to the library and read masses of books about children that went to boarding school and wore uniforms and played hockey, wishing I could be one of them. Stupid!'

No, it wasn't stupid. Leo's brief glimpse of the lonely child touched something inside.

'And your relationship with your family now?'

'I love my siblings, obviously. And my mother too. But our relationship has always been…complicated.'

'Why so?' Leo kept his voice deliberately neutral.

'A number of things.' Her sigh was short and sharp. 'I think she has always held me responsible for my father abandoning us.'

'But didn't you say you were just a baby?'

'Yes. But I was sickly and needy and screamed all the time. My father decided he'd had enough, leaving my mother to cope on her own. She was young, only nineteen.'

'But hardly fair to take it out on you?'

'Well, you can't help how you feel, I guess.' She tried for an accepting smile. 'And then later on there was something else…an unfortunate incident.' She stopped, pursing her lips together as if to physically prevent herself from saying any more. But there was no way Leo was going to let it rest there.

'What kind of incident?'

'It doesn't matter.'

'What kind of incident, Emma?' Leo heard the growl in his voice.

'Just a man my mother was seeing.' She lowered her eyes. 'He came on to me…and when I told my mother… well, let's just say she didn't take my side.'

Leo went very still, the primal, protective instinct inside him poised, ready to pounce. Emma's tone was even, clipped into neat sentences, but it was obvious how much this had affected her.

'When you say "came on" to you…' His hands curled into fists. 'What exactly do you mean?'

'It was my sixteenth birthday.' Another sigh, as if she was trying to make out it was all rather boring. *Like hell it was.* 'There was a party, the usual sort of gathering, people singing and dancing and drinking too much. Smoking weed. Not me, of course, I've never been into any of that. But this guy…my mum's boyfriend, he… he said he'd got a present for me, that I was to follow him. He led me into this copse, pushed me down and then…he threw himself on top of me.'

'*Cristo*, Emma!'

'It's okay.' She rushed to reassure him. 'I managed to get away. Luckily, he was really drunk, so I managed to wriggle out from under him.'

Leo felt his blood pressure soar. This scumbag needed to be tracked down and castrated.

'But when I told Mum, she didn't believe me. She said I must have led him on. That he had turned me down and now I was trying to make trouble.' Emma chewed the corner of her lip. 'So, the next day, when the guy left, she blamed me for that too. She said it was just like with my father...that I was a curse on her relationships...that I couldn't bear to see her happy. But it really wasn't like that.'

Her touching need to make him see she had done nothing wrong punched right through him. She didn't need to prove herself to him. Not in this instance. 'I was just trying to protect her, make her see the sort of man he really was.'

Dio santo. Leo had to take a moment to calm himself down. He already loathed this woman who had treated Emma so despicably. Instead of supporting her daughter, a vulnerable young woman who had just suffered a serious assault, she had turned against her, accusing her. What kind of mother did that? And as for that creature that called himself a man...

Instinctively he felt for Emma's hand, clasping it tightly in his. Too tightly, as Emma's wide-eyed surprise made clear. He forced himself to let go, to sit back, take a breath. But one thing was for sure. From now on, anyone who tried to hurt his wife would have him to answer to.

'And that was when you moved to London?' He needed to concentrate on the facts.

'Yes. I couldn't stay...not after that. We both agreed it would be best to put some space between us. I had signed up to do A levels at the local college, but those plans had to change. Moving to London meant getting a job as soon as I could and continuing my education in my spare time.'

'And I'm guessing that wasn't easy at such a young age.'

'No, but I survived. I'm tougher than I look.' Her brave smile killed him. 'And it was actually quite empowering. A whole new life.'

A life that Leo had torn apart. A life that she had been carefully constructing for years, brought down around her ears. By him. No! Leo corrected himself. Emma had brought this on herself. She deserved to be punished for that article, even if she had submitted it in error. The fault lay with her, no matter how much that innocent gaze might try and say otherwise.

He raised his eyes, ready to challenge the guilt that refused to be banished. The guilt that she had to be deliberately provoking with her guileless air. But, try as he might, he could see no sign of it in the glitter of her eyes. Instead he saw something infinitely more troubling. Along with her stoic acceptance, Leo realised that she was putting her faith in him to make things right. Not practically, he would have no problem with that. But emotionally. And that was what clawed at his throat. Because by looking for the good in him, she was searching for a man he could never be.

Leo tore his eyes away from her face. Suddenly the restaurant felt far too hot, stifling, oppressive, the other diners too loud, their chatter a cacophony of meaningless noise. He tugged at his tie, undoing the top button of his shirt to run two fingers around the inside of his collar.

Suddenly Emma's acceptance felt like deceit. Her faith like some sort of trickery to get inside his head. Why would she so easily forgive a man who had lost her her job, stolen her virginity, made her pregnant after one night of selfish indulgence? He had been taken in by her guile once, it wasn't going to happen again. Right now he needed answers.

'Why were you still a virgin the night we met?' The question shot from his mouth, harsh, interrogatory, as if *she* was the one who had done something wrong.

Emma gave him a defensive look, heavy lashes blinking rapidly. 'I don't know, I just was.'

'Not good enough, Emma.' The guilt inside him had sharpened like a blade and he would use it as a weapon. 'Why would someone who had never had sex before choose to do so with a man they had only just met?' *A man like me*. The words stayed silent in his head, but they were there, pressing down on him. *A cold, callous, son-of-a-bitch who took what he wanted and to hell with anyone else.*

'The simple answer is that I'd never met anyone I wanted to have sex with before.' Her frankness did nothing to ease his guilt. Far from gloating, it only increased his shame.

'And the complicated one?'

'Well, I guess if a psychiatrist got into my head, they might say I had "issues" about sexual relationships.' She gave another nervous laugh, twisting a strand of hair around her finger in that way she did. 'I was never comfortable with the whole "free love" thing that my mother subscribed to, different partners coming and going all the time. And then when that guy…did what he did…'

'He assaulted you, Emma. Why can't you just say it?'

'Okay, when that guy…' she took a breath '…*assaulted* me…it just turned me off the whole idea of sex at all. So I sort of closed myself down.'

Her softly flushed face stared back at him, open, innocent, torturing Leo still further.

'So I guess I should thank you.' A tentative smile
lit her eyes.

'Thank me?' The growl in his voice was meant as
a warning.

'Yes.' A warning she seemed determined to ignore.
'Because you made me realise I wasn't the hollow shell
of a woman I was starting to think I was. That the issues I had weren't insurmountable. You made me feel
for the first time, Leo. Really feel.'

Her hand fluttered down onto the table. For one
awful moment Leo thought she was going to reach
for his, take his balled fist and try and smooth it out
for comfort or support when he could give her neither.
But instead her fingers felt for the edge of her napkin,
smoothing over the linen.

A storm of conflicting emotions roared in Leo's
head. He had to get away. Right now. Put some space
between him and the bright blue eyes that were so innocently holding him to account. The softly seductive
curves that were still determined to torment his body.
But he would not give in to his desires. No way. Denial
would be his penance—even if it was too little too late.

'We should leave.' Scraping back his chair, he moved
behind Emma's so she would be in no doubt that this
was a command, not a suggestion.

'Of course.' He heard the surprise in her voice, but
she immediately gathered herself, standing up, flicking
her hair over one shoulder. Leo caught the scent of it,
soft and floral, assaulting his senses. His eyes strayed
to the pale skin of her neck left exposed. He swallowed
hard, fighting the urge to lean forward and press his

lips against that delicate flesh, to heat it with his breath, trail his mouth upwards. Lights flashed behind his momentarily closed lids.

She turned, so close now she had to be able to feel the heat emanating from him, sense the ache in his groin that refused to lessen. With a monumental effort he took a step back, his resolve tested beyond all limits when he caught the raw emotion glittering in her eyes.

Taking her arm, Leo hurried them between the tables of diners, heads turning in surprise at their rapid departure. Finally in the car, his hands gripped the steering wheel as he impatiently waited for Emma to put on her seat belt. With a roar of the engine he pulled the car out onto the road, grateful for Emma's silence. For the darkness all around him muffling his punishing thoughts.

CHAPTER EIGHT

'A GOOD STRONG HEARTBEAT.' The sonographer steadied the transducer over Emma's gel-covered abdomen. 'Can you hear that?'

Emma nodded, not trusting herself to speak. She *could* hear it—that remarkable pulsing, whooshing sound of a new life growing inside her. Standing close beside her, Leo had gone completely silent, not even appearing to breathe.

'You can make out the arms and legs quite clearly.' The transducer moved around. 'And here…this is the baby's spine.'

Emma stared at the blurry black and white image on the screen, emotion choking her throat. This was the most amazing thing she had ever seen.

'I'm just going to take a few measurements now, and then I'll be able to give you a predicted due date.'

Beside her, she felt Leo shift, clearing his throat before addressing the sonographer in Italian.

'Non ci sono problemi? E tutto normale?'

'Sì, tutto normale. Perfectly normal.'

The sonographer turned to smile at them both, before looking back at the screen. For a moment all went quiet as she clicked and dragged dotted lines over the images, concentrating on making her calculations, before finally pronouncing, 'February the fourteenth!' She beamed at them. 'A Valentine baby!'

A Valentine baby. Biting down on her lip to stop the wobble, Emma forced herself to smile back. This baby hardly epitomised love and romance, hearts and flowers. Far from it. Wild, uncontrollable passion in the moment, that couldn't be denied. But since then nothing but formal exchanges, polite, clipped conversations. It seemed to Emma that Leo was deliberately going out of his way to flatten their relationship. To douse the glimmer of any flame before it had a chance to catch hold.

But here was their baby, already so perfect, its tiny heart beating inside her, quietly preparing itself for its entrance to the world. And even though it had thrown her own world into chaos, forcing her to rush into a marriage with a man she couldn't begin to know, who refused to give anything of himself yet still threatened to undo her with his every glance, Emma knew this baby was the most miraculous, incredible thing that had ever happened to her.

Accepting the proffered paper towel, she rubbed the gel off her tummy, then straightened her blouse and swung her legs over the examination table. The sonographer was printing off the images of the scan, about to hand them to Emma, when Leo reached forward to take them from her.

'Grazie.' He didn't examine them but, folding the strip carefully, tucked it into the pocket of his white linen shirt.

'We will book you in for a twenty-week scan,' the sonographer continued. 'By then I will be able to tell you the baby's sex. Should you wish to know, of course.'

Back out in the bright sunshine, heading down the bustling street towards where their car was parked, Emma waited for Leo to say something. Anything. But instead he stared resolutely ahead, his lips firmly closed, and Emma felt the swell of hurt rise to her throat. Was he really not going to make any comment on the amazing thing they had just seen? Almost like he was pretending it hadn't happened. Eventually she could stand it no longer. As they stood on the edge of the kerb, waiting for the lights to change so they could cross several busy lanes of traffic, she shaded her eyes to gaze at his profile.

'So, what did you think?' She kept her voice level, non-confrontational, even though his lack of emotion made her want to beat her fists against his granite chest. 'The scan was remarkable, wasn't it? The way you could see so much when the baby is still so tiny.'

'*Sì.*'

Emma waited. *Was that it? Was that really all he had to say?* But despite the growing ache, like he was pressing on a bruise, despite the imperious profile that refused to turn her way, Emma would not give up. Because giving up meant admitting defeat. Admitting that not only did Leo have no time for her but he had no time for their baby either. And that was more than she could bear.

'How big did she say it was?' She swallowed down her hurt, her pride. 'One and a half inches?'

'*Sì.*' He was staring hard enough at the traffic to make it stop by willpower alone. A bus slowed as it went past, and Emma saw the two of them reflected in its dark glass windows. Leo, stony faced but still effortlessly cool in casual chinos, standing almost a foot taller than Emma, whose hair was blowing around her shoulders. They looked mismatched. They looked like strangers.

When the lights finally changed Leo took her arm and hurried her through the throng of pedestrians. On the other side, Emma hastened her stride to match his, even though the intense heat was making her sweat. She pulled in a breath, digging deep to find her last reserves of resilience. Determination, stubbornness, a blind optimism that she could start to make Leo start to thaw driving her on.

'Shall we find out the sex of the baby at the next scan?' The speed of their steps was making her breathless. 'Or would you rather keep it as a surprise?'

'I don't know, Emma.' At last he stopped, turning to address her, but his words were cold, irritable. 'And frankly now is not the time to discuss it.'

Emma met his dark stare. 'Why not?'

'Because I have a pile of work waiting for me on my desk, two conference calls to make, and a trustees' meeting to chair. So, if you don't mind, perhaps we can leave this conversation for another time.'

They had reached the side road now where Leo's car was parked, its lights flashing as Leo clicked the key fob.

Emma looked away, defeated. She was so tired of pretending. To herself and to Leo. Tired of trying to make out that everything was okay when it wasn't. Tired of swallowing down the knot of hurt, only to have it unravel inside her, wrap itself around her internal organs and squeeze ever tighter. She was tired of being brave, constantly having to fight off rejection. Rejection that hurt more with every passing day.

These past few weeks had been exhausting. Physically and mentally draining, until Emma wasn't sure she had a drop of resilience left. She had started this journey not knowing what to expect of her marriage, but that hadn't stopped her from nurturing foolish hopes. Hopes that she and Leo might start to get to know and like each other, take pleasure in each other's company, not just as prospective parents but as man and wife. In every sense of the word.

Ha! Bitterness tore through her. At her own naivety, stupidity. Because those hopes had been cruelly crushed. Not least on her wedding night.

She still cringed when she thought back to the meal in the restaurant. All done up in her posh frock, trying to be positive about a future she had no control over, optimism cloaking common sense. She had put on fancy underwear, for God's sake. Paused in front of the mirror to admire what the clever cut did to her silhouette. How it made her feel sexy. She had imagined Leo looking at her, wanting her, the way she wanted him, despite everything. Taking her...

Now her cheeks just burned with humiliation. For Leo had not wanted her. Despite her best efforts to play the part of his new bride, she had got it all wrong. As had been clearly demonstrated during the silent ride home, the curt nod of goodnight as the doors of the villa had closed behind them. The sight of his broad back striding away from her.

Alone in her bedroom she had stripped naked, balling the offensive underwear to hurl it into the corner of the room, hot tears pricking the backs of her eyes.

But a new day had brought a new perspective. Giving herself a stern talking to, Emma had thrown back the curtains, determined to face facts as they were. In short, she had to get real. Leo had only married her because of the baby. There was no secret about that. But she had married him for the same reason. In that regard they were quits. She just had to keep her head straight, swallow down the humiliation of that night and focus on what was important. Their baby. The baby was all that mattered.

Which was why this latest rejection was such a slap in the face. Leo might not be interested in her, but his lack of interest in the baby hurt—really hurt. And like a mother lion Emma felt her protective instincts rising up, heating her blood. She opened her mouth to tell him just what she thought of him, then stopped. What was the point? It would be like attacking a lump of granite with a rubber hammer. Exposing nothing but her own deeply held insecurities.

Instead she turned on her heel, marching off in the opposite direction as fast as she could, her sandals snapping on the pavement, hair flying. If she put enough space between them, she might just be able to control the turmoil that was threatening to engulf her. The hurt that was threatening to crack her apart.

But Leo was beside her in a second, his hand on her arm, turning her to face him. His shadow fell across her, his face a tight mask of annoyance. 'Where do you think you are going?'

'Anywhere as long as it's away from you.' Emma forced the words through a choking throat.

A muscle spasmed in Leo's cheek, his famous control slipping very slightly. 'Explain yourself.'

Just that. Cold, imperious. Emma tried for a dismissive stare, tried to start walking again but Leo blocked her way, waiting.

'How about you work it out for yourself?' Her breath heaved in her chest.

'I will do no such thing.' A dark scowl marred his face. 'You are coming back to the car and I am taking you home.'

'No.' Emma stood firm, although the quake in her voice was getting harder and harder to control. 'I will find my own way back, thank you very much. And it's not my home, anyway. I don't have a home.'

'What are you talking about?' Leo's fierce gaze scorched over her face. 'Of course you have a home. Several homes, in fact.'

'They are not my homes, they're yours. Everything is yours—the cars, the houses, even the clothes I am wearing were bought by you.' Her words rushed out, trying to beat the tears she knew weren't far behind. 'All I have is a baby you don't want.'

The air between them stilled.

'Now you are being ridiculous.'

'Am I?' Her voice finally cracked and she stifled a sob. 'Or am I just spelling out the truth?'

'Look, Emma…' She could see the effort it was taking to try and be reasonable in the set of his jaw, the grit in his voice. His hands found her arms, lightly running over her skin, leaving it prickling beneath his touch. Reaching her wrists, he pressed his thumbs against her ragged pulse. 'I can only assume this unreasonable behaviour is due to your condition.'

Emma took in a breath of scorched air. Shaking his hands from her wrists, she was ready to fly at him, but a woman was coming along the narrow street behind them, walking a tiny dog on a lead.

'It has nothing to do with my condition.' She hissed the words through clenched teeth. The woman was alongside them now, looking at them curiously. Even the little dog seemed interested. Fighting to compose herself, Emma waited for them to pass. 'And everything to do with your arrogant, overbearing attitude.'

'Is that so?' Leo shoved his hands into his pockets, his casual pose fooling neither of them. 'You are very quick to point out my failings, Emma.'

'It's not difficult.' Her eyes blazed.

'Then I am only sorry that I am not the man you want me to be.'

'No, you're not sorry.' Her words came out in a rush of hurt and fury and sheer frustrated impotence. 'You couldn't care less. You intend to carry on with your life exactly as you always have—working and travelling and doing deals and, and…bedding beautiful women too, for all I know.'

Silence fell between them like a held breath. Emma looked away, heat suffusing her body, sticking her hair to the back of her neck, constricting her throat. She heard Leo shift his position.

'No, Emma.' His voice was pulled taut. 'There will be no more women. I am married to you now. I have made my vows, and I will respect them. Always.'

'You say that now, but—'

'No buts.' Cupping her jaw with one warm, strong hand, he lifted her chin until she had no choice but to fall into the drugging intimacy of his gaze. 'I will be totally faithful, in the same way as I expect you to be to me.'

Emma blinked hard. The idea of her ever being unfaithful to Leo was so ludicrous it was almost funny. She knew in her heart that she would never want another man. No one could ever match up to Leo. He would be her one and only lover. She could already picture herself, old and alone, Miss-Havisham-like, pining for the man she could never have. Maybe minus the wedding dress…

And yet Leo's declaration, the sheer intensity of his grey stare, did not match her bleak, chaste vision. It was controlled and commanding, as always, but provocative too, searching for some sort of confirmation.

'Well, of course,' she mumbled beneath her breath. 'That goes without saying.'

'Then we have a starting point to work from.' Like a switch flicked, Leo's mood changed to one of quiet intent. With his head on one side, he raised his hand, his thumb and forefinger tracing along her jawline with a caress so soft it was almost not there. But Emma's eyelids still flickered with the unwanted tremor, her skin blazing in the wake of his touch. 'It is incumbent on us both to try and make this commitment to one another work.'

'As long as it's all on your terms?' Emma dug around for the last of her defiance, which was being seriously undermined by a dangerous heat that was creeping over her every nerve.

The effect this man had on her was astonishing.

'Terms to be arranged.' The words were businesslike but his swift, assessing gaze anything but. 'Now…' All brisk authority again, he dropped his hand, shoving it into the pocket of his trousers to retrieve the car key.

'Are you going to accompany me back to the car, or am I going to have to carry you kicking and screaming?'

Emma screwed up her eyes, refusing to let that image permeate her brain.

She felt Leo slip his arm around her shoulder, taking advantage of her confusion, shepherding her forward. And as she found herself obediently sliding into the seat beside him, studiously avoiding his imperious profile as he started the car, she wondered for the umpteenth time how on earth she had ended up in this crazy situation. And, more importantly, how was she going to find the fight to survive living alongside this man?

Leo took the scan photograph out of his pocket and laid it flat on his desk. Only now he was alone in his office could he trust himself to look at it properly. Being in that claustrophobic consulting room had him shut down. The shock of seeing the beating heart of his baby punching emotion right through him. Hard and deep. Raw. Stealing his breath in a way he had never experienced before.

Something about the look of expectation on Emma's face had been the final straw, pushing him over the edge. His only option had been to get out, take some time to process what was happening. Deal with it.

Now he studied the row of images in meticulous detail, his finger tracing the baby's skull, its profile, the tiny jut of its nose. His son or daughter. He felt the muscles in his gut knot in response.

Once upon a time, having a child *had* been part of his life plan. Back when he'd assumed he would be the next Conte di Ravenino, when he had agreed to marry Cordelia Moretti, he had seen producing an heir as part of the job, a duty he would have performed with due diligence, like any other task necessary for the good of his family.

Fool that he was, even after the title had been so cruelly snatched away from him, a misguided sense of honour had seen him prepared to go ahead with their marriage. Leonardo Ravenino was a man of his word after all. He didn't let people down.

What an idiot!

He still squirmed with horror at the look on Cordelia's face when he had gone to see her with his noble reassurance. Surprise, panic even, quickly masked by a cool detachment. That wouldn't be necessary, she had briskly informed him. Different plans had been made. After a respectful period of separation she would, in fact, be marrying his brother Taddeo, the true Conte di Ravenino. *Had no one told him?*

No, no one had. Because he hadn't mattered any more.

Betrayed by his mother, let down by his fiancée, Leo had resolved there and then never to trust a woman again. Cordelia may have hurt his pride more than his heart, but he refused to ever be manipulated by the fairer sex again. From now on he would remain firmly single. No more engagements. No emotional ties or complications. And definitely no children. He had been adamant about that.

Now look at him. Once again, the course of his life had been changed by a woman. But this time the consequences were far more serious than hurt pride. More serious even than losing the principality. This was momentous.

Leo tore his eyes away from the images of his child,

roughly raking a hand through his hair. His mind went back to Emma's furious outburst in the street earlier, tensing his muscles. The first time he had seen her temper, felt the flash of its fire. It had had a strange effect on him. Irritation, yes, but a sort of triumph, like her display of emotion had unlocked something between them, banishing his brooding mood. And arousal too—though that was never far from the surface with this woman.

But he would not allow Emma to think that having public tantrums meant getting her way. Or private ones, for that matter. He'd seen too many of them these past few years—accusations hurled at him from spurned lovers, women with quivering lips and flashing talons declaring what a bastard he was. Maybe they were right. Technically, they definitely were.

Emma's no-holds-barred article had certainly painted an ugly picture of him. Describing him like some modern-day Casanova, a philandering, heart-breaking womaniser, she hadn't held back with colourful adjectives, all delivered in that sanctimonious way that suggested she herself would never be taken in by such a man. That she was far too clever for that. Except of course she wasn't. Emma may have chosen to leave out the night they had spent together, but that didn't mean it hadn't happened. She couldn't erase the twist of their limbs, the collision of heated skin, the sweet deep shudders that had racked her body, culminating in the screaming of his name. No matter how much she wanted to. And she certainly couldn't erase the baby growing in her womb.

Then there were the toxic references to his background, her veiled suppositions about the Principality of Ravenino. That he had been stripped of his title because of some sort of infidelity, betrayed his fiancée, embarrassed his father, deemed unfit to rule because of his debauched behaviour. She had got it all wrong, of course, but that was no consolation.

He had had no choice but to pick up the phone and demand that Emma Quinn be fired from her position at the *Paladin* with immediate effect. He had been perfectly within his rights. Had he chosen to he could have brought the whole damned newspaper to its knees. But the dark truth was it was Emma alone he had wanted to punish. For holding a mirror up to his hedonistic lifestyle, reflecting an image he didn't want to see.

But even more so for having the audacity to poke about in his past, for trying to uncover what he'd been so determined to leave behind. Just the thought of her picking over the bones of his life felt like the worst sort of betrayal. Gleefully piecing together all the snippets of information she could find, the more heartbreaking, the more tragic the better, so she could cobble together that nasty piece of salacious trash.

At the time fury had overridden any other emotion. But time had turned that fury into a small, hard ball. It still sat within him, but no longer carried the same weight. Events had overtaken them. Other emotions had crept in. And one of them was guilt. For the way he had treated Emma that fateful night, and the way he was treating her now. An unwelcome visitor, it took Leo by surprise every time it sank its claws into him. And he didn't like it. Not one bit. It made him feel weak. Exposed. It meant he had to redouble his efforts to hold her at bay.

Which was why he had had to shut her down earlier, silence her chatter. His new wife had to learn that the more something mattered, the less he was going to talk about it. Circumstances had brought them together, but that did not give her the right to get inside his head. He would provide every possible comfort for Emma and the baby. Complete security. And complete faithfulness. But that was it.

Leo sat back in his chair, swinging it to one side, staring unseeing at the sprawling city of Milan far below. Everything had happened so fast he had never even considered the moral implications of his marriage. But he'd meant what he'd said. He would be totally faithful. Judging by the crazy way his body reacted to her, Emma was more than enough to fulfil his needs. When the time came, he would make damned sure he fulfilled hers. It would be his pleasure. Literally.

Physically he didn't doubt they could make this work. But emotionally Emma had to realise what she was working with. A man who didn't do feelings and who certainly didn't do love. She only needed to go back to her own article to find the truth. Leo Ravenino was a man with a heart of stone.

And the sooner she realised that the better.

CHAPTER NINE

IT WAS LATE by the time Leo arrived back at the villa. Work, when he had finally been able to put his mind to it, had provided temporary relief from the roar in his head.

There was no sign of Emma when he walked into the salon. Neither was she in the library or out on the terrace. A creeping sense of unease flooded over him as he paced from one empty room to the next. Where the hell was she?

Impatient feet took him in search of Maria, who informed him she had seen the *signora* less than an hour ago when she had returned her supper tray to the kitchen. Apparently, she had told the cook she was going to take a walk around the grounds before dark.

Leo slowly let the air out of his lungs. He needed to calm down, stop overreacting. Stop letting his wife's slender hands from metaphorically grabbing him round the neck.

He found her down by the lake, sitting on a bench that was catching the last amber rays of sunshine. Speaking into her phone, she hadn't heard Leo approaching and he paused, listening. It seemed to be an intense conversation, judging by the way Emma was twisting her legs around each other, her head bowed so that her hair fell forward, obscuring her face.

'Well, it's not as if you would have come to the wedding.'

Leo edged closer.

'But that's just it, I didn't want to be talked out of it. Leo and I both agreed we wanted to marry before the baby was born.'

She twisted a strand of hair tightly around her finger.

'I know that, Mum. I know there are alternatives. I've lived with the alternatives all my life. But I needed to do what was right for me. And for the baby.'

The catch in her voice carried on the air, stiffening Leo's spine.

'I'm not asking you to understand. I'm just telling you because I thought you'd want to know.'

Leo had heard enough. Throwing back his shoulders, he stepped out of the shadows.

Emma jumped, the phone almost falling from her hand. Glaring at Leo, she ended the call with a rushed goodbye.

'Has no one ever told you it's rude to listen in to other people's conversations?' She pushed back her shoulders.

Leo ignored her comment, sitting down beside her, making her edge further away.

'Your mother, I take it?'

'Yes.' Emma looked down at her fingernails.

'Passing on her congratulations, no doubt.' Sarcasm masked the vitriol he felt for that woman. Emma's account of the way she had treated her still burned a hole inside him.

'Not exactly. She doesn't believe in marriage. Especially to capitalist billionaires.'

Leo made a dismissive noise in his throat. He didn't give a damn what this hateful woman thought of him and his way of life, but the fact that she couldn't support her daughter really got under his skin.

There was a beat of silence.

'Why do you do it?' Leo turned to look at his wife. Wearing a bright yellow cotton dress, she made him think of sunshine. But her mood was grey.

'Do what?'

'Why do you let your mother get to you like this?'

'I don't know what you mean.'

'Yes, you do, Emma, you know exactly what I mean.'

Emma shrugged. 'Because she's my mother, I guess.'

'And that's enough, is it? That gives her the right to treat you like dirt for the rest of her life and for you to accept it?'

'No, of course not.' Flustered, Emma looked down at her lap. 'And I never said she treated me like dirt.'

She hadn't had to, it was obvious. Leo glowered into the fading light, his gaze travelling across the lake, at the golden rays rippling across the water, the darting shapes of the low swooping swifts.

'Well, I'm just saying it might be nice if your mother started to show you some respect. That's all.'

Emma's startled look twisted something inside him. Was it really such a shock that he was sticking up for her? It occurred to him that maybe she had never had anyone on her side. That she was still fighting her own battles now. And he had done nothing to help with that.

They hadn't exactly parted on good terms earlier in the day. The journey back to Villa Magenta had been conducted largely in silence, Emma staring resolutely ahead, her profile, when Leo had sneaked the occasional glance, very still, framed by the curtain of brown hair. Dropping her at the steps to the villa, he hadn't even gone in with her, turning the car and heading straight back to his office in the city. His parting words that he would see her later had been ignored in her hurry to get out of the car. His actions had seemed reasonable at the time. Now they felt harsh. Petulant even.

'And if she can't do that, you need to cut her out of your life.' He drove home his point with ruthless conviction.

But Emma's gaze had sharpened. 'Like you have with your family?'

Well, that would teach him. By trying to help, by starting to *care*, he had fallen straight into her trap. Suddenly his wife was no longer a wronged daughter but a prying journalist again.

'Still looking for a scoop, Emma?' his voice growled.

'No.' She shook her head. 'I'm not asking as a journalist. I no longer have that job, if you recall. I am asking as your wife. The mother of your child.'

'Yes, I do recall.' Bitterness tore at his voice. 'I recall the pack of lies you wrote about me, about my reasons for leaving Ravenino.'

'Then why don't you tell me the true story?' Her voice was soft but determined, designed to throw a cloak over his anger. But it didn't work. Especially when it was followed up by her next question. 'Why did you never inherit the title of Conte di Ravenino?'

Just hearing Emma use that title, *a title that should have been his*, felt like sandpaper scraping across his skin. His reaction was irrational, he knew that, but Ravenino had long since stolen the rational part of his brain. No matter how hard he had tried to ignore the place, to bury his resentment beneath the distractions of work, women, more work, more women, it still pulsed inside him like an angry beast, red and raw and very much alive. It occurred to Leo that Emma too was capable of robbing him of rationality. This was a bad combination. He needed to shut her down. Right away.

'My family is dead to me.' He turned his profile on her. 'That's all you need to know.'

'But why?' Still she pushed. Against the wall built of years of resentment.

A bruised silence fell between them, the sky darkening along with the mood.

'Because some things are best left to rot in the dark.' The effort to remain rational was costing him dear. Even then he had said more than he'd meant to.

'And some are better brought out to the light.'

'What's this, Emma?' His dismissive snarl was intended to wound. 'Some homespun pearls of wisdom from the little book of love and peace? Careful, your hippie roots are starting to show.'

'So what if they are?' Far from leaving her cowed, it seemed the more he turned against her, the stronger she came back at him. 'At least I had the courage to share my background with you. At least I didn't pretend it didn't exist.'

'Che diavolo.' Leo's curse split the air. Pitching away from her, he dragged a hand across the back of his neck. 'Very well. You win.' He aggressively pushed back his shoulders. 'My mother was a manipulative, adulterous liar. There, is that good enough for you? Does that satisfy your thirst for scandal?'

'I'm not looking for scandal. Just the truth.'

'I think you will find they are one and the same.'

Slowly he turned back to face her. 'I spent the first twenty-eight years of my life assuming I would inherit the title of Conte di Ravenino, only to discover just before my father died that I had no entitlement to it at all. Because I am not a true Ravenino.'

Emma blinked against the force of his words. 'But why? I don't understand.'

'*Certo*, that's the name on my birth certificate, the only name I've got, but Alberto Ravenino was not my real father.'

'You are the result of a love affair that your mother had with someone else?' He could see her trying to put the pieces together.

Leo gave a dismissive laugh. 'What a romantic you are, Emma. I appreciate your attempt to make my conception sound like the result of a romantic tryst, but in all probability, it was just as likely to have been a sordid fumble in a back alley somewhere. And no doubt a great inconvenience to all concerned. My mother duped Alberto into thinking he was my father. Lied to him all their married life. Only on his deathbed did he face up to his suspicions. The idea of meeting his maker while carrying the burden of doubt must have focussed his mind.'

So she had got it all wrong. Emma twisted her hands in her lap as silence settled between them, muffling the night. All those awful things she had written about him, that he had lost his birthright because of his own immoral behaviour were completely untrue. He had been wronged. By his family and then by her. Heat flushed her cheeks as she turned to him.

'I'm so sorry, Leo.'

Immediately Leo stiffened. 'I don't want your sympathy.'

No, of course he didn't. Leo Ravenino was all about strength, power, self-control. Sympathy was for the weak. For lesser beings than himself.

'I'm not offering sympathy.' She edged closer nervously. 'I want to apologise for those things I wrote about you. I'm very sorry.'

Leo's shrug did nothing to assuage her guilt.

'If I had known the truth, I would never have—'

'Spare me the excuses. I'm not interested.'

'But I want you to understand.' Shame lanced through her, choking her throat. 'I didn't know you then!'

'You still don't know me, Emma.' His cold, clinical voice was designed to flatten all emotion. 'I doubt you ever will.'

Emma bit down on her lip, determined to halt its tremor. He was right, they didn't know one another. Despite the intimacy they had shared, the consequences and the actions they'd had to take because of those consequences, they were little more than strangers. Emma had hoped, assumed even, that gradually they would learn about each other, learn to trust. *Maybe even to love.* But Leo had no such goal. Instead he was using the wall of his past like a barrier to keep her out.

Taking a breath, she turned away to look at the view, Leo's proud, resolute profile making it clear there was no point in prolonging her apology or offering anything else to try and make amends.

She forced her hands to unclasp, and instinctively they spread over her stomach, cradling the invisible baby. Their baby. Despite Leo's harsh manner, his hurtful refusal to let her into his life, she couldn't help but feel for him. For what he had suffered. Speaking with such bitter passion about his mother and the man he had thought to be his father, he had exposed just how hurt he had been. How wounded he still was. His contempt for the man who had fathered him, who hadn't been honourable enough to face up to his responsibilities, still pulsed like a living beast.

Emma was learning that Leo was all about honour. If you cut him open it would be written through him like a stick of rock. He may have broken many a woman's heart, but he didn't cheat. He was a hugely successful businessman, but he'd made his billions fairly, through hard work and intuition. And if you were foolish enough to get someone pregnant…you did the decent thing. Straight away. No questions asked. No matter how much your life might be inconvenienced by it.

Unlike her own father, he would never abandon their child.

His strong moral values should have been a comfort to Emma—they *were* a comfort. She knew that in practical terms Leo would be there for them for ever, come what may. She knew that they would want for nothing. But she also knew that she was walking on increasingly dangerous ground. Because the further she tunnelled inside Leo's head, the more she managed to discover about him, the more vulnerable it made her. Inch by inch, Leo Ravenino was winding his way around her heart.

She shifted in her seat, sitting on her hands to keep them still. Beside her Leo had gone quiet, staring sullenly into the night. But beneath the dark glower, the simmering hostility, some basic instinct made her want to try and ease his burden.

'So you don't know who your real father is?' She spoke cautiously into the dark.

'No. Neither do I care.' Leo's jaw clenched. 'Any man who turns his back on his unborn child, lets him be raised by another man, doesn't deserve to be called a father.'

'You don't know what the circumstances were at the time. Your father may not even have known of your existence. Maybe your mother had her reasons for not telling him.'

'There are no excuses. What my mother did was beneath contempt and the man I thought to be my father was too weak to do anything about it.'

'Yes, but—'

'No buts.' Leo's dark silhouette stiffened, his voiced laced with irritation. 'Why do you persist in trying to see the good in people when clearly there isn't any? My mother, your mother. By trying to justify their behaviour you are merely demeaning yourself.'

His words were designed to hurt but Emma refused to feel them.

'And if I look for the good in you?'

'Then you are a fool.' The reply whistled back, as cold as a bullet.

Leo turned away, but not before Emma had caught the flash of something raw before the night shadows took hold, sculpting his face like stone. And despite his rebuttal, she found herself reaching for him again.

'I'm just saying we all make mistakes.' Her hand found his arm, which was tightly folded across his chest. She felt his muscles flex beneath her touch, but he didn't pull away. 'It's easy to make bad decisions that we later regret.'

'Yeah, well, in my case this particular *mistake* meant that I lost everything.'

'Not everything, surely?' She could feel his skin beneath his shirtsleeve, warm, hostile.

'The Principality of Ravenino, the title of Conte, my home, my job—the role I had been groomed for all my life. Is that enough for you? Oh, and my fiancée. We mustn't forget her.'

Emma stilled. 'Cordelia?'

'Yes, Cordelia. Full marks, Emma, for remembering her name.' A long-held bitterness scoured his voice. 'But just to put the record straight, the engagement was not broken off because of my infidelity. It ended on the result of a single DNA test, along with the rest of my future as I knew it.'

Emma swallowed hard. *Cordelia Moretti.* She thought back to the images she had come across when doing her research on Leo. The wedding photos of Cordelia's marriage to Taddeo, Leo's younger brother, now the Conte di Ravenino. A fine, sophisticated woman with an aquiline nose, her dark hair swept back into a sleek chignon, diamond earrings dangling against the long sweep of her neck. She was everything that Emma wasn't.

At the time Emma had assumed Cordelia had been wronged by Leo, that he had treated her badly. Broken up with her. Broken her heart for all she knew. Now she saw how she had got everything the wrong way round. It was Leo who had been the victim. Had he also been the one with the broken heart? Was that why he still hurt so badly?

She let go of Leo's arm, feeling something coming apart inside her, something she couldn't control.

No wonder he had never shown any feelings for her. It all made sense now. She could never compete with a woman like Cordelia. Fevered thoughts piled one on top of the other, each more torturous than the last.

Oh, God, why did this have to be so hard?

'Nothing to say, Emma? No more questions you want answered? More details of my tragic past you would like to pick over?'

'No.' She fought against the swell of emotion pressing down on her chest. She fought with everything she'd got. She fought so hard it hurt.

Because she couldn't carry on like this, being slowly torn apart by Leo. She could never be Cordelia. She could never make Leo love her. But she was his wife. She was carrying his child. They were tied together for ever. So she had two choices. Either let herself be crushed with misery or stand up and fight.

She pulled back a little but refused to spare herself the weight of his gaze. She could do this, she told herself sternly. She was stronger than she thought. From the age of sixteen she had been on her own, working so hard to keep a roof over her head, food on the table, studying like crazy to get some qualifications, fighting for a career. She had moved countries to marry a man who was almost a stranger, come to terms with her shock pregnancy.

She had done all this without collapsing in a heap or running screaming for the hills. She wasn't going to start now. Fate had played some strange tricks on her, but fate didn't hold all the cards. She did have agency. She just had to use it.

'Actually, yes.' She changed her mind. 'I do have another question. What do you want from our relationship,

Leo?' She addressed him boldly, her eyes never leaving his face. The question took on a force of its own, spilling out in the silence that followed.

She saw the column of Leo's throat move on a swallow, his lips firm, then soften, before he finally spoke. 'I thought we had already established this.'

'No, we haven't. At least not to my satisfaction.' Emma held her nerve. Even if it felt like jumping on board a runaway train. 'What do you want from me? What is my role to be?'

'My wife. The mother of my child.' His eyes narrowed to dangerous slits of steel. 'Surely these are not difficult concepts to grasp.'

'Your lover?' Emma spoke the words like a dare, quickly, before her nerve failed her. 'Am I to share your bed?'

'Do you want to share my bed, Emma?' He turned the question around so fast she had no time to prepare for it. Like a mirror swung round to face her, she saw her own startled expression.

'I… I would like some clarity…going forward…'

'Clarity?' He reached out, his finger gently tracing a line along her lips, as if reading her question like Braille. 'Is that what you want?' With his head on one side he silently regarded her, like an interesting specimen. 'Or do you want sex, Emma? Hot. Wild. Passionate sex?'

Emma gave a sharp gasp.

'Because I can do that…' He whispered the words slowly, his thumb moving to stroke her cheek, his head lowering almost imperceptibly until his lips hovered just above hers. 'If that's what you want.'

Like a curse cast over her, or a drug she was addicted

to, she didn't just want it—she yearned for it, ached for it. She wanted Leo so badly at this moment she would have traded her soul. Her next breath.

'Say you want it, Emma.'

'I... I want it.'

His lips finally came down on hers, hot and firm. A commanding kiss that drove through Emma, turning everything soft and sweet. Calling to the growing ache in her core. Carrying away her fears and doubts, pushing them blissfully out of reach. At least for now. Because nothing felt more right than this.

The kiss ended and their arms loosened but still neither of them moved. Struggling to find a breath, to steady the thud of her heart, Emma looked into Leo's eyes, his wild stare pulling everything tight inside her. She took another gasp of air, air that was full of the scent of him, heady and potent. Her aching need for him screamed from every nerve, drowning the small voice that tried to tell her she needed to be very careful. Because being in Leo's arms felt like coming home. Like only he could make her happiness complete. And that was a very dangerous path to walk.

'I cannot be the man you want me to be, Emma.' Almost as if he could read her mind, Leo's voice was low. 'You need to know that.'

With a surge of boldness Emma rose to her feet, standing on tiptoe, her hand shaking as she slid it over the hard, flexing muscles of his chest, past the buckle of his belt, until it found the swell of his erection. She did have agency. She did have power. She refused to be the victim.

'Then I will take the man you are.'

Leo stared into her beautiful face, at the determined

line of her mouth, her eyes dark with desire. Reckless hunger pounded through him hot and hard. Like a dam about to burst he couldn't hold it back any longer. He had tried to do right by her, tried to make her see that man he was. But she had turned his warning into a promise. The words, falling softly from her lips, the most erotic thing he had ever heard. *I will take the man you are.*

So be it. He would give her that man.

Taking hold of her arms, he linked them behind his neck, tugging her towards him, her hair falling over her shoulders as she tipped her head back. His lips found hers again, the wet heat of her mouth slamming hot, hard arousal to every part of his body. Running his hands over her shoulder blades to the small of her back, he let out a guttural moan as his pounding erection met her soft curves. And when Emma returned the sound, writhing against him, Leo deepened the kiss, shifting his position so that his thigh was nudging between her legs. The dam had burst now. There was no going back. He had been waiting for this moment for too long. Far too long.

They fell apart with a shared gasp of breath. Unable to wait another minute, another second, Leo reached for her hand, hurrying them back through the gardens, tall black shadows marking their way before the villa loomed into view, brightly lit windows glowing against the dark. He opened the back door, pausing only for a second to glance at his wife, her tousled hair, her shining eyes. So beautiful. Tightening his grip on her hand, he silently led her along the long corridor that led to the vast kitchen, flicking the overhead spotlights on then off again, the brightness too much after the darkness outside.

He turned to kiss her again, relishing the bite of pain as Emma threaded her fingers into his hair, digging her nails into his scalp. With his hands cradling her head, the softness of her hair spread over his fingers, flowing over his wrists, like a river of silk.

Setting his hips in a rhythmic sway, he pulled her tightly against him, her eager response, the way she arched into his body driving him on. Driving him crazy. His hands slid over her bottom, bunching up the floaty fabric of her short summer dress until he was underneath, slipping his fingers under the skimpy panties, seeking her slick, wet core.

Emma gave a twitch of pleasure at his first light touch, which soon turned to a guttural moan as his fingers worked faster, more deliberately, his own need a bright light behind his eyes as he felt the thrill of her coming closer and closer to orgasm. With one arm locked around her waist, he backed her against the wall, his focus entirely on giving her the maximum pleasure, instinctively knowing what she liked.

And when her sharp gasp told him she was there, he covered her mouth with his own, his breath hot and fierce as he absorbed the shudder of her release, felt it ripple through his body, almost as if it was his own.

Which was not going to be far behind. For a moment they stood there, their breathing ragged as they gazed into one another's eyes. Never had Leo seen a more beautiful sight. All soft curves and warm skin, her eyes bright, her cheeks flushed, Emma called to him on some deeper level. Somewhere he had never been before.

But if he didn't get a grip, they weren't going to make it to a bedroom. Not that he minded. Such was his frenzy, his aching need to make love to Emma, he would have happily performed there and then, on top of the granite worktops or up against the vast shiny fridge he wasn't sure he had ever opened. But Emma deserved better.

Taking hold of her hand, he laced his fingers tightly through hers. He was going to get them upstairs, into his bedroom and into his bed if it was the last thing he did. He was going to make love to her, passionately, crazily, with everything he had. Until the ache in his soul was satisfied. Until he had made her his once and for all. Until he had finally found peace.

CHAPTER TEN

'*BENE...BENE.*' BEATRICE lifted up the pasta, inspecting it closely as Emma rolled it through the machine for the umpteenth time. 'You are definitely getting the 'ang of this.'

Emma smiled. Queen of the kitchen, Beatrice had taken some persuading to let her anywhere near her pasta machine, so the pressure had been on from the start. Making the dough had been stressful enough, Beatrice barking instructions in rapid Italian or broken English, both equally unintelligible, elbowing Emma out of the way when she did something particularly terrible, as if the sky might come crashing down because of it.

Nevertheless, Emma was enjoying herself. And she adored Beatrice. Small and plump, her smooth cheeks often dusted with flour, they reminded Emma of the soft balls of dough she so lovingly created. The mother of six grown-up children, Beatrice had been widowed ten years ago, forced to go back to work when her useless, incompetent husband had died leaving her penniless. You would never get her to admit it, but she loved her job at Villa Magenta. She even loved all the high-tech equipment, boasting about it to her friends. 'I say to Agnesia, *You no have the steam oven? You livin' in the Dark Ages.*'

'You think it is ready for the filling?' Emma stopped turning the handle of the machine.

'*Sì...sì...*'

They were making prosciutto and ricotta ravioli, Leo's favourite according to Beatrice, who seemed to know the food preferences of anyone who had ever crossed her path.

Emma had been living at the villa for two months now, two months that had stirred up such a complicated mix of emotions she didn't know how to begin to untangle them. What's more, she didn't even want to. Because to examine their relationship, to try and understand the sexual relationship they had embarked on, in all its intense, vivid glory, meant examining herself. Something Emma was studiously avoiding doing.

Starting that evening down by the lake, when they had finally fallen upon each other like starving beasts, tumbling into bed and making love with wild and deeply sensual craving, there had been no going back. Like some sort of crazy addiction, a mad, hedonistic ride of pleasure, it was hot and wild and raw. And totally uncontrollable.

It could happen anywhere, at any time, but mostly Leo would come to her bed late at night, running his fingers down her spine or moving her hair aside to kiss the nape of her neck. And Emma would find her body instantly on fire, her hands reaching for him, urgent, desperate, to take her to that place only he could take her, make her feel something only he could.

She had quickly learned how to give pleasure as well as receive. An innocent virgin no more, she had done things that made her blush in the cold light of day, made her shiver with excitement at the thought of repeating them. Like taking Leo in her mouth, closing her lips around the silky hot girth of him, revelling in the way she could make him feel. She loved turning him on like that. It was empowering, life enhancing.

But sexual intimacy was as far as it went. In all other ways their relationship was as sterile as it had ever been. Worse if anything. The wall that Leo seemed so determined to surround himself with grew taller and more impregnable with every week that passed. Like he was building it up, brick by brick.

On the surface he was polite, enquiring after her health, how her day had gone. But it was a distracted courtesy, like he was keeping her at arm's length, his mind already moving onto something else, something more worthy of his valuable time. There was a distinct lack of familiarity between them, any closeness solely restricted to sex. No cosying up on the sofa, chilling out together, enjoying each other's company, the way normal couples did. They had never even spent the entire night together.

Waiting until after she had fallen asleep, or using the excuse of work, always more work, Leo would extricate himself from her arms and disappear into the night. The bed beside her empty in the morning, the crumpled sheets, the scent of his body all that was left of the intimacy they had shared. A damning indictment of what could never be.

But it wasn't like he hadn't tried to warn her. *I cannot be the man you want me to be.*

Alone again, his words would come back to haunt Emma. But she only had herself to blame. She was the one who had initiated this shift in their relationship. She was a hopeless case, she knew that. Like a dog chasing her own tail, going round and round and getting nowhere. Ordering herself not to get emotionally involved but constantly obsessing over him. Determined to mirror his cool demeanour but thinking about Leo all the time. Dreaming of him. Falling in love with him...

No matter how hard Emma tried to ignore that traitorous word, it kept coming back to haunt her, niggling away at the back of her head, threatening to fall unbidden from her lips if she wasn't careful. So she made sure she was on her guard at all times. She would rather saw off her own legs than let Leo see as much as a chink of how she felt about him. He had made his feeling towards her quite clear—at least his lack of them. It was up to her to deal with the situation as it was. No matter how much it hurt.

'Buonasera.' Standing in the kitchen doorway, the room was suddenly full of Leo's presence, the air thick with the pull of him. Wearing a dark suit, the jacket slung over his shoulder and held by one crooked finger, his grey eyes flicked between Beatrice and Emma. 'What is going on here?'

'Beatrice is teaching me how to make pasta.' Emma gestured to the perfectly shaped squares of deliciousness, steadfastly ignoring the thumping of her heart. 'Prosciutto and ricotta ravioli.'

'My favourite.' Leo raised a dark brow a fraction and Beatrice gave Emma a complacent smile. 'I'll just take a quick shower and then we can eat.'

Supper was taken out on the terrace as usual. Even though summer had turned to autumn, the evenings were still gloriously warm and Emma for one was relieved the searing temperatures had dropped.

'*Delizioso,*' Leo declared, touching a napkin to his lips before scrunching it up and laying it on the table. 'Beatrice has taught you well. We will make an Italian mama out of you yet.'

Emma smiled. 'I don't know about that, but I love spending time with her. She's a fantastic cook. Where did you find her?'

'A restaurant I used to frequent in Milan. The food was great, so I went into the kitchen and told her to come and work for me.'

'Just like that?'

'*Sì.* I always find a direct approach works best.'

That was *so* Leo. You saw what you wanted, then you made it happen. Except, of course, when the circumstances were completely out of your control. Like finding out you are not the legitimate heir of the principality you had been raised to rule. Emma could see how hard that must have been for a proud man like him to accept. It was still there, held inside him, like a poisonous canker. But any attempts to broach the subject again, maybe try and talk it through with him, had been firmly shut down.

'Did you know that one of her sons, Giuseppe, has got a new job working for a big pharmaceutical company?' Emma speared a piece of ravioli. 'Beatrice is thrilled because their youngest child has some health problems that have been putting a terrible strain on the family's finances.'

'Yes, I heard.'

Something about Leo's guarded response made Emma suspicious and she looked up. 'You wouldn't have had anything to do with that, would you?'

'Put it this way…' Leo raised his wine glass to his lips, hooded eyes regarding Emma over the rim '… I like to reward my loyal staff if I can.'

'And their families.'

'And their families,' Leo repeated, setting down his glass. 'We Italians are all about families, you should know that.' The grey eyes glittered.

Yes, Emma did know that. It was the reason she was here, after all. *The sole reason.* And that thought stuck like a barb in her skin. No matter how much she tried to justify the bizarre terms of their relationship, tell herself that this was the way it was, the way it would always be, it was still so hard to accept.

She took a sip of water, carefully replacing her glass. She could sense that Leo was already itching to go. Manners prevented him from leaving the table until Emma had finished, but that didn't stop his foot from jiggling under the table, his fingers drumming very lightly on the top. Well, tonight he would have to wait.

'We have had a lot more applications from journalists on the website today.' She searched for his attention. 'The standard is very high.'

'Bene.' Leo surreptitiously looked at his watch.

'I'm confident we are going to get some really good people on board.'

'I'm sure you will.'

Emma sighed. Bored with sitting around with nothing to do, she had asked Leo if she could get involved with some of the many charities that Raven Enterprises supported. But in typical Leo fashion he had escalated her request, suggesting they started a foundation in her name.

It was an exciting idea, if a bit daunting. Deciding she would like to use her experience in journalism somehow, and maybe focus on youth unemployment and homelessness—if nothing else, living at Villa Magenta had made her aware of just what a privileged life she was leading—she had taken these ideas to Leo and he had made them happen. Constructive journalism was key, he told her, taking a solution-focussed approach.

And so the foundation Read All About It had been born. Financial support for young journalists to work with charities and highlight the issues they faced. The idea was simple but brilliant.

Heading up a small team of people, Emma was really enjoying the challenge, the feeling she was making a difference. But there was disappointment too, because Leo had dissociated himself from the project as soon as it had been launched.

'Would you like to look over some of the figures?' She already knew the answer, but she couldn't help herself.

'No need. The foundation is in your name, you have complete control.'

'But it's your money.' She persisted. 'Don't you want to make sure it is being spent wisely?'

'The lawyers will do that. That's their job.'

Emma sighed. It was great that he trusted her to just get on with it, but the way he was distancing himself from any involvement felt like he was distancing her. Still further.

'Okay, if you're sure.' She put down her fork. 'Have you finished?'

'*Si, grazie.*'

'Then I will get the dessert.' With a determined air, Emma rose, collecting up the bowls.

'Dessert?' The surprise in his voice was not exactly encouraging. To be fair, she had never seen him eat anything sweet.

'Yes. Beatrice asked me to show her how to make a traditional English pudding. I didn't have exactly the right ingredients, so I had to make do.'

'Well, I look forward to seeing the result.' *No, he didn't.*

'Wait there.' Emma stretched out an arm, as if to physically prevent him from escaping. She was determined not to let him cut and run. 'I won't be a moment.'

The pudding, as Emma removed it from the oven, was not all she had hoped it might be. Rather more solid than she'd intended, it was distinctly burnt on the top. And there was no sign of Beatrice to save it. Presumably she had abandoned it and Emma to their fate. Still, ever the optimist, Emma decided she could blag it. It wasn't as if Leo knew how it was supposed to look.

'Ta-da!' She placed it on the table before him.

'Is this a family recipe?' Leo regarded it with suspicion.

Emma didn't have any family recipes. She hadn't had that sort of family.

'No, it's more like an old-fashioned English dish. But these retro puddings are all the rage now.' She tried to dig the spoon in to serve Leo a portion, but it was surprisingly difficult.

'Need any help?'

'No, no.' Emma ignored the smile in his voice, leaning forward to get some more leverage. 'There you are.' She placed the bowl in front of him.

'Interesting.' Leo turned a burnt corner over to peer underneath. 'What is this delicacy called?'

'Bread and butter pudding.' Emma popped a bit in her mouth. It tasted as bad as it looked. 'It was meant to be made with slices of white bread, but I had to use ciabatta.'

'Very ingenious.' His jaw worked with exaggerated force.

'But I'm not sure it's quite the same.'

'Possibly not.' Leo raised laughing eyes to meet hers, a curve shaping the firm lines of his mouth.

Emma looked down before her face betrayed her. Leo smiled so little that when he did it was like a full-on assault to the heart.

'It's disgusting, isn't it?' She risked looking up at him again.

'Assolutamente disgustoso.' He stuck in his fork which remained standing defiantly upright. 'Though all is not lost. I dare say it could be used to fill some gaps in the walls.'

'Oi!' With a laugh Emma balled up her napkin and threw it at him but it missed, knocking over his wine glass, sending red wine spraying over Leo's shirt. 'Oh, God, I'm sorry.' She rushed round to pat at his shirt but immediately he was on his feet, trapping her in his arms. 'You need to take that off right away. It will stain.'

'Or you could do it for me, *cara*?' He placed her hands on his chest, where his heart thudded beneath the damp fabric. Immediately Emma felt the familiar coil of desire, the pulsing clench of her core.

Her fingers started to work at the buttons, driven on by slumbering eyes darkening with desire. But their progress was halted by the persistent buzz of Leo's phone in his trouser pocket.

'Aspetta. Wait.' He slid his hand down between them. 'Let me turn this off.'

But that never happened. One glance at the screen and Emma saw his features pull tight, his whole body stiffen. '*Mi scusi.* I have to take this.'

It wasn't even a proper apology. More a distracted mutter that he didn't care if she heard or not. With his shoulders high he turned, his stride wide as he left the room with the phone clamped to his ear.

So that was it then. With a heavy sigh, Emma watched him go. Once again, she had been abandoned in favour of whatever deal he was doing, a business negotiation that was clearly far more important than she was. She glanced back across the table, at the offending pudding curling up before her eyes. Her gaze rose to the horizon, looking for inspiration, strength, a miracle—she didn't know which.

Rising to her feet, she went over to the sunbed further along the terrace, picking up the book she had left there earlier. Stretching out on the padded cushions, she found her page. It looked as if this was the only company she would be having this evening.

'Emma?'

She must have closed her eyes for a minute because the book on her lap had fallen to the floor. She leaned to pick it up. 'Yes?'

'Something has come up.' Leo strode towards her, his silhouette dark, forbidding. 'I have to go away.'

'Oh, right.' Emma collected herself, smoothing down her hair, drawing up her knees. She could tell from the tone of his voice that this was no ordinary business trip.

'I will be gone for some time.'

'When you say some time…'

'I don't know exactly. As long as it takes.' Impatience simmered in his tone.

'And when will you be leaving on this trip of indeterminate length?' She hid her despondency behind a mask of sarcasm.

'Tonight. Straight away.'

'Tonight?!' Emma swung her legs over the edge of the sunbed. 'But it's my twenty-week scan tomorrow. Surely whatever it is can wait until after that?'

'No, Emma, this can't wait.' His jaw was set as firmly as his words.

'But—'

'It's not as if I need to be there, Emma. You are the one that is pregnant.'

His words were like a shot to the heart. Like he was tearing her apart, bit by bit. There was no arguing with his merciless logic, but that didn't make it hurt any less.

'Very well. I'll see you when I see you, I guess.' She opened her book again, making a great show of finding a page she wasn't going to be reading. Anything to try and hide the hurt clawing its way to her throat.

'I will ring you in due course when I have a clearer idea of the length of my stay.'

'Fine.' She bent back the spine of the paperback. 'Whatever.'

She heard him take a few steps away, then stop.

'Indulging in petulant behaviour is not going to help the situation, Emma.'

Very deliberately, Emma placed the book beside her and lifted her face to meet his.

'I didn't realise there was a "situation".' She fought back with everything she had. 'How could I when you haven't told me where you are going or the reason for your trip?'

'Ravenino.' He forced the word through clenched teeth. 'I have to return to Ravenino.'

Emma stared at him in astonishment. That was the last place she had expected him to say.

'It's my brother. He's had an accident.'

'Oh, I'm sorry, Leo!' Immediately on her feet, Emma rushed towards the solid wall of Leo's cool restraint, all petulance gone. 'Is it serious?'

'Head injuries. He fell off a horse. He's in an induced coma.' The unemotional information was delivered in bullet points.

'Oh, no! Of course you must go to him straight away.'

'I'm not going to sit by his bedside, Emma.' Irritation growled in his voice. 'They need me to take over the running of the principality. Cordelia is insistent that I'm the only person that can do it.'

Cordelia. Just her name on Leo's lips produced a sharp jab of jealousy.

'So that was Cordelia, was it?' Emma asked casually. 'On the phone?'

'*Sì.*' Distracted, Leo looked down at another message that had buzzed in. 'The jet has been put on standby. I need to leave for the airport.'

Emma swallowed down the horrible surge of jealousy. So Leo's assertion that he would never visit Ravenino again had been reversed by a single click of his ex-fiancée's elegant fingers. But this was an emergency, Emma reminded herself. Her own father had died in a riding accident, what if Leo's brother suffered the same fate? This was no time for petty jealousies. A sudden idea came to her.

'Why don't I come with you?'

Leo looked at her in surprise. 'To Ravenino?'

Yes, of course to Ravenino. Where else?

'Yes.' She kept up the bravado. 'I can postpone the scan for a week or so.'

'What would be the benefit in that?'

'Well, I would love to see where you come from and—'

'This is not a little holiday, Emma. I have a job to do. I don't need the encumbrance of a pregnant wife tagging along.'

Emma stilled, watching the wave of hurt coming towards her , crashing over her like a tsunami, dragging her under, drowning her breath.

She turned, her feet taking her back across the terrace, away from him. Tears choked her throat, but her eyes remained dry. She stared ahead, trying not to think, trying to hold the misery at bay. At least until he had gone.

Behind her Leo made a gruff sound in his throat. She heard him coming towards her and her shoulders stiffened, her whole body following suit, going rigid with tension. She couldn't do this. Not any more. Moving further away, she forced her vocal cords into action.

'Just go, Leo.' Her weary words floated into the night. 'Just go.'

CHAPTER ELEVEN

'THE QUARTERLY FINANCIAL budget projection needs to be finalised.' The secretary swiped at the tablet in his hand. 'The record of the legislative assembly agreed. And don't forget you have a meeting with the French ambassador on Tuesday.'

Leo nodded, dismissing his secretary, relieved the morning briefing was over.

He spanned a hand across his forehead, massaging temples that felt as if they had been constantly throbbing for days.

The pressure of work was enormous. Running the principality as well as his own business interests meant there wasn't a spare minute in the day. Rising at first light, he started the day with a five-mile run, ending it with a punishing session in the gym, desperately trying to ease the knots in his muscles, persuade his brain to switch off and let him sleep. Which rarely happened.

He slid his hand across his closed lids, pinching the bridge of his nose. He had always thought he thrived on pressure. On pushing himself harder and harder. It was what he did. So why was there no sense of satisfaction? Just hollowness inside. He was back in Ravenino, doing the job he'd thought he'd always wanted, albeit only as a proxy. He had fully expected to be hit by any one of a number of negative emotions that had to be lying in wait for him on his return to his homeland. Resentment, hostility, envy.

What he had never expected to feel was...nothing. Not then, when he had first set foot on Ravenino soil. And not now, three weeks in, when his authoritative command had steered the principality away from the brink of uncertainty, calmed the financial markets and reassured the investors. He was doing a good job, he knew that. He would leave the principality in a better shape than he'd found it. Whenever that was.

He leaned back in his chair, stretching out his spine. Yesterday they'd had good news. Taddeo had been brought out of his coma, and all the signs were that he would make a full recovery. It would just take time. Leo thought back to Cordelia's face when she had come in to tell him. Not just shining with relief but love too. She had clearly married the right brother after all. Leo gazed out of the window. Funny how things turned out.

Immediately his mind conjured up an image of Emma, the way it always did when he stopped working for as much as a second. Which was a good reason not to stop. Because he didn't want to be reminded of her—not when his last memory was of the hurt on her face before she had turned away. Anguish. Sorrow. All inflicted by him.

Since then a few brief phone calls had done nothing to repair the damage. Polite enquiries about one another's health, updates on Taddeo's progress, Emma's voice noticeably devoid of emotion, even when he had asked her about the scan. All was fine apparently. That was all he could get out of her. It was like a light had gone out. She never asked when he might be coming home. Perhaps she didn't care. Perhaps she was glad to see the back of him. He wouldn't have blamed her.

But he'd had to be firm. He didn't want Emma here in Ravenino. But neither did he want to examine the reasons too deeply. This place, the land that he had once loved so much, that he would have devoted his life to, given his life *for* if necessary, in a heartbeat, had become his nemesis.

He turned to look out of the window, where the principality was laid out before him. Tree-covered hills, clusters of houses, a sparkling sea, all representing nothing but failure. His failure to be the right son, the true heir. His failure to be the man he had always thought he was.

Was that why he couldn't bear to bring Emma here? He tried to push the thought away, but it refused to budge. Was it because he couldn't bear the idea of her witnessing his failings that he was so determined to keep her away? Because he didn't want her to see him for the man he really was? Because her opinion of him mattered. She mattered. Too much. In fact, the jolt of realisation hit him square between the eyes.

Emma was the only thing in his life that mattered at all.

The phone on the desk rang and with some relief Leo reached forward to answer it. The work might be all-consuming, but it was also his friend. It kept the demons at bay.

The thud of her heart sounded in her ears as Emma's first sighting of the principality of Ravenino came into view.

Jagged cliffs covered in dense greenery fell to a turquoise sea dotted with small white boats. Hundreds of pastel-coloured houses clung to the vertiginous rocks, white sandy coves fringed the shore. And then, as the aeroplane banked, ready to land, there it was—the magnificent Castello Ravenino, perched right on the water's edge, grand and proud, a symbol of power and rule, of centuries of history.

Pulling her bag down from the overhead locker, Emma joined the queue to exit the plane, her fellow passengers chattering noisily as if just arriving here was cause for celebration in itself. Holidaymakers or residents, or probably a mixture of both, they eagerly stepped onto the tarmac, dragging their suitcases, holding on to the hands of their children, hurrying towards passport control.

But Emma could find no such cause for celebration. Far from it. Only nerves, batting inside her like the wings of a bird, a mouth so dry she feared she might never be able to speak again.

But somehow the taxi driver understood her instructions to take her to the Castello and now, as she stared up at the imposing stone walls, she knew there was no going back.

Her decision to come to Ravenino had been made in the middle of another sleepless night. Another night when Leo had dominated her thoughts, stealing into her dreams, waking her with his hands squeezed around her heart. Standing under the shower one morning, she had started to formulate her plan. She couldn't carry on like this. She couldn't pretend any more. She wasn't prepared to live this sort of half-life any longer. His wife in name, but with no power, no role. His lover when it suited him, but only ever on his terms, at his command.

Which meant she only had one option. She had to confront Leo and tell the truth.

Taddeo's accident had only highlighted the dire state of their relationship. At a time of crisis, when most couples turned to their partners for help and support, Leo had pushed her away. Totally shut her out. Cruelly rebuffed her.

Emma understood how hard returning to Ravenino was for him, even if he had refused to show her any emotion. Despite his cool demeanour, she had seen it in the taut lines of his face, heard it in the gravel of his voice. In retrospect, that should have been enough to warn her off but, no, she had jumped in with both feet, suggesting she go with him, driven by an innocent desire to ease his burden. No, not just that. In truth she had been driven by a desperate need to prove that she meant something to him.

Fool that she was.

The cold look he had given her was etched for ever on her mind. His cruel words were still ringing in her head: *'the encumbrance of a pregnant wife tagging along.'* It was all there in those damning words. Their whole relationship encapsulated in a few bitter words. If she had worried she meant nothing to him, she'd been wrong. She did mean something to him—nuisance, burden, responsibility. A thorn in his side. And one he was stuck with for ever.

Well, not any more. If it suited Leo to pretend that she had no feelings, or he was just too damned selfish to care if she did, she was going to put him straight. Because Emma was beset with a whole surge of feelings, tormenting her day and night. Stealing her sleep, her appetite, the glow from her cheeks and the light in her eyes. Stealing her dignity and her self-respect.

These past few weeks she had barely been able to look at herself in the mirror, repelled by the face that stared back at her. The face of someone too weak, too feeble to stand up for herself. Who had allowed herself to be used by a man who cared nothing for her. Who pined for a man in his absence when his presence only gave her pain. Worse, far worse, to fall in love with this man. Because, yes, Emma had had to face up to that torturous fact too. Only by doing so would she ever be able to move on.

Which was why she was here. This was it. Do or die. She was going to tell him how she felt about him. *Really felt*. And if that was like signing her own death warrant, then so be it. Because maybe a quick, clean kill would be easier in the end. Put her out of her misery. Anything had to be better than being eaten away by the agonising torture of staying silent, hiding her true emotions, pretending she didn't love him...

Walking up the long flight of steps, she felt her heart grow heavier with every tread. Her hand trembled as she reached for the bronze bell button, hearing it echo inside, the sound of a dog barking. Hunching her shoulders, she waited, half expecting a colony of bats to appear, flapping around her head to warn her off.

But there were no bats, just a polite butler who enquired her name, registering no hint of surprise when she had announced herself as Signora Ravenino. Escorting her into the cavernous hallway, Emma gazed around at the sweeping stone staircase, the polished marble floor, the heavy brass chandeliers. So this was where Leo had grown up, the place he had thought would always be home. A lump formed in her throat. For Leo's loss. For her own loss. Feelings, she told herself sternly. Just more feelings.

Beside her the butler was trying to usher her into a salon, telling her he would inform Signor Ravenino of her arrival. But Emma stood firm. She didn't want Leo to have any advance warning that she was here. Surprise was the only weapon she had in her armoury. It was why she hadn't told him she was coming. A skilled negotiator when it suited him, she didn't want to give him time to prepare his reaction. This exchange had to be raw, real. That was the whole point. She had to look into his eyes when she told him the truth. She had to see what was really there. No matter how painful that might be.

Pasting on the most winning expression she could muster, she explained to the butler that her visit was a surprise. That she would like to arrive unannounced. After a moment's hesitation he informed her that the Signor was working in the library and that if she would like to follow him, he would show her the way. A flight of stairs led them along a dark corridor until they finally stopped outside an enormous pair of panelled oak doors.

With a small bow the butler left her. Taking in a huge breath, the bravest breath of her life, Emma grasped the twin handles and pushed.

'Not now.' Leo didn't look up from his paperwork. The day had been beset with problems and he didn't need anyone coming in with any more. What he needed was to be left in peace.

The faint sound of a breath stilled his hand, locking his muscles in place. *No. It couldn't be.* Very slowly he lifted his head.

'Hello, Leo.'

A smack of shock hit him between the eyes. *Emma!* He swallowed hard. But still the shock reverberated through him, thrumming in his blood. Something almost like panic set in. This reaction was too extreme— he had to take measures to control it.

'What are you doing here?' He made no attempt at courtesy, cursing the thud of his heart, the fact she looked so small and slight standing in the doorway. The way it pulled at something inside him.

'I had to come and see you.'

'The baby?' With of jolt of horror he jumped to his feet. 'Something is wrong?'

'No, Leo, the baby is fine.'

Relief washed over him but still the pounding of his heart refused to be tamed.

'Then what?' His hands gripped the edge of the desk. 'What is so urgent that you couldn't tell me over the phone?'

'What I have to say needs to be said face to face.'

Leo's mind raced with possibilities, none of them good. His brows drew into a scowl.

Emma advanced into the room, the anguished determination written all over her pale face punching him low in the gut.

She stopped six feet away from where Leo still stood behind his desk, unable to move. Scarcely able to breathe. 'I have to tell you…' She paused, then swallowed. 'That I can't carry on with our relationship. Not as it stands at present.'

Leo stilled, ice flooding through his veins. What nonsense was this? He drew in a steadying breath, searching for the measured response that had to be there somewhere.

'If you mean because I have to be here in Ravenino, then frankly, Emma, I would have expected more understanding from you.' He firmed his lips. 'This situation is not of my making. I didn't *ask* my brother to fall off a horse. I didn't *ask* to take over the ruling of the principality. But these events have happened and now I am left to deal with them.'

'I'm not talking about your being here in Ravenino.' Slowly she took another couple of steps towards him, her voice low, her eyes too bright. 'I'm talking about our relationship as a whole. All of it. Me and you, man and wife. It's not working.'

He heard the curse fall from his lips and, turning his back, made himself count several beats before facing her again.

'Emma.' His voice was laced with warning. 'I refuse to play these stupid games.'

The slight shake of her head did nothing to tame his blood.

'Of course you will carry on with our relationship. We are man and wife. And that's an end to it.'

But her infuriating silence suggested otherwise, more inflammatory than any words.

Something inside Leo leapt and growled. Anger? Alarm? Or fear?

'I don't have time for this.' His voice grew harsher. 'Whatever your problem is, it will have to wait. There are far more pressing issues I need to deal with.'

'No, Leo. It won't wait.' When she finally spoke, he could hear the defiance, see its shimmer in her slender frame. Two more steps and she was on the other side of his desk, her shoulders back, her head high. She was holding on to her composure, but her gaze was wild, tearing into Leo, producing a surge of emotion he couldn't even put a name to. 'This needs to be said now and I am going to say it.'

'Very well.' Leo forced his clenched jaw to unlock enough to say a few words. To affect an air of indifference. 'If you must.'

He heard her take a breath, saw the way it swelled her breasts beneath the loose-fitting silk blouse.

'When I entered into this marriage I thought I could deal with it the same way as you. Purely as a deal to secure the future of our unborn child. I thought I could cope with that. That the security you were offering would make up for the lack of…of emotional attachment. But now I find that it doesn't. And that changes everything. Now I find I have to be honest, both with myself and with you. And I need you to be honest in return.'

'I have never been anything but honest, Emma.' Impatience clawed at his voice.

'Then perhaps I am at fault for looking for something that isn't there.' Her hands fluttered to her abdomen, smoothing over the slight swell beneath the blue fabric before letting her hands rest there, possessively, protectively. As if she needed to guard their unborn child from him. 'And that is the problem I have to address. The reason I am here.

'I can't carry on the way we are any longer. I can't pretend that I am fine with your brisk efficiency, your lack of emotion. The way you would come to my bed but then sneak away before morning, as if what we had just done was wrong, sordid. You made me feel used, ashamed. You have taken the intimacy between us, something precious, special, at least to me, and turned it into something dirty. Shameful.'

'That was never my intention…'

'And then when you were called here to Ravenino, the place that means so much to you, you pushed me away again. Shut me out.'

Leo dragged a hand through his hair. Why was she persisting in raking over this when no good would come of it?

'You erected barriers right from the start, enforced boundaries to keep me out. To keep me in my place. And it worked for a while. I thought I could stick to the rules. But now I find I can't. It's too hard.'

Holding himself totally still, Leo's mind whirred to find ways to put an end to this misery. If Emma was unhappy, and clearly she was, he would renegotiate the terms, strike another deal. This was what he did. What he was good at. Even if right now it felt as if a heavy boot was pressing down on his chest. He just had to fight harder to maintain control. He had no choice.

'And what exactly is it that you find so hard?' He used sarcasm to mask his growing agitation.

But then Emma's lip trembled, taunting him, driving him nearly mad.

'Everything.' Her shuddering sigh racked her whole body. 'I know the last thing you wanted was to have our marriage complicated by messy emotions. And I'm sorry for that. Truly I am. But I can't help it.'

'Can't help what?'

'I can't help being in love with you.'

The words bloomed inside his head, spreading hot and thick, pounding through him.

Emma was in love with him? How was that possible?

He had worked so hard not to let their relationship fall into this trap. Keeping himself emotionally sterile at all times. It had never been a problem before. Distancing himself from the many women that had graced his bed in recent years had been easy. Impervious to their simpering flattery or declarations of ardour, his heart had been left completely untouched. It only went to prove what he had known all along. He wasn't capable of love. His mother's betrayal had killed his heart stone dead.

But with Emma it was different. Somehow, she had managed to creep beneath his impregnable defences. So he had redoubled his efforts to keep her at bay, cutting short the time they spent together, working even longer hours than were absolutely necessary, dragging himself from her bed when all he wanted to do was pull her into his arms, feel her skin against his as they drifted off to sleep, wake to see her head next to him on the pillow. Even though every night tearing himself away from her was more difficult than the one before.

But he had done it. He had been strong, for Emma's sake. And he'd thought he had succeeded. That his effort hadn't been in vain. Until now. Until this.

He could feel Emma's eyes locked on his face, tracking every twitch of muscle, seeking out the turmoil that lay just beneath the surface. Well, she would not find it. He refused to expose his emotions to her. He had no intention of laying his feelings bare. He didn't even understand them himself, except to know they were raw and powerful and pulled his skin too tight. No, this situation needed to be calmed and contained, and the sooner the better. Before things got completely out of hand.

He twisted away, taking a second to compose himself, to steady the pounding of his blood. Turning back on a sharp intake of breath, he was ready to face her again.

'I agree this is an unfortunate situation.' But not her eyes. He couldn't look into those pale blue eyes for fear of coming undone. Instead his gaze hovered somewhere over the top of her head. 'But perhaps you are mistaken.'

'I am not mistaken, Leo.'

'Is it possible the pregnancy is confusing your emotions?'

'Don't, Leo.' She flashed him a murderous look. 'Just don't.'

'Mi dispiace?'

'Please don't patronise me by suggesting I can't interpret my own feelings. At least do me the courtesy of acknowledging that what I say is the truth. My truth. I have been in love with you for weeks, months, maybe since the first time we met. Those are the facts.'

'And what am I supposed to do with these facts?' The twist in his gut turned to anger, something he could deal with. 'You turn up here uninvited, unannounced, making wild announcements about not being able to carry on with our relationship. How exactly do you expect me to react?'

'I just want honesty, Leo, that's all. The same honesty as I have shown to you.'

'Very well.' He ground down on his jaw. 'You need to know that I will not be blackmailed.'

'Blackmailed?' The bitter word turned to astonishment on her open lips.

'Yes, blackmailed, Emma. In my experience, the only reason a woman tells a man she loves him is to goad him into responding. Because she wants to hear the words back. Because that gives her power.'

A look of disgust crossed Emma's face. Bizarrely this brought relief. Disgust he could cope with. It was so much easier to deal with than the sight of Emma hurting.

'I suspect you have had too much time on your hands. Perhaps you have found these last few weeks at Villa Magenta rather boring. Your charity work not enough to occupy you. The novelty of having your every need catered for, every comfort at your disposal wearing off so you have looked around to find something to account for your dissatisfaction. And that something was me.

'But I will not be blackmailed, Emma. By you or anyone else. I will not be tricked into sharing sentiments I don't feel, just to make you feel better.'

He paused, the weight of his words swinging like lead between them. Up until now he had managed to avoid the full glare of her eyes, his gaze flitting lightly over her face, knowing there was no safe place to land. But he could avoid them no longer. He had to deal with whatever horror he saw. Because deal with it he would. Quickly and efficiently. A clean kill. It was kinder in the end.

Her silence was total, not as much as a breath stirring the air. But the eyes he finally met were wide, unblinking. And dry. Bone dry. Dead.

Tears he had been expecting. He could have dealt with them. Many a woman had tried to use them as a weapon against him when things hadn't been going their way, only to find they'd left him completely unmoved. But Emma's steady stare tore him apart.

'You have nothing further to say?' Leo could stand this cruel silence no longer. He had to bring it to an end.

'No.' She shook her head, her fingers finding a lock of hair over her shoulder, smoothing it down. 'I came here looking for honesty to try and make sense of our relationship and find a way forward. And you have given me that honesty. For which I thank you.'

She was thanking him? For being a cold-hearted brute?

'I will leave you in peace now. I have arrangements to make.'

'What arrangements?' His voice growled with suspicion.

'I am going to go back to the UK. I need some time to sort out my head.'

'You will do no such thing.'

'I don't need your permission, Leo. I am your wife, not your possession.'

'And as my wife I order you to stay here.'

'Here, as in Ravenino? The place you were so determined I should never even visit?'

'Here, as in Italy. You will return to Villa Magenta.'

'And what will you do? Have Luigi follow me around again, making sure I don't escape?'

'I will put my entire security team onto it if necessary.' Frustration clawed at his throat. *How had it come to this?* 'You are not only my wife but you are carrying my child. I absolutely forbid your returning to England.'

'You can't stop me, Leo.' She tightened her jaw. 'Unless you intend to physically restrain me, of course. No doubt there is a dungeon around here somewhere you could throw me into.'

Leo seethed with impotent rage. *There was.* And he *was* tempted.

'So what exactly do you intend to do in England? Go back to your family and their squalid little encampment in a muddy field? Start making daisy chains for a living?'

'No.'

'Have that delightful mother of yours tell you what a miserable failure you are?' He was building up a head of steam now, a rush of white noise in his ears. 'Do you think she will welcome you back, Emma? Or will she be locking away her latest boyfriend for fear you might get your claws into him?'

The flinch of pain that marred Emma's beautiful face slashed into his soul, hard and deep. But panic drove him on. He would not lose her. He could not lose her.

'And don't think for one moment I will let that toxic woman anywhere near my child. I expressly forbid any contact with her. Ever.'

His frantic gaze ran over her body, alive to every small movement. As if she might vanish before his eyes.

'I will return to London.' The struggle to hold on to her composure cracked in her voice.

'To live where, exactly?'

'I don't know, Leo.' A dreadful weariness weighted her words. 'But I will find somewhere. I have done it before.'

'For how long?'

'Two or three months? I need some headspace, time to think things through.'

'Very well.' He raked a hand through his hair. He had to assume some sort of control if he was to get through this. 'But I have two conditions. Firstly, I will be the one to arrange accommodation for you in London. And secondly, you will return to Italy before the baby is born.'

Emma's pause was mercifully short before she gave a brief nod.

'I have your word?'

'Yes, Leo, you have my word.'

'Because if not…'

'I *said* you have my word.'

Leo allowed himself to breathe.

'In that case I will have the jet put on standby for you. The flight will go via Milan so you can collect your belongings from Villa Magenta.'

He moved back behind the desk, his eyes cast down, his hands shuffling the papers he no longer gave a damn about.

'I will be in touch in due course.'

He waited for sounds of movement, for Emma to leave, slamming the doors behind her. Or stay…coming towards him to affect some sort of reconciliation. To tell him that she had overreacted. To beat her fists against his chest. To scream at him what a bastard he was. But hearing nothing he flicked his eyes upwards to find her still standing there, her hands clasped under the slight swell of her bump, wide eyes staring at him from beneath that fringe.

Leo swallowed. Goddamn the woman.

'I will say goodbye, then.' Her voice was very small.

'Goodbye, Emma.' He looked back down at the paperwork.

'Oh, one more thing.' With some effort he raised his head again. When was she going to be done torturing him?

'When I had the scan…they asked if I wanted to know the baby's sex.'

'And…?' Leo felt his heart rate spike dramatically.

'I said yes.' Emma held his gaze, strong and blue. 'It's a boy, Leo. You are going to have a son.'

CHAPTER TWELVE

EMMA WAITED FOR the pain to kick in, almost welcoming it. Because anything had to be better than this frozen inertia. Like she had been drugged. Anaesthetised. She knew the agony was there, that Leo's cruel words had ripped her wide open, his reaction more brutal, more merciless than her worst fears. But she couldn't feel the wounds. Yet. Maybe her poor body was refusing to process them.

But at least she had managed to stand upright in front of Leo. She hadn't collapsed in a heap of misery. She had remained coherent, conducting herself with decorum in the face of more heartbreak than she had ever thought possible. At least she had walked out of that library with her head held high. Even if she had no idea how she'd done it.

But now the corridor seemed to be closing in on her, the musty smell of the books in the library lingering in her nostrils suddenly making her feel nauseous. She felt for the wall to steady herself. The dimensions of the space seemed to be changing, surging and retreating. Someone was coming towards her, a tall slight figure, gliding rather than walking, surrounded by white light. Emma half closed her eyes.

'*Dio mio!*' The figure had her arm around her shoulders now. Bony but warm, flesh and blood. So she was real, not an apparition. 'Emma? It is Emma, isn't it?'

Emma nodded weakly, letting her head rest against the woman's shoulder.

'Here, let me help you to a chair.'

A couple of staggering steps took them to a nearby seat.

'I should send for a doctor?' The woman crouched down beside her, taking Emma's hand in hers.

'No.' Emma tried to shake her head but it felt as if her brain was loose inside. 'No, I'll be fine in a minute.'

'Is it the baby?'

'No.' How did this person know she was pregnant? 'Well, it does make me feel a bit dizzy sometimes.' It was such an effort to talk. 'But, really, it will pass.'

'Then wait here. I will fetch Leonardo.'

'No!' The vehemence in Emma's voice sent a look of surprise across this woman's face. She was very beautiful, Emma realised as her senses started to return. Fine-boned, wide dark eyes searched her face. *Cordelia.* Of course, it had to be. 'Please don't tell him.'

'Well, if you are sure?' She stood up, her puzzled gaze travelling down the corridor until a member of staff appeared, as if she had conjured him up by thought alone. Rapid instructions were issued before she turned back to Emma. 'Are you well enough to move into the salon?'

'Yes, I think so.' Emma struggled to her feet to prove a strength she was far from feeling. Sandwiched between Cordelia and the servant she was guided into a grand salon and gently lowered onto a gilded sofa.

'Giovanni will bring you some water. Is there anything else you need?'

'No, I will be fine now, thank you.'

'Would you like me to stay with you? I was on my way to visit my husband in hospital but...'

'No, really, you go.'

She had reached the door before she turned to look back at Emma with an apologetic smile. 'Forgive me, I didn't even introduce myself. I am Cordelia. Your sister-in-law.'

'How do you do?' Emma gave her a faint smile. 'And thank you for looking after me. You must think me very feeble.'

'On the contrary...' Cordelia's dark eyes swept over her. 'You are married to Leonardo. That in itself takes strength and courage. He would never choose a wife who didn't possess such qualities.'

Emma looked down, swallowing hard.

'I appreciate that coming back to Ravenino has been very hard for him. Frankly his mood has been quite black. Which is why I am so pleased to see you. I'm sure having you here will be a great comfort to him.'

'I doubt that.'

'Don't underestimate yourself, Emma. He has missed you a great deal.'

'He...he said that?'

'Not exactly.' Cordelia adjusted the handbag over the crook of her arm. 'Leonardo is not a man to voice his emotions. But you forget that I know him. And I know when a woman has finally won his heart. Congratulations, Emma, I hope you will both be very happy.'

Stepping out onto the balcony, Emma took a lungful of fresh air. Having been fussed over by various members of staff for the past hour, she desperately craved solitude, time to think.

The view, at least, was calming. Sea and sky stretching in all directions, the shape of the mainland just visible on the horizon. A fishing boat headed towards the harbour, excited seagulls squawking in its wake. Everything about this place was so steeped in history and tradition you could feel it in the very air you breathed. A living history that Leo had been written out of.

Emma bit down on the tremble of her lip. How many times must he have stood gazing at this view? How many times must he have visited his beloved Ravenino in his head? And what must it feel like to be back here now? To have everything he had lost tantalisingly placed back in his hands, but only for a short while. Just long enough to rub salt into the wounds.

Leo's treatment of her couldn't have been more brutal. But beneath the cruel words, the arrogant authority, had she caught a glimpse of something else? Something that looked like torment. Like he was being pulled in two directions. Like being here was ripping him apart.

Cordelia's voice sounded in her head. '*He has missed you a great deal.*' Was that possible? '*I know when a woman has finally won his heart.*' She was wrong, she had to be. But her words had been enough to make Emma pause. To cancel the flight that had been put on standby for her, at least for today. Because running away no longer seemed like the answer. Staying and fighting did. Fighting for what she believed in. For happiness that could only be found in Leo's arms, in his bed, in his heart... Fighting for the man that she loved.

Her first thought had been to flee. To put some space between her and Leo in the desperate hope that if she returned to the UK, she might be able to patch up her broken heart enough to come back stronger in time for the birth. But the rules would have to change. She would be adamant about that. She would insist that she and the baby have their own apartment. Live separate lives. Leo could have unrestricted access to their child, but that's all. She couldn't go back to the arrangement they had shared at Villa Magenta. It was too painful. Too degrading.

Her head had told her this was the only way forward. But her heart refused to agree, twisting inside her now, telling her to fight for what she wanted, goading her into action. Condemning herself to such a cold, sterile existence would never make her happy. She would be existing rather than thriving, trapped in the twilight of a half-life where the sun would never shine. Living alongside the man she loved but who could never be hers. Who only ever came to her in her dreams.

Strength and courage. Did she possess enough of those qualities to try one more time? One last attempt to get inside Leo's head, to break through the protective wall and expose the turmoil that lay beneath. Because she was pretty sure that what was inside was broken, hurting. And despite everything, she knew she wanted to help him. To heal him. Even if it turned out to be her parting gift.

A strange sensation fluttered in her stomach and Emma grasped the stone balustrade. She hoped she wasn't going to feel faint again. But no. She spread her hands over her belly, waiting. There it was again. The baby. Their baby. Moving inside her, like it was trying to tell her something. Too gentle to be called a kick, yet more powerful than the mightiest blow. Emma closed her eyes against the swell of emotion. Here was the strength she needed. Now all she had to do was use it.

The cobbled streets of Ravenino greeted Leo like an old friend, twisting and turning their way down narrow alleys, opening up into ancient piazzas, ascending long flights of steps to white-painted churches. Leo knew every inch of the place. It was written into his DNA. As kids, he and Taddeo had treated the town like their playground, taking every opportunity to escape the walls of the Castello in search of freedom.

With Leo the brains of the operation and Taddeo egging him on, they had often been found stripped half-naked splashing in a fountain when they should have been in lessons, riding a donkey through the town with the Castello security team in hot pursuit. There had been punishments, of course. Harsh physical punishments, largely taken by Leo, the elder brother. The one who should have known better. But he hadn't minded. Taller and stronger than Taddeo, it was only right he'd taken the brunt of it. Besides, he'd loved his brother. He would have done anything for him.

But as the years had gone on their relationship had changed, responsibility settling on Leo's shoulders, seeing him start to obey the rules, take his lessons seriously, frequently travelling abroad for months at a time to further his education. Taddeo, meanwhile, had discovered women, lots of women. And partying. Frequently crashing home drunk when Leo had already been behind his desk, preparing for another day of dry instruction. Words had been exchanged. Leo informing his brother it was time he grew up, Taddeo demanding to know when Leo had turned into such a crashing bore.

By the time their father died they had become very different people. But the shock of finding out he was to be the next Conte had hit Taddeo almost as hard as Leo. Neither of them had handled it well, and Taddeo's arrogant assumption that Leo would take on much of the responsibility behind the scenes, effectively leaving him to carry on with his hedonistic lifestyle, had sent Leo into a storm of fury. Tempers had flared, voices had been raised. And when Taddeo had got wind that Leo had tried to honour his pledge to Cordelia and she had turned him down, he had used that to full advantage to get under Leo's skin. To taunt him in a way that only siblings could. And that, for Leo, had been the final straw. He'd wanted nothing more to do with Ravenino. Nothing more to do with Taddeo.

Turning the corner, he found himself in front of the town hall, the clock just starting to strike the hour. On either side of the dial, bronze figures took aim at the bell beneath, swinging their hammers with never diminishing strength.

'You and me, Leo,' Taddeo had once said, gazing up as he had linked his skinny arm through his brother's. 'One day we will be strong, just like them.'

But were they? Not Taddeo, incapacitated by an accident, lying in a hospital bed. And Leo himself? Sometimes it felt as if the stronger he was determined to be, the weaker he became. Certainly as far as Emma was concerned.

Emma. The memory of her standing there in the library, so upright, so proud, cut through him like a blade. But she shouldn't have come here. And she certainly shouldn't have declared her love for him.

He turned away, retracing his steps to the Castello.

Being summoned to Ravenino had been a cruel blow, but Leo had counted on there being *one* positive outcome. Being away from Emma would give him time to clear his head, order his thoughts. But that hadn't happened. Emma was permanently there—no matter where he was, what he was doing. A receptor in his brain, a tug in his gut, a pulse in his groin. He carried her with him wherever he went. Sometimes it felt as if she was attacking him on all fronts, just by existing. Just by being Emma.

Which was why his reaction had been so hostile when she had turned up this afternoon, out of the blue, talking about love. She was disobeying his orders. She was breaking the rules. She was messing with his head. She had even found out the sex of their baby without his permission.

A boy! His son! Pride reared up inside him again, constricting his throat. A daughter would have been just as joyous, but he couldn't help the way the thought of a son puffed out his chest, called to him on some primal level. And the fact that Emma had discovered it first no longer mattered one jot.

Inside the Castello grounds now, Leo gazed up at the imposing fortress, the granite walls, the towering turrets. A symbol of strength and power through the centuries, it epitomised everything he'd thought he'd stood for. Everything he had thought he'd wanted. And yet now…now he realised he had been mistaken. By coming back to the principality, he had been forced to face his nemesis, only to find it was no such thing. Ravenino was his past, not his future. It was not preventing him from moving on. He alone was doing that.

It was a shocking revelation. Leo looked around him,

breathing deeply, searching for the emotion that had to be there. Testing himself. Almost willing himself to feel what he had told himself he had to feel. Loss, regret, anger, bitterness. Because to deny it was to make a mockery of the last three years of his life. Years when he had skated over the surface of his life. Never standing still enough to examine the motives behind his behaviour. Never stopping to look at what lay beneath for fear it would be too hard.

But Emma had challenged him right from the start. From the moment she had put her slender fingers on the keyboard and composed that article. From the flash of her eyes that night in London, the shock revelation she was pregnant, the torment of trying to live alongside her at Villa Magenta.

And now this. By declaring her love for him. Always inside his head. Always Emma.

He started walking again, his feet taking him around the side of the Castello, towards the family chapel and the graveyard that was the final resting place for generations of Raveninos. He followed the grassy path that led to his mother's grave, set against the wall, catching the quiet rays of the afternoon sun. He had been here many times over the years, Taddeo by his side, placing flowers in the vase beneath the headstone, paying their respects to their mother who had died before her time. But now there was another grave, a newer headstone.

Alberto Leonardo Ravenino
May he rest in peace

A simple inscription sharply carved into the black granite.

Leo squatted down beside the grave. He now regretted refusing to attend Alberto's funeral. Regretted not having been there to pay his last respects to the man who had raised him. The man who Leo had thought to be his father for twenty-eight years. At the time he had been too consumed with rage to think straight. He had hated Alberto for being so weak—for daring to love a woman who had betrayed him in the worst possible way. For keeping the lie to himself until the very last moment. Leo had raged against the selfishness of his final act—casting him aside, just to ease his own conscience.

Now that anger had gone, replaced with understanding, sympathy even. He truly hoped Alberto was at peace. As a ray of sunlight flickered from one grave to the other, he realised he even wished the same for his mother. That they had found eternal happiness together, if ever such a thing were to be found.

Whatever had happened to him?

Emma. That was what. Emma had changed his whole perspective on life. Changed his priorities. Made him come alive. Made him feel. Not the shallow emotions shown to the faceless women who had shared his bed. Not the hatred and bitterness that he had harboured for so long. Nurtured even. Afraid that if he let go of it there would be nothing left of him. That his antipathy had made him the man he was.

With a rush of adrenaline his mind cleared. His fractured thoughts finally shaped into a clear picture.

Emma was his tormentor and his liberator. The light to his dark. She was everything to him. And yet he had sent her away...

Rising to his feet, Leo pushed back shoulders that

were locked with tension. Cowardice, denial, stupidity, he could think of a host of reasons for his behaviour. But none that excused it. Because the truth was he had panicked.

Emma's brave, beautiful, astonishing words had shaken the world beneath his feet. She had forced him to face the unthinkable. Not the knowledge she had fallen in love with him. That truth he held against his heart like the most precious jewel, warm and safe. Nothing and no one would take that away from him.

But the way her confession had flayed him, laying him bare, ripping him open for all to see. Showing him he was not the man he had told himself he was—clinical, unemotional, controlled. Making him feel what he told himself he could not feel. Did not want to feel. *And yet he did.* More deeply, more passionately than he could ever have imagined. *Love.* So powerful it hurt. So strong it burned. *He loved Emma.* That was an absolute, indisputable fact. One that he had realised the second Emma had made her confession. One that he had most probably always known but had stubbornly refused to acknowledge.

And so he had gone on the attack. Fought back. Because when you were exposed, that's what you did. When the outer layers had been stripped away, leaving you nowhere to hide, what other choice did you have?

But of course there were other choices. Honesty, for example. Sincerity, truth. Things that he had prided himself on. Things he would have said he stood for, until now. Until Emma had exposed him as a charlatan.

He had to explain—right away! He had to take her in

his arms, hold her, feel her, inhale her. Make her a part of him. Never let her go. *But first he had to find her.*

Furiously cursing himself for ever sending her away, he set off between the gravestones at a rapid pace, small birds taking flight as he disturbed their peace. But then reality kicked in and he stopped. Emma had gone. She would be in Milan by now, maybe back at Villa Magenta, packing her bags. He glared at his watch as if he could halt time. He needed to get the jet back here as fast as possible to take him to Emma before she instructed the pilot to fly her to London.

He tugged his phone out of his pocket, frantically making the call, holding the phone to his ear, scuffing the earth at his feet. *Come on, come on.*

'Leo.'

Emma. His Emma.

It took a second for him to realise the voice—*her voice*—had not come over the phone.

His head jerked up, his heart thudding in his ears. Standing about ten feet away she was framed between two gravestones, motionless, but so very alive amongst his sleeping relatives. Warm flesh and soft lips and a heart bigger than any he had ever known. And if that wasn't enough, if that wasn't far more than he ever deserved, she was carrying his child. His son. The next generation. Not the next Conte di Ravenino, he didn't give a damn about that any more, but something far more precious. His own family. *His own future. Dio*, what a fool he had been. A huge surge of emotion flooded through him, a tidal wave more powerful than anything he had ever felt before.

'Emma.' He couldn't keep the tremor from his voice. 'You...you came back.'

'I never left, Leo.' She twisted her hands in front of her. 'I couldn't.'

'Emma… I…'

'No, let me speak.' Determination lifted her chin, fixing her gaze on his. *Dio*, he loved her so much. 'I know you don't want me here, that you thought I had gone…'

'No… I…' He started towards her, but she took a step back, holding her hands out before her as if to ward him off.

'But I couldn't leave before trying one last time…'

'No, you don't understand. You don't need to try anything. You don't need to do anything.'

'Oh, but I do, Leo.' She gave a small shake of the head. 'Because I will never forgive myself, never find peace if I don't give you the opportunity, one last time, to tell me what you feel in your heart. About me. About us.'

'Oh, Emma.' His voice choked, Leo tried to close the space between them, but for every step he took forward, she took one back, stumbling over the long grass at the side of the pathway. *'Attenta!'* He stretched out a hand but dared come no closer. 'Please, be careful.'

'I'm fine.' She steadied herself, pushing back her shoulders, taking in a gasp of breath.

But she wasn't fine. She was fragile, sensitive, delicate. Flesh and blood. Skin and bones. And yet still she'd found the strength to confront him. Because she was also brave. The bravest person he had ever known. And for some unknown reason this perfect woman, this woman so beautiful, both inside and out, loved him.

He wasn't worthy. The thought struck him like a blow. He would never be worthy of such a woman.

Doubts crowded in, drawing down his brows into a scowl. And Emma noticed, biting down on her lip to stop the tremble. But still she pressed on.

'So I am going to ask you this, Leo. And I will accept your answer with all its implications.' Her chest rose on a brave breath. 'Do you think there is any chance that you could ever find it in your heart to love me?'

Oh, Emma. Darling Emma.

'More than a chance.' He felt the swell of love crowding his chest, filling his lungs. 'A certainty.'

Emma stared at him, that soft mouth opening in surprise. 'A...a certainty?'

'*Sì.*' Leo struggled to find the words trapped so deeply inside him. 'Because I already love you, Emma. In fact, I think I always have.'

They were the right words but the wrong tone, the struggle to stop his voice from cracking making them sound harsh, unfeeling.

Uncertainty flickered in Emma's eyes. 'Please don't say that if it isn't true, Leo.' Her hands strayed to the swell of her belly. 'I only want the truth.'

'Then hear this as the truth. *Ti amo.* I love you, Emma.'

He wanted to take her in his arms, to crush her against his chest. He wanted to kiss her, fiercely, with everything he had. He wanted to show his love in a way that words could never do. But he knew he had to be cautious.

One step at a time he stole the space between them, holding Emma still with his eyes, scared that one wrong move, one wrong word might see her bolt like a startled horse. Because she still looked totally stunned. Disbelieving.

Finally, she was in his arms. But her posture was stiff, her arms down by her sides. Her eyes, when he caught her chin to raise them to his, wide and blue as the sky.

'I love you, Emma.' He repeated the words, a soft whisper of breath against her face. 'With all that I have, all that I am.'

'Leo... I...'

'Hear it in my voice. See it in my eyes. And if that's not enough...' He reached for her hand, so small, chilled, despite the warmth of the late afternoon, and raised it to his chest. 'Feel it in my heart and know that it is true.'

'Oh, Leo.' Eyes shining, she raised her face to his gaze, and Leo could only stare in wonder at the woman he loved so much. The upturn of her nose, the fine cheekbones, the line of her closed lips. He loved every inch of her. Every single molecule that made her who she was. He squeezed the hand against his chest, warming it, willing her to feel the thud of his heart. But to his dismay tears had started to spill from her eyes, silently rolling down her cheeks, a flood of them.

He had never seen her cry before. Not once. Not after everything he had put her through. As his fingertips touched the dampness of her tears his heart splintered into a thousand pieces.

'Don't cry, Emma. Please.' He fell to his knees, down in the dirt where he belonged. Wrapping his arms around her waist he buried his face in her belly. 'I know I have treated you very badly, that I don't deserve you, but please don't cry. Please find it in your heart to forgive me.'

'There is nothing to forgive.'

'Oh, but there is. But I will make it up to you, I promise, if you will give me the chance. If you just—' His words were suddenly stolen by the most remarkable thing—a flutter against his cheek where it was pressed to Emma's belly. Their baby! Leo scrambled to his feet, his hand to his face as if he could somehow keep hold of the feeling.

'The baby! I felt it move!' He stared at Emma in wide-eyed astonishment, and she smiled at him. The most beautiful smile. Taking his hand, she pressed it back down on her belly.

'I know. It's amazing, isn't it? And before long he will be with us. A new life. A new start. That's what I want, Leo. Not forgiveness. No looking back. Just forward towards the future.'

'My darling Emma.' He brushed his hand against her cheek. 'When did you get to be so wise?'

'Well, one of us has to be.' The twinkle in her eyes warmed his heart, dried the last of her tears.

'*È vero.*' He smiled back, brushing her hair away from her face. He wasn't going to argue with her. 'And I promise to be the best man I can possibly be.'

'You already are that man, my love.'

'And the best father.'

'I have no doubt of that.'

'I love you, Emma Ravenino.'

'And I love you too, Leonardo. More than I can say.'

'Emma?'

'Mmm…?'

'Stop staring at me.'

Emma shifted the position of her elbow. She had been gazing at Leo ever since he'd closed his eyes, studying the beautiful face she loved so much while she had the chance. Thick dark lashes fringed his closed lids. Two fine grooves between his brows indicated his tendency to scowl with scrutiny or impatience. Straight nose, perfectly drawn mouth, jawline covered in a dark shadow of stubble. She could still feel the burn of that stubble against her face. Against her breasts, against her inner thighs…

'You are still doing it.' His eyes flickered beneath lids that were still firmly closed.

'So what if I am?' Emma teased. 'You can't stop me.'

'Hmm… Is that a challenge?' The eyelids slowly opened. 'Because you know I can't resist one of those.'

'So what are you going to do about it?'

'Let me think.' The lids half closed again. 'Ah, yes, this…'

With a rush of movement she was in his arms, her breasts crushed against his naked chest, her lips crushed beneath his.

When the need for air eventually forced them apart, Emma gazed at him again with laughing eyes. 'Okay, you won that, but only because you played dirty.'

'Not half as dirty as I'd like to be.' Leo's leg slid between her thighs, his head moving to nuzzle her neck and shoulder, pushing aside her hair until his lips found bare skin.

'Stop that, you.' Reluctantly Emma shoved him away. 'We really should get up, you know.'

'I don't see why. We can do whatever we want.' Leo moved a strand of hair away from her face. 'And right now I want to be in bed with my wife.'

'But we have been here for hours. People will be wondering where we are.'

'Who cares?'

'Cordelia maybe?' Emma swept her fringe out of her eyes.

'Cordelia is too preoccupied with Taddeo to be worrying about anything else.'

'I've met her, you know. Cordelia,' Emma admitted softly.

'You have? When?'

'After I left you in the library. I started to feel a bit faint and she helped me into the salon.'

'*Cristo*, Emma. Why didn't you say? Why didn't she come and tell me?'

'Because I asked her not to. Begged her, in fact. I couldn't face seeing you again. Not after...'

'I'm so sorry, Emma.' Leo cupped her face in his hands. 'So sorry for all the hurt and pain I have caused you. For saying that hateful thing about your mother and her boyfriend...it was unforgivable.'

'It doesn't matter.'

'Yes, it does.' He dropped his hands, raking them through his hair, his anguish clear. 'It matters that you were brave enough to open up to me about something so painful in your life and I threw it back in your face in a moment of selfish anger. It was despicable of me.'

'Then I forgive you.' Emma gazed at the storm in his eyes, instinctively wanting to take the suffering away.

'I will support you in any way I can—you do know that? Do anything within my power to make amends. I'll even try and get on with your mother, if that's what you want.' His lips twisted with a wry smile. 'We could stick her on a desert island. Buy her a commune, whatever you think best.'

'Hmm, I don't think that would work. I'm not sure you have fully grasped the principles she lives by.'

'Nor will I, until she loves you the way you deserve to be loved.'

Emma's throat tightened. She reached for Leo's hand, linking her fingers in his to bring it down on the covers between them. 'Let's just take it a day at a time and see what happens. Miracles don't happen overnight.'

'Some do.' Leo moved their hands to her stomach, his eyes shining with love.

'Yes.' Emma gazed back at him. 'They do, don't they?'

Pushing himself up against the pillows, Leo folded his arms across his chest. Bronzed skin, sculpted muscles, hard, dark nipples. So beautiful. 'If you let me, I would like to try and give you some sort of explanation for my behaviour.'

'No…really…it's not necessary.'

'Please, Emma, let me say this.'

'Okay.' She snuggled beside him. 'If that's what you want.' But her teasing tone was met with a firming of the jaw, a swallow of the throat she could hear as well as see.

'This is not an excuse, nowhere near, but the reason I was so intent on pushing you away was because I was convinced I could never be the man you wanted me to be. That I could never give you the happy ever after you deserved.' The seriousness in his eyes broke her heart. 'I thought I had to protect you.'

'From what? I don't understand.'

'From me. From the man I was sure I was. Deep down. I thought that if I were to let you love me, if I allowed you into my heart you would see it for what it was.'

'Which is?'

'Something small and shrivelled and black.' His mouth twisted with distaste.

'No! Why ever would you think such a thing?' Shock shadowed Emma's gaze as she reached for his hand again, clasping it to her breast.

'Because that's what it felt like. I was so consumed with bitterness and hatred over losing Ravenino I was convinced it had become all I was. I took my mother's betrayal and used it as a weapon, a protector, resolving to never let a woman close to me again. Then you came along and everything I thought I knew was thrown into doubt. You shook the very foundations of my ordered life.' He gave a soft laugh.

'And to make matters worse, I found out you had issues with your own mother. But instead of railing against her, you were still trying to build a relationship with her. I couldn't understand why you would do that, why you would carry on letting her hurt you. Now I know it's because you are a much better person than me.'

'Not better, Leo, just different.' Emma clutched his hand tightly to ward off tears, testing a watery smile. 'Okay, maybe better.'

But Leo's return smile only drew his features tighter. 'You unwittingly showed how I had let my own mother's mistake dominate my life. But I was still too stubborn to acknowledge that I was wrong, and you were right. That forgiveness is so much better than bitterness. That the dead weight I was carrying around inside me was of my own making.

'So what did I do? I fought against you as hard as I could, distanced myself, tried to convince myself you meant nothing to me. For your sake as well as mine. But it was useless. No matter what I did, you were still there in my head, smashing through my defences, driving me crazy.'

'Oh, Leo.' Emma kissed the hand she held in hers, then moved her lips to his face, laying the softest of kisses against his mouth. But Leo edged away, determined to meet her eyes.

'When you turned up today, out of the blue, I went into a kind of shock. And that was before you told me you loved me. It was like I couldn't process the enormity of my feelings for you.

'So I walked the streets in search of vindication, fully expecting the sense of loss to kick in, for the hostility and resentment I had nurtured for so long to take over. To validate the way I had treated you. But nothing happened. All I could think of was how I had hurt you. So I had to try harder.

'I went to the graveyard, sure that the graves of my mother and Alberto would trigger the old bitterness and anger. But still there was nothing. That's when I realised the ache in my gut had nothing to do with Ravenino any more, and everything to do with you. I was about to go chasing after you when you found me. I can't tell you how it felt to see you standing there. To know you hadn't given up on me.'

'We have Cordelia to thank for that. She told me I had won your heart. I didn't believe her, but it at least gave me the courage to stay and ask you one last time.'

'Then I owe her a great debt.'

'We both do.'

'But nothing compared to the debt I owe to you, *cara*. For being strong enough to smash through the walls of my stubbornness and fear and allow me to finally see the truth.'

Emma took a breath, ready to make a confession of her own. 'You know I always thought you were still in love with Cordelia?'

'Whatever made you think that?' Leo's brow furrowed in surprise.

'I decided you could never love me because your heart still belonged to her.'

'Tesoro mio.' Leo touched her cheek with his free hand. 'I agreed to marry Cordelia out of duty, then made the mistake of thinking I should honour the agreement, even when I lost the principality. My pride was hurt, I'll admit, but I never loved her.'

For a moment they just stared into one another's eyes, the spilling of confessions laying them bare.

'You know I would never have accepted that description of your heart, even if you couldn't love me.' Emma's solemn words broke the silence. 'I have seen your kindness and generosity time and again, even when you have tried to hide them from me. The way you have helped Beatrice and her family. The respect you show your staff, the employees of your companies. The charities you support.'

'Supporting people financially is easy.' The backs of his fingers smoothed over her chin, down her neck. 'My mistake was thinking I could do that with you. That that would be enough. And when I found it wasn't, that I wanted all of you, not just your company, your body, your lovely face across the table from me at breakfast, but your heart and your soul as well—then I knew I was in deep trouble.'

'Darling Leo.' Emma gazed at him. 'You have all of those things. Plus my undying love. Now and for ever.'

'Then I have so much more than I deserve.'

'I love you, Leo, so very much.'

'And I love you. So much more.'

Enveloping her in his arms, Leo lowered his head, finding her lips to deliver the sweetest, most tender kiss in the world.

EPILOGUE

'DO YOU THINK we should go and rescue them from our son?' Behind him, Leo could hear Emma moving around the room, collecting up their belongings.

He looked out of the bedroom window to where the small group had settled themselves under the shade of an ancient oak tree. A rug had been laid out, the remains of an impromptu picnic scattered around them, and baby Carlo was being tossed in the air by his doting uncle. Even though Leo couldn't hear it, he knew his son would be chuckling uncontrollably. Leo loved that chuckle. It was the most joyous sound in the world.

Joining him, Emma rested her chin on his shoulder, sliding her arms around his waist.

'No, let's leave them to it.' Leo squeezed her hands. 'They look like they are having fun. Besides, it's good practice for Taddeo.'

'No! What…? You mean…?'

'*Si, cara,* it's true.' He turned to smile at his wife. 'Taddeo told me this morning. Cordelia is pregnant.'

'How wonderful!' Emma's face lit up. 'A little cousin for Carlo! I'm so pleased!'

They both watched as Carlo was passed to Cordelia,

who confidently straightened his little sun hat, redid the ties, then kissed him on the nose.

'So we could have the next Conte di Ravenino in the making?' She posed the question lightly, but Leo could sense the tinge of anxiety.

'We could indeed. And there's no need to look like that, *amore mio*. I have fully accepted that Taddeo is the rightful Conte, and his son will carry on the line.'

'No regrets?' Her gaze searched his face.

'None whatever. How could I when I have you and Carlo? You are so much more precious than any piece of land or title.'

Emma smiled, touching her finger to his lips. They had been living at the Castello on and off for almost nine months now. Carlo had been born here. But they both knew their stay was only temporary. And despite Leo's reassurances, a little bit of Emma still worried that he would find it hard to leave.

'Do you think Taddeo will cope on his own? Without you to support him?'

Leo shrugged. 'I'll still be available if he needs me, but it's time he stood on his own two feet. And you know what, I think he'll be fine. The accident was the best thing that could have happened to him.'

'Leo!'

'I mean it. It seems to have finally knocked some sense into him.'

'I'm not sure he'd see it like that. But he told me himself that he feels much more confident now. Ready to rule.'

'About time. But if he dares to use that phrase on social media, I will kill him.'

'Don't be such a grouch.' Emma laughed. 'He's very

grateful, you know, for everything you've done while he's been recovering.'

'I know. But it's time to hand over the reins now. We have our own lives to get on with. And to be honest, I can't wait.'

'Me too.' Emma gazed up at his handsome face. Grey eyes stared back at her, clear and bright. Shining, not with doubt or regret but with love. It was time to stop worrying.

'Speaking of which, what time are we flying back to Milan?' She crossed back into the room, where an array of Carlo's adorable baby clothes were spread on the bed. 'I need to get on with this packing.'

'Staff are employed for that job.' Leo walked behind her. 'I need my wife for far more important activities.'

'Such as?'

'Well, if Carlo is being entertained elsewhere it seems a shame to waste the opportunity.'

'Leonardo Ravenino, you are incorrigible.' Her stern voice didn't fool either of them. 'I'm sure you must have matters of state to discuss with Taddeo before we leave.'

'The state can wait.'

'Another quote for social media?'

'Ha!' Laughing, Leo smothered her in his arms, pressing the length of his body against hers. So tall and strong, taut muscles beneath warm flesh. Closing her eyes, Emma moulded herself against him.

'Oh, I nearly forgot.' Leo loosened his hold. 'I saw something in the press this morning that will interest you.' He moved into the bedroom, searching around. 'Where did I put it? Ah, here it is.'

He held up a newspaper in his hands and the two of them exchanged a glance. It was a copy of the *Paladin*.

'Not another reporter getting into terrible trouble by submitting the wrong article?' Emma came to stand beside him.

'No, not this time. Although that didn't turn out so badly in the end, did it?' Leo turned to face her, love shining in his eyes.

Sitting them on the edge of the bed, he turned over the pages until he found what he was looking for, a report on a recent G7 conference on homelessness. 'Here, listen to this: *"World leaders agreed that much more needed to be done, both nationally and internationally. The charitable foundation Read All About It was cited as an excellent example of an innovative approach to raising both awareness and funding."'*

'Ooh, that's great publicity for us.' Emma took the newspaper from his hands to read it for herself. 'I'll make sure the team know about this.'

'Never mind the publicity.' Leo stopped the hand that was reaching for her phone. 'How about taking a minute to give yourself some praise? What you have achieved is incredible. I am so proud of you.'

'Thank you.' Emma reached to touch his lips with her own. 'I'm proud of myself too. Though technically it was your idea.'

'But you made it happen.'

'Yes, I did, didn't I?' She rested her head on his shoulder.

'And you don't regret not working for the *Paladin* any more?'

'No, of course not!' Emma sat upright, turning to take Leo's face in her hands. The face she loved so much. The newspaper slid to the floor. 'How could I possibly regret anything now that I have you and

Carlo? My life has never been more perfect. It never could be.'

It was true. Finally Emma felt like she belonged. Not the lost child trying to fit in with her chaotic family in the wilds of the countryside. Not in London, struggling to make ends meet, or trying to prove herself at the offices of the *Paladin*. But with Leo, as a wife and a mother. And not only that but she had a career she loved too and the full support of a husband to make it happen. No longer Emma Quinn but Emma Ravenino, she finally knew who she was.

'I'm so glad.' Leo removed her hands, kissing her knuckles. 'I would hate to think I might have to start trying to make it up to you again. You know where that leads.'

'Mmm…yes, I do.' Emma felt herself being lifted up onto the bed, gently laid back across the pillows. 'It's a penance I have to bear.'

'And can I say you do it with great fortitude.' Leo lay down beside her, putting his arms around her again, drawing her to him, lightly kissing her forehead, her cheeks, her lips.

'Thank you. I do my best.'

'*Ti amo, mia bella* Emma.'

'And I love you too, Leo. Always and for ever.'

Emma had just enough time to say the words before Leo's mouth was on hers again. For a moment they both caught the light in each other's eyes before the power of the kiss took over, and their lids closed in surrendered bliss.

* * * * *

QUEEN BY ROYAL
APPOINTMENT

LUCY MONROE

MILLS & BOON

For my bestie and sister-of-my-heart, Carolyn.
I'm just so grateful to have you in my life.
Much love!

CHAPTER ONE

LADY NATALIYA SHEVCHENKO stood outside the private reception room in the Volyarus palace, feeling more like she was entering a war tribunal than going to the family meeting her "uncle," King Fedir, had decreed she attend.

And she was the one about to be on trial for Acts Against the State.

Only, legally, she'd done nothing wrong. Morally, she hadn't either, but she did not expect "Uncle" Fedir to agree.

King Fedir wasn't actually her uncle. He was her mother's cousin, but the two had been raised as close as siblings and he had always called himself Nataliya's uncle.

Taking a deep breath and centering herself, calling on a lifetime of training and all her courage, she indicated with a nod of her head for the guard to pull the ornate door open. His very presence indicated that there were more people in that room than her family.

Unless palace security had changed drastically, family only meant guards at either end of the hall, which there were, so this one meant more dignitaries inside.

Two guesses for who those dignitaries were and she would only need one.

Head held high, Nataliya walked into the luxuriously appointed room. No one would mistake this space with its silk wallpaper, and gilt and brocade furniture, for anything other than a royal's.

Her heels clicked against the marble, before stepping onto the lush carpet that filled the center of the room.

King Fedir sat in an ornate armchair that might as well have been his throne, for all his regal bearing. Except that glower he was giving her. That didn't look so much regal as just really, really annoyed. To his right sat Queen Oxana, her expression entirely enigmatic.

Nataliya's own mother was there too. First cousin to the King and Oxana's best friend, Solomia, Countess Shevchenko, nevertheless occupied a seat of no distinction.

Further from the royal couple than the youngest son of Prince Evengi of Mirrus, the other major player in this farce of judgment, Nataliya's mother sat in an armchair away from everyone else. Whether that had been by her choice or the King's, Nataliya would figure out later.

Right now, she surveyed the other occupants of the opulent room. Prince Evengi, former King of Mirrus, and his three sons sat opposite King Fedir and Queen Oxana. Although Prince Evengi had abdicated his throne to his eldest son, Nikolai, nearly a decade ago, there was no doubt that he was the driving force behind the contract Nataliya and her parents had signed.

A contract that stipulated, among other business and private concerns, that Nataliya would wed the second son to the House of Merikov, Konstantin.

Rumored to be descendants of both Romanov and Deminov blood, the Russian family had established their kingdom on an island between Alaska and Russia, like Volyarus, but Mirrus was in the Chukchi Sea.

They had another thing in common with Volyarus. The basis of their economy had started with mining rare minerals and was now just as profitable a worldwide concern, if not quite as stable as Yurkovich-Tanner, the company that supported Volyarus' economy.

Despite the Ukrainian heritage of Volyarus and its not so amicable history with Russia, King Fedir was determined to cement a family and business alliance with Mirrus, even ten years after that draconian contract was signed.

The only other two occupants of the room were her

"uncle's" sons, Maksim, Crown Prince, and his elder brother, the adopted Prince Demyan.

There was a time that their families had been very close.

Although, Nataliya worked for Demyan and saw Maks and his wife on occasion when they were in Seattle, that closeness had been gone for many years.

Breaking protocol, Nataliya ignored the assembled Kings present and smiled her first greeting to her mother. "Hello, Mama. You look well."

"Thank you, Nataliya. It is always good to see you." Mama smiled back, but the expression did not reach her worried eyes, the same warm brown as Nataliya's.

Nataliya was not surprised her father had not been summoned. He was, for all intents and purposes, a nonentity in her life and still very much a persona non grata in Volyarus.

Fifteen years ago, his decision to abandon his Countess and their child to pursue marriage to his most recent mistress had broken the cardinal rules of discretion and putting duty to country above personal considerations.

He had brought ugly attention to the royal family and the throne, and for that, Nataliya doubted he would ever be forgiven.

After greeting her mother, Nataliya gave King Fedir and Queen Oxana her full regard, dropping into a perfect curtsy between their two chairs. "Uncle Fedir, Aunt Oxana, it is a pleasure to see you again."

That might be stretching the truth a bit. And under the circumstance, she had no doubt the man who was in actuality her first cousin, once removed was regretting not rescinding the courtesy title of uncle long before now.

"Nataliya..." King Fedir actually looked at a loss for words, for the first time in Nataliya's memory. He certainly hadn't been the last time they'd spoken.

That time during a phone call, she'd had to schedule two weeks in advance.

She might call him *uncle*, but she didn't enjoy family privileges any longer.

When the silence had stretched, Queen Oxana gave an unreadable look to her husband and stood.

In a move that shocked Nataliya, the Queen approached her in order to give Nataliya the traditional kiss of greeting on both cheeks. "My dear, it is good to see you." The Queen's voice held no insincerity. "Come, you will sit beside me."

The Queen gave a look to her son Maksim, indicating with a regal inclination of her head a couple of equally elegant flicks of her wrist what she wanted done. Despite being Crown Prince, Maks immediately jumped up and oversaw the moving of chairs so that Nataliya's mother sat on her other side, thus cementing in the minds of everyone present just where the Queen stood on the issue to be discussed.

Nataliya's scandalous behavior that had not in fact been scandalous at all.

The King did not look pleased by this turn of events, but Nataliya did not care.

His lack of true concern for her and her mother had been shown fifteen years ago, when they had been forced to emigrate to the States to *protect the good name of the royal family*. Though neither were responsible for the gutter press dragging their names through the mud.

No one spoke for several interminable minutes while both of the older Kings looked on at Nataliya in censure. King Nikolai had a better poker face than even Oxana, however.

Nataliya had no idea what the current King of Mirrus thought of the proceedings and what had prompted them, but even his unreadable regard did things to Nataliya's insides she wished, for the hundredth time at least, it did not.

And because she never lied to herself, she did not try to believe she did not care what that was. He was not the man she was supposed to marry, but he was the only man in the House of Merikov whose opinion carried any weight with her.

When she did not let the clearly strategic silence force her into speech, King Fedir frowned. "You know why you are here?"

"I prefer not to guess."

"You signed a contract promising marriage to Prince Konstantin."

"I did." Though if any man did not live up to his name, it was the one she was not engaged to, but still expected to marry one day. "Ten years ago," she added, letting her tone tell them all what she thought of a decade-long wait for that contract to be fulfilled and yet her being here because she'd done what? Gone on a few dates?

Not that she hadn't wanted just this reaction, but seriously?

Get real.

A very unroyal-like sound came from Prince Evengi. "Then explain yourself."

Nataliya stood and gave the King a curtsy, acknowledging him formally, before returning to her seat. One must observe the niceties. "What would you like me to explain?" she asked.

"Do not play obtuse," he barked.

King Nikolai said something in an undertone to his father and the older man yanked his head in acknowledgement.

Prince Konstantin, current heir to his brother's throne, frowned at Nataliya. "You know very well why you have been summoned here, why we have all had to take time from our busy schedules to deal with this mess."

"What mess might that be?" she asked, unimpressed.

Had she curtsied to him? No, she had not and the ice cap on Mount Volyarus would melt before she did.

This man lived and breathed the company that made up the majority of his country's economy. The time he'd taken for his affairs had been negligible and Nataliya had felt no actual envy toward the women he'd taken to his bed and done nothing else to romance.

Ten years ago, she had signed that draconian contract for two equally important reasons. Ten years in which this man had not even made enough time in his schedule to announce the engagement. Ten years during which Nataliya had lived in a stasis that had not upset her all that much, honestly.

Her mother's limbo, she was not so sanguine about. Because one of the clauses of the contract was that Countess Solomia would be able to return to Volyarus upon the marriage of her daughter to the Prince of the House of Merikov.

Without the formalized engagement, much less a marriage, that had not happened.

Her second reason had been no less successful. Nataliya had hoped that by agreeing to marry Konstantin, her inappropriate feelings for his married brother would go away.

While she'd gotten over Nikolai, it wasn't because of her commitment to Konstantin.

"This mess." Konstantin threw down the fashion magazine that had run the "50 First Dates for a Would-Be Princess" article.

"Are you hoping to claim that in the past ten years, you have not dated anyone, Prince Konstantin?" she asked him, with little interest in his answer and aware that the term *date* was in fact a misnomer. "Only I have a whole file full of pictures that would indicate otherwise."

"You had me followed?" he asked with fury, surging to his feet.

Only his brother's hand on his arm kept the angry Prince across the room.

She should probably be intimidated, but anger and posturing held no sway with a woman who had endured years in her father's household. She could have told her erstwhile intended that.

His position as Prince was no more impressive to Nataliya. She'd been raised as part of the royal family of Volyarus until the age of thirteen and had never ceased being the daughter of nobility.

"Perhaps you would like to explain, Uncle Fedir?" she prompted, her own anger a wall of cold ice around her heart, making her voice arctic.

And she did not regret that. At all.

The King of Volyarus winced as his own family and that of the other royal family present gave him varying looks of anger and condemnation.

"Of course we kept track of Prince Konstantin, but it was in no way nefarious." He made a dismissive gesture. "I have no doubt you had your interests watched, as well." He indicated Nataliya with a tip of his head.

She wasn't offended being referred to in that manner. The King's ability to hurt her had passed years ago.

"You shared your investigator's findings with your niece?" Nikolai asked, his voice laced with censure, but no shock at the other royal's actions.

If he'd given a bit of that censure to his brother, Nataliya would have respected him more. And something in her expression must have told him so because he gave her a strange look.

"I did not," King Fedir denied categorically.

"Then how?"

"I believe I can answer that," Prince Demyan, who had remained silent up until then, said.

Interesting that her mother and Queen Oxana were the only other women who had been invited to this ludicrous tribunal.

King Fedir stared at his other son. "How?" he barked.

"You know I use hackers to watch over our interests,"

Prince Demyan said, clearly unafraid of making such an admission in the rarified company.

Not one of these royals would voluntarily share *anything* being said in this room right now.

King Fedir nodded with a single jerk of his head.

"Nataliya is one of those hackers."

"The best one," Nataliya added. "Not to put too fine a point on it."

Demyan actually smiled at her, but then they were still friends, if no longer as close as siblings. "Yes, the best one."

"You did not assign her to watch over her own errant fiancé," the King asked, obviously appalled at the idea.

"He is *not* my fiancé," Nataliya said fiercely.

"No!" Demyan said at the same time.

"Then how?" Her uncle looked at her. He had asked her the first time she'd brought the photos to his attention.

She'd avoided answering then, not wanting a lecture about her actions to derail the reason for their discussion. She'd still hoped he would put her happiness somewhere in the realm of his priorities three months ago. Now she had no such illusions.

She shrugged. "I like to practice my skills. I was looking through files and noticed one with his name on it."

Everyone in the room seemed shocked by her actions.

"You hacked into your King's private files?" Nikolai asked, nothing in his tone indicating what he thought about that.

But his deep voice reverberated through her being nonetheless. If she could have chosen one person *not* to be here for this farce, it would be King Nikolai of Mirrus.

"Not exactly. I hacked into Demyan's files." She frowned. "In fact, I was looking for security breach points. To shore them up. I *like* Demyan. I did not want him to be vulnerable to other corporate or politically motivated hackers."

"Thank you," Demyan said amidst gasps and condemnation by others.

"And so because you were angry my son had not paid you enough attention since signing the contract, and in a misguided fit of jealousy and feminine pique, you thought to embarrass him into action?"

She stared at the old King of Mirrus, flabbergasted at his interpretation of her actions.

"You think I was *jealous*?" she asked in icy disbelief she made no effort to soften.

"Naturally," Konstantin said, ignoring her tone as he had her person for the past decade. "Only you miscalculated my reaction."

"Did I?" she asked, doubting very much that she had.

"Your weekly online auction of the items I sent to you in my effort to court you prior to announcing our formal engagement made me look the fool."

The *wooing* gifts had started arriving exactly one month after her appeal to King Fedir to renegotiate the terms of the contract, no doubt prompted by him. Konstantin's attempt at courtship had been as impersonal as the greeting between strangers at a State function and with even less effort put behind it.

"The proceeds go to a very deserving charity," she pointed out, not at all unhappy with the direction this conversation was heading, and not particularly bothered that Konstantin had found her disposal of the gifts inappropriate.

Maksim swore, a pithy Ukrainian curse that shocked the people around him. But he was looking at Nataliya with reluctant respect. He knew.

Nataliya couldn't help smiling at the man who had been as close as a brother until she was thirteen years old, and her entire family was ripped from her. She even winked.

He laughed.

"You find this amusing?" Prince Konstantin asked with angry reproach.

"I find this situation laughable, yes," Maksim said without apology in his manner, or tone.

And Nataliya wondered if the future King of Volyarus was more reasonable than his father and understood how over-the-top everyone's reaction was.

Not that she had not relied on that extreme reaction, but she still found it archaic, chauvinistic and not just a little ridiculous. Her manipulations would not have been possible if a gross double standard did not exist in the minds of almost every male in this room.

"You think your cousin is amusing, though her actions have destroyed our families' plans of a merger?" Konstantin asked furiously.

"Oh, there will be a business merger," Demyan said before his brother could answer. "Both our countries will benefit, but more to the point, Mirrus cannot afford to back out. The repercussions would be devastating for Mirrus Global and your country's economy."

"I will not marry her," Konstantin said implacably.

His father looked pained, and his brother, the King, frowned, but Nataliya felt elation pour through her. She had won. Because regardless of what the rest of the people in this room wanted, his words had just released *her* from her promise. And ultimately, that was all that mattered to her.

She'd only been eighteen, but she'd signed the contract in good faith and had been unwilling to simply renege. Her integrity would not allow it. She was not her father.

King Fedir suddenly looked old, and tired in a way she'd never noticed before. "That is exactly what you wanted, though, wasn't it?" he asked her.

"I could have done without the name calling and disgusting double standard, but yes."

King Fedir shook his head, clearly confused by her reaction. "I thought you wanted your mother settled back in her home country."

"Ten years ago, I wanted that more than anything. *I* wanted to come home, or at least be able to visit often."

"And that has changed?" King Fedir asked, sounding as fatigued as he looked.

"My mother has finally found peace with her life in America."

Queen Oxana looked wounded. "You don't want to come home?" she asked her best friend of more than thirty years.

Mama drew herself up, her dignity settled around her like a force field, making Nataliya nothing but proud. "My home is in America now."

"You do not mean that." Queen Oxana had the effrontery to sound hurt when she'd done nothing to stop Mama and Nataliya's exile fifteen years ago.

"I do."

"She does," Nataliya said with satisfaction, and was so happy about that she could cry. "You and your husband exiled my mother and me for the sins of my father. And though he knew how important that clause in the contract was to us both, he made no effort to press for fulfillment of the marriage merger." Now it would not happen at all.

Queen Oxana's expression was troubled. "You were too young to tie down to marriage when it was signed."

"But not too young to sign it? Not too young to be used as a political and business pawn?" Nataliya shook her head in disbelief.

"We all have duty we must adhere to," the Queen said, though with less fervent conviction than she used to.

"Our duty included exile. Looking back, I realize that asking more of my daughter was obscene." Mama could do regal disapproval as well as any queen.

"You know why we had to ask the sacrifice of you," King Fedir said to his cousin.

But Mama made Nataliya so proud yet again when she shook her head. "No, I never understood your decision to sacrifice me, a woman who was a better sister to you than Svitlana ever was. I spent years grieving the loss of my homeland, but I grieve no longer."

"And so you decided to break the contract?" Nikolai asked, this time his opinion clear for any to hear the disapproval and disappointment in his tone.

Nataliya met his gaze squarely. "My mother told me five years ago that she was not sure she would move back to Volyarus permanently, even if she could."

His brows drew together in a thoughtful frown. "Then what prompted your dating and the very public rejection of my brother's attempt to court you?"

"There is so much wrong with that question, I don't even know where to start." Was he as draconian as his father?

Nataliya had never believed it of Nikolai.

"Try. Please."

It was the *please* that did it.

"One, I was *never* engaged to your brother. I was contracted to be engaged and married at a later date, which was never specified. Not exactly good contract negotiations," she criticized King Fedir. "So, I *could* have been dating all along."

Heck, she could have been sleeping around. She'd had no legal or moral obligation to go to her marriage bed a virgin, and the stipulation of her chastity or lack of romantic social life until the marriage had not even been alluded to in the contract.

She'd read it through, all thirty-six pages of it, before embarking on the dating article.

"But you did not date before this." Nikolai's words made it very clear that his family had in fact had her watched.

She shrugged, not particularly caring that a *lady* was never supposed to be so dismissive. "I did not want to risk developing an emotional attachment that would have made keeping my promise difficult, or possibly even impossible."

Nikolai nodded in approval of her words. "Very wise."

"So, by converse, you consider that your brother has been foolish?" she asked, unable to resist.

Konstantin cursed.

Nikolai looked at his brother and then back to her. "Considering the outcome of his choices, I would say that is a given."

"My choices?" Konstantin demanded with umbrage. "I was doing my best to protect and expand the business interests of our country so that we did not lose our independent status. How does that make me the bad guy here?"

Nataliya might have agreed with Konstantin, except for two things. One, he'd had affairs, if not dates. Two, he'd acted like an ass about *her* innocent dating.

If he hadn't, she might have even felt compelled to honor the contract.

But Nikolai ignored him. "You said *one*, there are other things wrong with my question?"

"Second, it is obvious that what prompted my actions was my desire *not* to marry a man who so obviously had no more personal integrity than my father."

"I am not like your philandering father." The Prince took clear offence with the comparison. "We were not engaged!"

Nataliya looked at Konstantin with a frown. "If that is your attitude, then how do you explain refusing to marry me because I *dated* other men while you were having *sex* with other women?"

Konstantin's mouth opened and closed without him saying anything.

"Anything else?" Nikolai asked her.

"Do you believe that waiting ten years to fulfill the terms of a contract is keeping good faith in that contract?" she asked instead of answering.

"There were circumstances," Nikolai reminded her, almost gently.

She nodded in agreement. "Your father's heart attack, followed by your own ascension to the throne and your brother having to take over more business responsibility."

"Yes."

"That was eight *years* ago."

"Our family was in mourning," Konstantin said snidely. "Surely you did not expect a formal announcement during that time."

He was referring to the death of his brother's wife, the new Queen, and trying to make her feel small doing it, but Nataliya wasn't going to let anyone in this room make her feel less than. *She* wasn't the one who had dismissed finer feelings or responsibilities.

"It is customary to observe a period of mourning for one year."

And it had been five. It didn't need to be said. They all knew. Again, the timing did not justify the ten-year wait.

For her, or her mother.

"No one from Volyarus approached me about formalizing the engagement," Konstantin pointed out, like that was some kind of fact in his favor.

"Are you saying that you only fulfill the terms of a contract when you are pushed into doing so?" she asked, not impressed and letting that show.

Konstantin glowered. "You have all but admitted you don't want the marriage," he accused rather than answer her question.

She wouldn't deny it. "I do not." While she'd never actually *wanted* to marry this man, she had wanted Mama to be able to return to the bosom of her family.

Nataliya had come to realize both she and her mom were better off without a family that could eject them from their lives so easily, but that was not how it had been ten years ago.

"If you had realized you didn't want to marry my son, surely you should have taken less scandalous steps to insure it." Prince Evengi sounded more baffled than angry at this point. "You could simply have reneged on the contract."

She cast a glance at her uncle before answering. "I approached King Fedir with my desire to do just that."

"And?"

"And he threatened to remove financial support of my mother."

"You are not worried he will do that now?" Nikolai asked her with a frowning side glance toward King Fedir.

"He could try, but I think everyone in this room is aware of how far *I* am willing to go to protect her."

"Are you threatening me, child?" King Fedir asked her, sounding more hurt than worried.

She gave him a cool look, hoping it conveyed just how very little she cared about his hurt feelings after all he had put her mother through. "I am telling you that all actions have consequences and I guarantee you do not want to live with the ones that would come from you doing something so reprehensible."

"Solomia, talk to your daughter!" King Fedir demanded, his shock palpable.

"I am very proud of you, Nataliya, you know that, yes?"

"Yes."

The King frowned. "That is not what I meant."

"You are upset because she carries the ruthlessness that is such a strong trait in our family?" Mama asked her cousin, their King.

Nikolai looked at Nataliya, his expression assessing. "But you did make a promise. *You* signed that contract," Nikolai said.

"I did." Nataliya could wish she hadn't been so eager to *make up* for her father's sins at eighteen, but she couldn't deny she had signed the contract.

"And you take your own promises very seriously."

"I do." Hence her need to get Prince Konstantin to back out of the contract.

Nataliya might no longer feel it was her responsibility to compensate for her father's behavior, but she still understood duty only too well. And she may have been exiled, but her integrity as a member of the royal family was still very much intact.

"She was willing to renege on the contract," Konstantin pointed out. "Her personal ethics cannot be that strong."

King Fedir drew himself up, his expression forbidding. "On the contrary, my *niece* came to me and asked me to negotiate different terms, sure that if the suggestion came from me, you would be more than willing to do so. At no time did she intimate our family should simply *renege*."

Nataliya didn't know what the point was of her cousin harping on how he thought of her as a niece. She would have thought King Fedir would want to distance himself from her at this point. Just as he'd done fifteen years ago.

Nikolai nodded his understanding. "But you refused?"

"I did, more the fool I."

Personally, Nataliya agreed with him. Her uncle had been a fool to think that she would sit meekly by, when in her estimation, she should never have been asked to sign the darn thing in the first place.

"But we raised a lot of money for Mama and Aunt Oxana's favorite charity," she pointed out, not entirely facetiously.

The charity that helped families stay near their children receiving treatment for cancer and other life-threatening illnesses was very dear to Nataliya's heart, as well. However, no one else seemed to find that the benefit she did, if all the gloomy faces were to go by.

"All that aside, you still consider yourself bound by the terms of the contract, do you not?" Nikolai asked her.

She stared at him, not sure what he was trying to get at. "Prince Konstantin has verbally repudiated his willingness to abide by its terms in front of witnesses."

"He did."

She smiled, relief that the current King of Mirrus wasn't going to try to push her to marry his brother despite either of their desires.

"The contract, as it is written, still stands," Nikolai said, his tone brooking no argument.

Shock made Nataliya lightheaded as dread filled her. "Your brother denounced the contract," she reminded him, even though she shouldn't have to, because Nikolai had just agreed that was the case. "I am under no obligation to marry him now."

"But you *are* under obligation to marry a prince of the House of Merikov," Nikolai said implacably.

Gasps sounded, his father demanded what he meant, but Nikolai ignored it all, his attention focused entirely on Nataliya.

Her brain was whirling, trying to parse out what he meant. Her gaze skittered to the youngest Merikov Prince. Dimitri, called Dima by his friends of which she counted herself one, though they'd met on only a few occasions, they had chatted more via text and email than she had with Konstantin in past years.

Not even out of the university yet, Dima was looking with utter horror at his eldest brother.

"I will not enter into such a bargain with a child," Nataliya vowed, knowing being called a child would prick her friend and unable to pass up the chance to tease him.

"You were four years younger when you signed that con-

tract ten years ago," Nikolai pointed out without correct-
ing her use of the term *child*, earning a frown from Dima.

"And still desperate to return home. I'm not that teen-
ager any longer either." And she would not allow done to
Dima, what had been done to her. She *liked* the twenty-
two-year-old Prince.

"Regardless of what your reasons were for signing the
contract, you did so. And while you were only eighteen,
you were not a minor. You are obligated to its terms unless
both parties agree to different ones."

"I will not marry either of your brothers."

"I am glad you did not include me in that categorical
refusal." His smile was more like an apex predator baring its teeth.

CHAPTER TWO

"You?" Nataliya asked faintly.

No, Nikolai could not be saying what Nataliya thought he was saying. "You're not a prince." The contract stipulated a prince. "You're a king," her voice rose and cracked on the word *king*, but seriously…?

He had to have lost his mind.

Ten years ago, she would have jumped at the chance to marry this man, but he had only had eyes for the beautiful socialite he had ended up married to. Naively believing that marriage to his brother would cure Nataliya of her adolescent feelings for the unattainable Crown Prince, she'd signed that stupid, bloody, awful contract in good faith.

"But you were married." To the beautiful, sophisticated woman who had become his Queen. Perfect for him in every way, she'd died tragically in a skiing accident. Only later had anyone realized the new Queen had been pregnant at the time.

"And left a widower five years ago."

A widower who would always love the wife he had lost. The fact that he had shown no interest in another woman since the young Queen's death showed that. Nataliya could not imagine a less appealing marriage to her.

"But…" She didn't know what to say. This was insane.

"You cannot want to marry this woman," Nikolai's father said, voicing Nataliya's own thoughts.

And probably the thoughts of everyone else in the room.

Only Demyan was nodding and Maksim looked satisfied. King Fedir looked astounded. Queen Oxana looked enigmatic, like always. But Nataliya's mom? She looked worried. And that, more than anything, solidified the sense of impending doom settling over Nataliya.

Her *mom* thought he was serious.

"I cannot?" Nikolai asked imperiously.

"She's made a spectacle of herself with that ridiculous article and the accompanying blog posts." Prince Evengi almost looked apologetic in the glance he cast at her. "She's dated no less than ten men, that we know of!"

"She has not had sex with any of them."

"How can you know that?" Prince Evengi asked.

But Nataliya wanted to know too. She *hadn't* had sex with any of them. Or anyone at all. But how could Nikolai know that?

She'd made sure that even if she was being followed by someone on behalf of the House of Merikov, like Demyan had kept tabs on Prince Konstantin, circumstances would be ambiguous enough that no one could be certain. She'd let two of her dates stay the night. On the sofa, but they hadn't left her apartment until morning.

So, there was no way he could *know* she hadn't had sex. Only he seemed arrogantly sure of himself.

King Nikolai gave her a measuring look before returning his regard to his father. "Because her integrity would not allow her to do so when the contract is still in place."

"You heard her—she doesn't consider the contract a deterrent," Prince Konstantin said derisively.

"She knows *you* didn't consider it such—that does not mean she has not."

"You expected me to be celibate the last decade?" Konstantin asked, shocked.

Before Nikolai answered, the old King cleared his throat meaningfully. "This is not the place, or time, for this discussion." He turned to his eldest son. "You are not obligated to fulfill the contract on behalf of your brother."

"On that, I do not agree."

And something became very clear to Nataliya, besides the fact that being spoken about like she wasn't there was *extremely* annoying. But this man had an entirely different code of ethics and standard of integrity than his brother.

In truth, Nataliya had never doubted it, but then she'd always thought the best of the man who had become King to save his father's life. The man who she had fallen in love with at age fifteen and had only stopped pining for when she was about twenty.

Funnily enough, it had been his wife's death that had finally severed Nataliya's unrequited yearning. She'd hurt for him. Grieved from afar on his behalf at the loss of his beloved wife and unborn child and somewhere in the grief, she'd been able to put away her own longing.

It had just felt so selfish. So wrong.

"I can't marry you," she said in a voice much weaker than her normal assertive certainty.

"Oh, but you can, and you will."

The room erupted into pandemonium.

Even Queen Oxana voiced her disbelief at the turn of events.

But Nikolai? Just sat there, looking immovable.

"The contract stipulates a prince of your house," Nataliya reminded him, ignoring everyone else. "You cannot insist I fulfill it by marrying you."

"I was a prince when you signed it, therefore the terms referred to me equally to my brothers."

"No. That's not right."

He just looked at her.

Suddenly, Queen Oxana stood and put her hand out to Nataliya. "That is enough discussion on this topic for present. You and your mother can join me in my apartments."

Nataliya might have argued, but her mother stood and somehow she found herself swept out of the reception room between the two women.

* * *

"I can't believe they made you sign that contract!" Gillian, wife to Crown Prince Maksim, exclaimed. "You were just a baby."

"I was eighteen."

"Too young to sign your life away."

"Welcome to life in the royal family," Nataliya said.

She'd left Mama and Oxana to themselves, knowing the two women needed to have a talk that had been fifteen years coming, and had searched out Gillian and her adorable children, finding them taking advantage of the summer sunshine in the palace gardens.

Nataliya loved watching the children play, knowing that the *normalcy* surrounding this very royal family was all down to Gillian's influence.

Gillian frowned, her expression going rock stubborn. "My children will be forced into that kind of agreement over my dead body. They won't be making any decisions about marriage until they are mature enough to do so."

"And when might that be?" Maksim asked drolly as he walked up. "When they are fifty?"

"If they aren't ready to make the decision before then, then yes!" Oh, Gillian was mad. "It's despicable that Nataliya was pressed into signing away her life at such a young age."

On Nataliya's behalf. And Nataliya couldn't say that didn't feel good.

Even her beloved mother had wanted her to sign that contract ten years ago.

Maks looked at Nataliya, something like apology in his brown eyes. "I offered to renegotiate the contract on more favorable terms for Mirrus Global if your participation could be removed from it."

"And?" Gillian demanded when Nataliya remained silent.

"His Highness refused. He considers it a point of family

honor for him to fulfill the contract. He's livid with both his father and his brother for the way they spoke to you."

"So, he doesn't agree with the whole misogynistic double standard?" Gillian asked, having gotten the whole story from Nataliya.

"No. He says that neither Nataliya, nor Konstantin were under constraint not to date before a formal engagement was announced."

"Nice of him to absolve his brother too," Nataliya couldn't help saying.

"Did *you* expect him to be celibate?" Maks asked, sounding like he thought it was unlikely.

"I was," Nataliya reminded him.

Maks opened his mouth, but Gillian forestalled him. "Think very hard before you speak again, Maks, because my respect for *your* integrity is on the line here."

He stared at his wife, like he couldn't believe she'd said that.

"I know you are arrogant, but are you seriously going to try to say that Nataliya should have been happy to live in limbo while Prince Konstantin was not?"

"No. That's not what I was going to say at all. I agreed with King Nikolai that neither Nataliya, nor his own brother were under constraints not to date."

"But if I had slept around, what would you have said?" Nataliya couldn't help asking.

Maks's mouth twisted wryly. "That would have depended on the results, wouldn't it?"

"What do you mean?" Nataliya asked.

Maks looked to where the children played, a soft smile curving his usually firm mouth. "Our firstborn child is testament to how unexpected results can come from a night of passion."

"And if the little surprise had been the result of one of

Konstantin's many…" Nataliya paused, unsure what term she wanted to use.

Indiscretion implied that Konstantin shouldn't have been having sex with those women. And she wasn't sure she wanted to imply that.

She only knew she didn't want to marry a man who had had so many sexual partners during the ten years he had not made any move to fulfil the terms of the contract they had both signed. Whether Konstantin liked it, or not, to Nataliya, that indicated a man who was both a womanizer and who did not keep his promises. Like her father.

"Sex partners?" Gillian offered, bringing a gasp of outrage from her royal husband.

Gillian rolled her eyes. "Don't be a prude, Maks."

"You are a princess now, Gillian. Maybe you could remember that."

"And this is the twenty-first century. Maybe *you* could remember *that*."

Nataliya found herself grinning despite the stress of the day. "She's got your number, Maks."

"And does King Nikolai have yours?"

"What do you mean?"

"He's completely convinced that you will adhere to the contract."

She didn't want to admit that he might be right. Integrity and honor were every bit as important to her as they were to the King of Mirrus. "I just don't understand why he's saying he wants to marry me."

"Well, he has to marry again at some point," Maks pointed out prosaically.

"But *me*?"

"Perhaps, I could answer that." Nikolai's voice hit Nataliya in the center of her being.

She spun and found him watching her with an implacability that sent a shiver through her.

"I wish you would. This idea that you have to fulfill the contract in place of your brother is ridiculous."

His enigmatic regard turned forbidding. "My honor is not a matter for ridicule."

"But it's not *your* honor in question."

Satisfaction gleamed in his steely gray gaze. "So, you acknowledge that it *is* a matter of honor."

"Prince Konstantin was the Prince referred to in that contract. Everyone knows that," she said, sidestepping the honor issue.

The King settled quite casually onto the fountain rim beside where Nataliya sat. "But it was not in fact, my brother who signed the contract."

"Why wasn't it?" She'd been required to sign on her own behalf and had only noticed that the former King had signed it on behalf of his son, when she'd read it before embarking on her dating campaign.

"In contracts of that sort, it is quite natural for the reigning sovereign to sign on behalf of his house. When I was crowned King, all promises made by my father in matters of state became mine to fulfill."

"So, renegotiate the contract." He had just said he had the power to do so.

"After leaving you and your mother's lives in limbo for ten years? I think not."

"But I don't mind."

"I do."

"I'm not queen material."

"If you marry me, you will be a princess. The title of Queen is bestowed only at my will."

And of course the wife he didn't love wouldn't be worthy of the title, not like the woman he had married and lost. "You know what I mean."

"But I do not agree."

"I'm a computer programmer, not a princess."

"You are a member of the royal family of Volyarus."

Like she needed reminding. "Not so you would notice. Not for the last fifteen years."

Maks made a sound of disagreement, but Nataliya just gave him a look. "When your father exiled me and my mom for my dad's indiscretions, we effectively lost our family. It's no use pretending anything different."

"Nevertheless, you *are* of royal blood, a lady in your own right," Nikolai pressed.

"No one calls me Lady Nataliya." At least no one in her current life.

"I'm sure that's not true. Protocol is observed here in the castle."

"I don't spend time here."

"And yet here you are."

"To answer for crimes that were not in fact crimes at all."

His smile did not reach his eyes. "No, not crimes, but you knew exactly what you were doing when you embarked on that article."

"It was for a perfectly respectable fashion magazine, not a scandal rag."

He nodded. "Well written and the tie in with fashion that you do not in fact have a great deal of interest in was clever."

"My friend thought so."

"Your friend?"

"The contributing editor who wrote the article and blog posts."

"I wondered how you had arranged the article."

"Jenna wanted to do the article but she's in a committed relationship, so she couldn't do the dates."

"Commendable."

"I thought so."

"Yes, you would."

"What is that supposed to mean?" she asked belligerently.

He spread his hands in a gesture of no offense. "You are a woman of definite integrity. Your standards for acceptable behavior match my own."

"How can you say that?" she asked, shocked by how he viewed her. "I hack computers for a living."

"But not for nefarious purposes or your own gain."

"No, of course not." What did he think, she was a criminal?

No, she realized. It was that very certainty that she had *standards* that made her appealing to him.

"Plenty of women who would love to be a princess have integrity," she pointed out dryly.

"But you are the one who signed a contract promising to marry a prince of my house."

"But you aren't a prince."

"We've been over this."

"I just don't understand how you can say you want to marry me."

"Ten years ago, you were vetted and found acceptable."

"For your brother!"

"For any prince of the House of Merikov. That was the way the contract was written."

"That's not how I read it."

"It is standard language for such a contract," Maks pointed out, almost apologetically.

"But that's draconian." Gillian sounded shocked.

Neither the Crown Prince or the King looked particularly bothered by that condemnation.

Nikolai brushed the strands of hair away that the gentle wind had blown across Nataliya's face. She wondered if he even realized he'd done it, but she'd noticed. To the very core of her, a place she'd thought dormant.

Nataliya no longer thought about him *that* way.

But the simple act of him sitting down beside her, close

enough she could feel the heat of his body, sparked undeniable sexual desire.

She realized he was watching her as the silence stretched. One of the children started to cry and both Maks and Gillian went over.

Nataliya and Nikolai weren't alone, but it felt like they were.

"You agreed that you signed the contract in good faith." His words didn't register at first.

She was too busy staring into his gorgeous gray eyes, but then her brain caught up with her mouth and she said, "And your brother reneged in front of witnesses today."

"But not on behalf of our house, only himself."

Nataliya surged to her feet. "I'm not eighteen anymore—no one is pushing me into fulfilling that darn contract."

"If you are the woman I believe you to be, you will convince yourself of the rightness of doing your duty."

"To marry you?" she asked in disbelief that simply would not go away.

"To marry me."

"Good luck."

His smile was even more dangerous this time. "I never leave anything to chance."

Ignoring manners and protocol, she turned on her heel and headed back into the palace without another word.

A blooming orchid with tiny buds indicating more flowers to come was sitting on the table in her room when she reached it. Nataliya stopped and stared.

What was this?

She picked up the card sitting beside it and felt a shiver go down her spine at the slashing writing.

With my compliments, Nikolai.

In his own hand. Not typed like the ones she'd had delivered from Konstantin.

She recognized the orchid too, from the very distinctive pot it was planted in. She'd been to the castle in Mirrus for the funeral of Nikolai's wife.

There was an orchid room where his mother used to grow the plants, now overseen by a world-renowned horticulturist. All of the orchids in that room were planted in the same style of pot with the Merikov crest in fine gold against the eggshell white of the ceramic.

Nataliya had spent a great deal of time in the orchid room during her three-day stay at the castle five years before. And she had learned that every orchid growing there had a special history and most were incredibly rare specimens.

Nikolai had caught her there more than once, because as he'd told her, he found comfort in the room his mother had spent so much time in.

Nataliya had offered to leave, but the young King had refused, asking her to keep him company. And that's what she'd done, sitting in silence with a man who was grieving the loss of his wife and unborn child.

Nataliya could not make sense of the orchid being here. As gifts went, it was very special. But he couldn't know that she'd started growing orchids after that visit. Nothing nearly so impressive as the Merikov collection, but lovely plants that gave her peace and joy caring for them.

Even if he had known something almost no one else did, Nikolai could not have gotten the plant delivered since the recent confrontation. Not even with a helicopter or the palace's personal jet.

Nikolai couldn't have known he planned to take his brother's place before the meeting today, so why the orchid?

Whatever the reason, the plant was beautiful and she knew how very special it was that he'd given it to her. She grabbed her phone and texted the number no one but his closest family and advisors was supposed to have.

Thank you for the orchid. It's beautiful.

His reply came back only seconds later.

I'm glad you like it, my lady. It was one of my mother's favorites.

Why did that *my* feel like it should be bolded? Like he was staking claim? And his assertion this had been one of his mother's plants? How was Nataliya supposed to feel about that?

Special. She felt special. And that was very, very dangerous.

Nataliya had the very distinct feeling that if the King decided to court her, it was going to be a different prospect than the past two months' worth of impersonal gifts sent via Konstantin's staff.

Nataliya remembered that fleeting thought a week later when she looked up from her computer to the sight of Demyan looking amazed.

It was not a look she'd ever seen on her imposing cousin's features before.

Needing a chance to come to terms with Nikolai's demand she fulfill the contract, *with him*, Nataliya had left Volyarus on her cousin's private plane before dinner the night of the big confrontation.

She'd been really grateful that Maks hadn't even blinked at putting his plane at her disposal. He'd assured her that he would smooth things over with his father and their royal visitors.

"You're still my family, Nataliya, and I can only apologize for not realizing that the exile to America was not voluntary on your mother's part. Had I known I would have redressed the issue."

She'd stared at him. "You were like my big brother. I thought you didn't care."

"My father told me that you and your mother needed space and distance to overcome the humiliation from your father. I believed him."

And then Nataliya had found herself being hugged by her cousin for the first time in over a decade and it had been all she could do not to break down and cry.

Demyan had come to her to say much the same thing when he got back from Volyarus, adding that he'd never stopped considering her a close member of his family.

Now he stood there, with a really weird expression on his face.

"What?" she demanded.

"You got a new computer."

"So?" She hadn't asked Demyan for new hardware though.

"It's from King Nikolai."

Well, that was…*different*. "He gave me a computer."

Demyan nodded.

"Why do you look so weird?" she demanded.

"It's a prototype. Even I couldn't get my hands on this build with the new chipset."

That stopped her. "How did you know?"

"Because I had to sign an NDA just to take possession and you've got one to sign too. The company rep is waiting in the conference room."

This was crazy, but she couldn't pretend she wasn't excited. She *loved* new technology and like Demyan had said, this was something even he hadn't been able to finagle out of the manufacturer before early release.

There wasn't just one computer waiting for her in the conference room. There were two. The second was top of the line of available technology and came with a note. *Raise some more money for a very worthy cause.*

Okay, she was impressed. Not just that he'd chosen a gift she would love, her own prototypical, super-slim, ultrafast laptop, but because he'd seen what no one else had. How much she'd enjoyed raising money for the charity she'd chosen. And he was telling her, he wasn't intimidated by the idea she would auction off his gifts.

He expected it. But he provided gifts *to* auction. Over the next two weeks, every gift she received from him came with a personally written note and some kind of duplicate or equivalent item for her to put in the online charity auction.

He also texted her, several times throughout the day. Some innocuous texts. Some even funny. Others surprising, like when he asked her opinion of Dima's desire to take a gap year between university and graduate school. Apparently, when Prince Evengi abdicated his rule to his son, he'd abdicated all major family decisions, as well.

And then there were the texts that drove her batty.

How many children do you want?

Do you object to living in the palace after we marry?

As if her agreement was a foregone conclusion. It annoyed her, but there was this tiny frisson of excitement too. Nikolai was a really special guy and he wanted to marry her.

She knew he wasn't emotionally attached in any way, wasn't even sure if he found her sexually desirable, but he definitely hadn't backed down on his stance.

She knew his father wasn't happy about it. Konstantin wasn't happy. Demyan had told her, and he'd heard it from Maks. But Nikolai was a king and a king who apparently wasn't going to let anyone else dictate his future.

Not like he was doing his best to dictate hers, Nataliya reminded herself.

When the couture gown, shoes, jewelry and handbag arrived along with its auction equivalent and an invitation to dinner and a play two days hence, Nataliya could do nothing but stare in consternation at the boxes littering her desk.

Demyan stood, leaning against the doorjamb. "So, he's finally moving this courtship into the dating stage."

"Can you date a king?" she asked, a tinge of hysteria touching her voice.

"I guess you're going to find out."

"He thinks that stupid contract has me all sewn up."

"No, he thinks your sense of duty and integrity has you all sewn up. But give the guy his due, he's setting the rest of his life up to fulfill his own sense of honor."

"I know you think duty is all there is to life—"

"Not since I married Chanel, but I won't pretend duty didn't play a big part in that."

"And that duty nearly destroyed your marriage." She'd been invited to the wedding. She'd seen the other woman's reaction before Chanel had disappeared from the reception without her groom.

And frankly, Nataliya had known all along what was going on. She was nosy and she had more ways than most of finding out what she wanted to know.

"We all make sacrifices for family and the good of Volyarus."

And she knew that despite how close he'd come to losing his wife, Demyan still saw duty in all capitals when he thought about it. Chanel just made sure that there was more to his life than a single concept.

"I made my sacrifice ten years ago, to provide a way for my mother to return home."

"And now she no longer wants to return to Volyarus full-time."

"But my sacrifice is still there, hanging over my head."

"Maybe it won't turn out to be such a sacrifice after all."

He could say that. Demyan's own sacrifice had led to the love of his life and children he adored. Hers could lead nowhere but heartache. Nikolai would never love her as he'd loved his first wife and even if she no longer felt the same things for him she once had, Nataliya didn't want to be trapped in a marriage to a man whose heart was locked in the past.

CHAPTER THREE

NATALIYA WAS NOT at all surprised when her phone dinged with a text ten minutes before the limo was supposed to arrive for her.

Nikolai had texted updates on his schedule and arrival throughout the day.

Like he wanted to make sure she was ready, like he worried she might get the time wrong, or something. Or maybe, he just wanted to be sure she was going to show up. After all, not once had he actually asked her to join him for dinner and the play. No, just the delivery of the dress and tickets which she doubted very sincerely they would have to show to take their seats.

She had no doubt that between him and his security detail, they were taking up an entire box at the theater.

As a king, he was used to getting his way. And she'd been, oh, so tempted to simply not be here tonight, but the truth was, she and Nikolai needed to talk.

Nataliya needed him to understand that his honor would not be compromised by renegotiating the contract.

A sharp knock sounded at the door and Nataliya smoothed the opalescent gray designer dress down her long body. She had to admit that Nikolai had good taste in women's fashion. Though considering the perfectly coiffed fashionista he'd been married to, Nataliya should not be surprised.

"Showtime," said Jenna, her friend who had written the "50 First Dates for a Would-Be Princess" article.

She'd come over today to help Nataliya prep for her date with a king, doing Nataliya's makeup and hair, styling her so that Nataliya looked better than she had for any of those first dates.

Because Nataliya had not wanted to look like a consolation date in any of the pictures that were bound to be taken by the paparazzi.

Not because she wanted to try to look her best for Nikolai.

Nataliya opened the door to her condo and stepped back in shock that the King stood on the other side, two of his security detail hovering in the background. The others were no doubt securing the building.

"You didn't need to come up," she said, unable to hide her surprise at his presence.

Wearing a light custom-made charcoal gray suit that accentuated his six-foot-four, well-muscled frame, his presence sent a hurricane rioting through her senses.

Every part of her body suddenly felt more alive, more *present* and it was hard to take each new breath.

"May I come inside?"

She jolted, realizing she was letting the King of Mirrus stand in the hall like a salesman. "Of course."

Nataliya stepped back and he followed her inside, one of his security men accompanying him to do a routine sweep of her condo while the other pulled the door shut behind them to stand at attention on the other side.

Neither Demyan, nor Maks practiced such heavy security protocols when they were in Seattle.

But then, Nikolai was a king already, despite being only thirty-five years old.

"The dress looks every bit as beautiful on you as I thought it would." He took her in, his gray eyes going molten with an expression she had never expected to see in his eyes.

Desire.

"Thank you." She swallowed. "You could have sent a car for me to meet you at the restaurant."

Who had ever heard of a king calling for his date in person?

She'd made the mistake of telling him how impersonal and detached she'd considered his brother's overtures. And Nikolai had assured her, his would not be.

But seriously? Could he say *overkill*?

"Surely not." He reached out and brushed a proprietary finger along her collarbone. "This will be our first public appearance together. Calling for you at your door is only the most basic courtesy."

Heat whooshed through her body from that one small touch and Nataliya was momentarily unable to respond.

"Well, I'm impressed," Jenna said forthrightly.

Nikolai turned to acknowledge the other woman. "Jenna Beals, former college roommate and good friend of my intended as well as contributing editor for the fashion forward magazine that ran the article on my future betrothed, I believe."

Jenna gave a credible curtsy. "It's a pleasure to meet you, Your Highness."

Nikolai smiled, his gray eyes warm. "I liked the article and blog posts."

"You did?" Jenna asked in clear shock. "Really?"

"It was a clever concept, showing the fashion side of the modern dating game."

Jenna gave Nataliya a significant look. "He doesn't think you should be shamed for going out on a few dates."

"Not at all, but all future dates will be with me," he said with arrogant assurance.

"Because you have so much time to spend with me," Nataliya said with unhindered cynicism.

"And yet, here I am."

"But this is a one-off." Wasn't it? He was a king, he didn't have time to woo her.

Woo. What an old-fashioned word, but what else fit?

His honor demanded he fulfill the contract on behalf of his family and he was determined to convince her that marriage to him was what she wanted. Ten years ago, it wouldn't have taken any convincing.

But that was then and this was now.

The multi-Michelin-star restaurant he took her to for dinner was one she'd heard a lot about, but had never tried. The simple, elegant modern Japanese-style decor went perfectly with the Asian Fusion food on offer.

Among the diners on the way to their table, she recognized two prominent politicians, a football star and a television star.

Even the notable patrons' attention caught on King Nikolai and his entourage as they walked through the restaurant. Security took tables on either side of the one she and Nikolai were led to.

He held her chair for her, himself, his closeness impacting her in ways something so simple should not have.

Disconcerted, she blurted, "You don't have to do this over-the-top stuff. I'm a computer programmer, not a princess."

"You are Lady Nataliya and when we are wed, you will be The Princess of Mirrus."

"As opposed to *a* princess?"

He settled into his own seat across from her at the intimate table for two. "It is the distinction given to the wife of the King."

"I haven't said I'm going to marry you," she said quietly, not wanting to be overheard.

The expression on his chiseled features was untroubled. "On the contrary, you signed a contract that said that very thing."

She looked around and though no one was looking at them, that did not mean none of the other diners were listening. Though the acoustics in the restaurant and table placement made it unlikely.

"Why?" she asked him.

"Why?" He paused. "What?"

"You know what I'm asking. You turned down Maks's offer to renegotiate the contract at favorable terms for Mirrus Global."

"But I do not wish to renegotiate the contract. There are not terms more favorable than the ones we have now."

He could not mean what it sounded like he meant, that marriage to *her* was the most favorable term.

"You can't want to marry me." This she whispered nearly inaudibly, paranoid about being overheard as only the daughter of the notorious Count Shevchenko could be.

"You are mistaken."

That was all. *You are mistaken.* No explanation, but then this was not the place to have this conversation.

She should have brought it up in the limousine, but she'd been fighting entirely adult sexual feelings she had never experienced before. And he'd been happy to keep up the conversation with a charming urbanity that only increased his attractiveness to her.

Not one of the fourteen men she'd dated so far for the article and its accompanying blog posts had been even remotely as interesting, even the computer programmer who had developed an app that she loved to use.

"I am still obligated to go on thirty-six dates for the article," she apprised him, surprised at her own reticence about doing so.

"Thirty-five." His smile was way too appealing for her peace of mind.

"Thirty-five?"

"Tonight is one."

"But the photos of my style." That was the whole point of the article.

And technically, it *could* work, because Jenna *had* styled her.

"I will take care of it." He called one of his security people over with a jerk of his head.

A few low-spoken words and the other man went back to his table, his phone already out.

"A photographer will be here before we are finished with our dinner."

"I'm sure Jenna will appreciate that." Because honestly? Nataliya had made up sixteen different excuses for not scheduling a date the past two weeks.

"I will make sure we have a photographer on hand for the remainder of our dates."

"You're not going to take me out thirty-five more times." No way did he have the time.

"Some of those dates will have to happen after our wedding, but I fail to see why you are so surprised at the idea. You did not imagine that we would lead separate lives?"

"What do you mean *after* our wedding? When do you think we are getting married?" It took at least a year, usually two, to plan a royal wedding.

"Three months from now Mirrus is hosting a summit for small countries and monarchies. I would like the event to culminate in our wedding."

"Maks and Gillian did that, but she was pregnant. There was a reason for the rush."

He tilted his dark head in acknowledgment. "You have waited ten years for my house to fulfill its part of that contract. That is long enough."

"You're really stuck on this honor-of-your-house thing, aren't you?"

She expected him to get angry, or at least annoyed, by her snark.

But Nikolai smiled. "Yes, in fact, I am."

She sighed, acknowledging if only to herself, that he

would not be manipulated as easily as his brother. "You're not going to be reasonable about this, are you?"

"If by reasonable, you mean change my mind, no."

She felt her own usually even temper rising. "You do realize you are a king, right?"

"And as such, I am accustomed to getting my own way."

She'd just been thinking that very thing, but still. "You're not supposed to admit that."

"I should lie?" he asked arrogantly.

"I don't know. Can you really see me as your Queen? Excuse me… I mean your Princess?"

"I have no trouble picturing that eventuality at all." The expression in his eyes was all male approval.

And it did something to her insides she did not want to admit. "I don't like dressing up."

"Yet you do so very well. I will never be anything but proud to have you stand by my side."

She frowned. He couldn't mean that. "I blurt stuff out before I think about it," she warned him.

"Do you? Thus far, I've noticed you being very careful about what you say and where you say it."

That was true in certain circumstances, like the few in which they'd met, but not always. "When I'm comfortable, I lose the filter between my brain and my mouth."

"I will look forward to you growing comfortable with me then."

"You don't mean that." How could he?

He didn't quite smile, but amusement lurked in his usually steely gray gaze. "You think I only want people around me who say what I want to hear?"

"You're a king."

"We've established that."

"You don't like people disagreeing with you."

"Disagreement is healthy." He gave her a look she

thought might be intended to intimidate. "Disrespect is something else."

She wasn't intimidated, but she was curious. "What if you think I'm being disrespectful when I'm only being honest?"

"What if you think I'm being neglectful when I am only busy?" he riposted.

"I don't know."

"Neither do I. Marriage requires trust and compromise from both sides."

"Is that what you had with Tiana?"

Nothing changed in his expression, but there was a new quality of stillness about him and rigidity to Nikolai's spine. "My first marriage is not something I like to discuss."

"Okay."

His eyes widened fractionally. "Okay?"

"I don't like talking about my childhood either." Everyone thought they knew what her life had been like because her father had been in the tabloids so much.

No one but she and her mother knew about the Count's violent rages, about the mental and physical scars both she and her mother bore because of them.

His final desertion had embarrassed the royal family and torn their lives apart, but it had also come as a terrible relief. Once they reached the States, her mother had taken out a restraining order against her estranged husband and renewed it after their divorce became final.

Living in the States, she'd finally stood up for herself and her daughter in a way she'd never been willing to do when their lives were wrapped with the Volyarus royal family.

"Hearing you say that makes me very curious, *kiska*."

He could be as curious as the proverbial cat, but she wasn't talking about those dark years when her father had lived with her and Mama in Volyarus.

Not for anything. "I'm not a kitten."

"Oh, I think you are. You've proven you have sharp little claws, but you are not vicious with them and I am very
much looking forward to petting you."

She choked on the wine she'd been sipping. "I can't believe you said that."

"I am a king, not a eunuch."

"But you don't want me."

"Don't I?" His heated expression belied her claim.
Suddenly, the air around them was charged and she
pressed her thighs together under the table. "I don't look
anything like Tiana," Nataliya blurted.

Dark brows raised, he said, "You look like yourself and
I find you very attractive."

"Oh." She really hadn't expected that blunt declaration,
much less the truth he'd have her believe was behind it. Unexpected heat suffused her face.

"Nothing to say back to me?"

"What do you want me to say?" she asked in a tone that
was way too breathless.

"You could tell me if the attraction is one-sided."

"Of course, I'm attracted to you." He was smart, powerful, gorgeous, strong and just downright sexy. "Who
wouldn't be?"

"I think I'm flattered." But he didn't sound too sure
about that fact.

And for some inexplicable reason, that made Nataliya
happy. She didn't like him taking her attraction to him for
granted, despite the fact he had to know that most women
would find him pretty much irresistible. "Don't be. You
know who and what you are."

"Yes, but I was beginning to wonder if *you* appreciated
my attributes."

He had to be joking. "I find that hard to believe."

She was no actress and right now, Nataliya couldn't stop
thinking how much she wanted to kiss him and try things

she'd never tried before with another man. It was all his fault too, the King who talked bluntly about stuff like *attraction*.

Which naturally sent her thoughts in a direction they never went. Except around him. And that had been a long time ago.

Only this was now and although she was no longer in love with him, Nataliya apparently still found Nikolai sexually irresistible.

And the King's expression said he knew it too!

A smile more predatory than amused creased his gorgeous lips. "The look on your face says that our wedding night will be very satisfying."

"Like you'd allow it to be anything else," she blurted with more honesty than common sense. "You're the guy who always wins."

"It comes with the territory."

Satisfied with how their evening had gone so far, Nik slid into the limousine, taking the seat beside his future bride rather than the one across from her.

Although she was more stubborn than he'd given her credit for, Nik had no doubt that she would eventually agree to marry him.

Because Nataliya was that rare commodity in his world—a woman of honor.

When she made a promise, she kept it. Not like the faithless socialite he'd made his Queen. He'd made the mistake once of bestowing political and social power that rivaled his own on his wife and lived to regret it.

Nataliya had waited ten years on a contract that should have been fulfilled in half that time. And she had not allowed herself to consider getting out of her obligation to marry a prince of his house until she had discovered Konstantin's propensity for one-night stands.

Nataliya had very exacting standards and a highly developed sense of honor, both for herself and others. In her view, Konstantin hadn't lived up to those standards.

Nikolai understood, even if he did not agree fully. Her attitude was to his benefit.

And it was those traits that had first made Nik realize she would make his ideal wife. The low-simmering attraction he'd recognized in the agonizing days after his pregnant wife's death was also welcome. He had no desire to have an icy-cold marriage bed, but even he had not realized how deeply that attraction ran until he started spending more time with Nataliya.

He'd even been turned on during the confrontation at the Volyarussian palace.

Not that he would ever acknowledge such a thing.

Nor would ever lose control of his desire or allow it to drive his decisions.

He would not make the same mistakes with his second wife he had made with his first.

Starting with choosing a woman who had bone-deep integrity and absolutely no tolerance for infidelity.

Nataliya allowed Jenna to put the finishing touches to her makeup for the fifth date in three weeks with Nikolai.

He had stayed in Seattle that first week, managing to see her every day he had been in town.

The next week he had flown in to take her to the big technology expo. That would have been amazing enough, especially with the VIP treatment attending it with a king had provided. Yes, even Nataliya in all her pragmatism had been impressed. But somehow he had managed an invite for her to the super-secret hackathon she'd been trying to get into for the last three years.

And the King of Mirrus had not complained even a little when she'd immersed herself in learning new hacking technologies and going up against some of the biggest names in her industry for hours.

Tonight they were attending a fund-raiser ball for the children's charity she'd been donating the proceeds of her *Courtship Gifts for a Would-Be Princess* online auction to.

It was being held at one of the swankest hotels in Manhattan and Nikolai had arranged for a private plane to fly Nataliya, Jenna, the photographer and even Jenna's boyfriend to New York.

Jenna and her boyfriend were excited about going out on the town after Jenna finished styling Nataliya for her date and getting the information the junior fashion editor needed for her blog post.

"My boss is beside herself with joy in the amount of hits we're getting on the blog from this series," Jenna said with satisfaction as she stood back.

Nataliya smiled at her longtime friend. "Good. You deserve recognition for your creativity."

"But it's your life that's making this possible. Everyone is keen to follow the courtship of a king and his would-be princess."

Nataliya was unwillingly enthralled herself. She spent too much time wondering what his next move would be and thinking about him between frequent texts and phone calls. "I think he's still expecting the wedding to take place month after next."

"Has he said so?"

"I got the mock-up invitations to approve this afternoon." But so far, she had not actually agreed to marry him.

He acted like it was a foregone conclusion. Because she'd signed that darned contract.

Jenna tried to stifle laughter but wasn't successful. "He's very confident you're going to agree, isn't he?"

"The word is arrogant."

"I'm pretty sure kings are allowed."

Nataliya smoothed a tiny wrinkle in the skirt of her dress. "And I'm *very* sure that he would be just as arrogant if he were the third son of the King's second cousin."

Jenna's laughter burst out and Nataliya couldn't help joining her, but she hadn't been joking. Not entirely.

Nikolai was always sure he was right and she'd yet to find an instance in which he was not. She couldn't even deny that she *would* ultimately agree to marry him.

She would like to say that was all due to her sense of duty and the contract she'd signed at the age of eighteen. And she could not deny that it did play a part, but that crush she'd gotten over?

Not so much in the *over* department.

Nikolai treated her like a person in her own right, not just an adjunct to his life. He didn't dismiss her job or put her down for loving what she did. Nor did he criticize her for having no personal clue about the latest fashions or being mostly ignorant of pop culture.

Nataliya wasn't interested in being *seen*, nor did she have any interest in playing on her current A-Lister status as Jenna called it.

Nikolai approved of her and supported Nataliya's interests and opinions in a way even her mom found challenging, Nataliya knew.

She was nobody's idea of perfect royalty.

So why did this King want to marry her?

What could *she* bring to the Royal House of Merikov? Other than her womb.

No question she would be expected to provide heirs *plural* to the throne. He'd been very frank about that fact. Just as he'd been, oh, so open on that first date about being attracted to her.

And yet he hadn't even kissed her. Not once. No kisses, no heated embraces.

Did he expect to use artificial insemination, or something, to get those heirs he was so keen on?

The thought was really lowering, but what else was she supposed to think?

He was so incredibly polite. And she? Wanted to kiss him and try all the things she'd ever read about with him. Sometimes he looked at her with what she thought was desire, but he never acted on it and she couldn't help thinking she'd got it wrong.

But did that stop her wanting him?

No it did not.

Stifling a sigh at her thoughts, Nataliya obediently looked in the mirror to check out Jenna's handiwork.

The dress was from an established design house but far from classic. Black lace over a nude slip that stopped midthigh, one shoulder was entirely bare and the other sleeve reached to her wrist. When she shifted, the slit that went right to the bottom of the slip showed her leg. The cut and style made the slit look like it went higher, but it did not in fact show anything but the pale skin of her thigh.

Thank goodness she did her muscle-toning elliptical every morning, or she would never show so much of her leg.

Biting her lip, Nataliya met Jenna's expectant gaze in the mirror. "It looks so risqué."

"But nothing that shouldn't be showing is."

"You can see the side of my breast."

"No, you think you can but the fashion tape and cut of the gown are both clever enough to keep you covered."

"Nikolai is going to have a fit."

Jenna rolled her eyes. "His Highness has been mixing with the glitterati for years while you've been happily moldering away at your computer keyboard. He's seen much more daring gowns."

More daring? What were they, see-through? When she asked, Jenna just laughed. "It has been known."

"This one looks like it's see-through."

"But it's not."

"The nude slip is an exact match for my skin tone."

"That was done on purpose," Jenna revealed with a tone of pure satisfaction. The clothes being provided by the fashion houses for Nataliya's dates were a serious coup for her friend. "The in-house designers were happy to provide a personalized gown for this event for you. You're an A-Lister now, hon."

"Only because I'm dating a king."

"Um…you do realize you just said that, right?"

Nataliya shook her head, but the image in the mirror was a woman who *could* date a king. Even she knew that. "You did good, friend."

"I had a great canvas to work with."

Now if only Nikolai would not just see Nataliya as a woman who could date a king, but one the said King would want to kiss. And perhaps do other naughty things with, *she* might feel like crowing.

CHAPTER FOUR

NIKOLAI'S INITIAL REACTION was all that Nataliya could have wanted.

Steel-gray eyes turned molten with hot desire and she prepared herself for a kiss to blow her socks off.

Good thing she wasn't wearing any socks because no kiss was forthcoming and the King's expression shuttered almost immediately.

"You look beautiful," he told her, oh, so politely.

And Nataliya wanted to scream. "Thank you," she replied in kind, however, none of the frustration she felt bleeding into her voice.

"Once we are married, however, you will not be styled so provocatively." He gave her another cursory glance before leading her out of the hotel suite. "It is a good thing you are not enamored with this type of fashion. That will not be a loss for you."

Every word he spoke stoked the annoyance simmering inside Nataliya until she felt like a fizzing teakettle.

"*When* we are married?" she asked delicately. "Having you dictate how I dress won't be a hardship for me?" she inquired with even more precise syllables.

He stopped in the elevator, his gaze flicking to the security detail before coming to settle on her. "Naturally, my opinion on how you dress will be important to you."

"Oh, really?" she asked sweetly. "Because, and I know this is going to come as a surprise to you, but I have been dressing myself for years now and I have never once needed a man's opinion on what *I* choose to wear."

"You will be my Princess, and with that honor will come certain responsibilities," he said repressively, the buttoned-down King she'd gotten to know early on making a full appearance for the first time on one of their dates.

Somehow, with all the worries she'd had about the responsibilities of becoming a princess, none of them had ever centered around her wardrobe. "Responsibilities like letting you tell me how to dress?"

"Be honest—would you have chosen that dress on your own?" he asked, sounding like he knew the answer already.

"I don't wear high-end designer gowns on a regular basis, full stop."

"You could, though, if you wanted. I have never seen your mother wearing anything but."

"She accepts an allowance from her cousin." Hush money Nataliya had no interest in. "I live on the money I earn."

"Admirable, but when you are *The* Princess of Mirrus, you will dress in the top designers' creations and I do not believe that *you* will choose clothing as provocative as the dress you are currently wearing."

She had this crazy urge to wear nothing but sexually provocative clothing for the rest of her life. Comfortable, or not. "Let me make something very clear, Your Highness."

He waited without saying anything, his manners impeccable.

"I will wear the clothes *I* like regardless of who I am married to. That means that if I want to wear jeans from a department store, I will and if I want to wear dresses just like this one, I will. No one, not even a king, is going to dictate my choices like a petty fashion tyrant."

One of the bodyguards made a suspicious sound that could have been humor, but a look at their faces showed only impassive regard.

When Nikolai opened his mouth to speak, his eyes narrowed in clear irritation, she held up her hand.

"I am not finished."

"Then by all means, continue."

"You have not asked me to marry you. We are not engaged and speaking to me like that is a done deal when you haven't even given me the courtesy of that one small tradition is *not* making the outcome you so clearly want more likely." With that she set her not-so-happy gaze on the bodyguard nearest the door. "Open the doors—this discussion is over."

She'd noticed the elevator stopped moving, but the doors had remained shut. His security detail was always one step ahead of any potential problem. She admired that kind of cunning even if right now she wanted off that lift more than just about anything.

A small jerk of his head meant the doors remained closed. "Hardly a discussion when you have not allowed me to speak."

"No, you are right, it is *not* a discussion when the man who intends to marry me, despite having never gotten my agreement to that eventuality, starts laying down the law about the way I will be dressing in the future. I don't remember you asking my opinion on that, you are right."

With that she gave the bodyguard a look letting him know she meant business, but was sure the King had given his tacit approval, or the doors would not have swished open.

Uncaring of the why, Nataliya swept out of the elevator, heading for the front doors, certain their limousine would be waiting for her outside.

They were in the car and moving through city traffic before he broke the silence between them. "It was not my intention to offend you with my remarks."

"Wasn't it? But I'd always believed you were a top-drawer diplomat," she said with no little sarcasm. Just what exactly had he intended if not to offend?

His mouth firmed. "I assumed that certain things had been made clear to you at finishing school as you were supposed to be prepared for eventual marriage to a prince of my house."

"Newsflash, I did not agree with everything my mentors said in finishing school and found the university far more to my liking." In fact, she'd only attended said finishing school so she *could* attend university and pursue a degree in computer programming and software design.

Something even her mother had insisted was unnecessary and would end up being useless to Nataliya later in life. Solomia had wanted her to get a liberal arts degree if Nataliya insisted on going to college. But Nataliya had fought for the future she'd wanted, while believing that part of that future was out of her control and had been since she was eighteen.

"The reports from the school do not mention a tendency to rebellion."

She wasn't at all surprised Nikolai had read Nataliya's progress reports from finishing school. She had no doubt he'd also read her college transcripts and all relevant commentary from professors and teachers alike.

"The fact I became a computer hacker rather than following a far more acceptable pursuit for a future princess didn't enlighten you?" she asked, revising her view of his powers of observation.

And not in a positive direction.

"Funnily enough, no."

"Because I never rebelled against the medieval contract I signed when I was eighteen?" she guessed.

The infinitesimal shift in his expression said she'd got it in one.

"I can't really explain that in terms of my sense of independent thought. It was just there, this knowledge I had promised to marry Konstantin."

"A prince of my house, not Konstantin per se."

"Well, he was the one I thought I was marrying and honestly? I wasn't keen to date or fall for someone and get hurt like Mama had been by my father."

"Theirs was a love match?"

"On her side, though their parents *were* instrumental in bringing them together." And like so many times in her mother's life, it was obvious *her* parents had placed their own social standing and prestige above what was best for their daughter.

Her grandparents hadn't argued against Mama's and Nataliya's exiles any more than anyone else had. Both had died, their daughter never restored to her place of birth.

"So you had family precedent."

"I'm a member of the royal family of Volyarus—of course I had precedent. Aunt Oxana married my uncle to give him heirs and he never let his mistress go. She made marriage for duty look easy." And somehow *right*.

Her aunt had never been *happy* in her marriage. She couldn't have been, but Oxana had never complained, had never shown regret for becoming Queen and giving birth to the heir to the throne.

"Your attitude has changed though?" he asked, not sounding happy.

"Not exactly." She may not have enjoyed finishing school, but Nataliya had been taught from birth to put duty to the royal family first.

She simply intended to do that without losing herself in the process.

She tried to put that into words and was surprised at the understanding that came over the King's features. Not only understanding, but approval.

"You have a strong sense of integrity and duty, but also an equally strong sense of self. Believe it, or not, Nataliya, I think that is a good thing."

"Even if it means I wear provocative couture one day and jeans off the rack the next?"

"It will be *my* preference that my wife dress appropriate to her station on all the days, but how to define that will naturally not only be for me to determine."

She wasn't sure she believed him. The guy who thought he didn't have to *ask* her to marry him despite her spelling it out to him. And she wasn't all that impressed with his belief it was *not only* his to determine, rather than *hers* in full.

Despite the argument that Nikolai insisted on referring to as a lively discussion, Nataliya enjoyed herself very much at the charity ball.

She was thrilled Nikolai had purchased an entire table's worth of tickets and then rather than filling the spots with dignitaries, he'd held a lottery for the employees of the charity to fill the seats. Each seat came along with the privilege of bidding on auction items up to a set amount that the House of Merikov would pay. In every way, he gave the seat winners a fairy-tale evening.

It was brilliant PR, but even with that aspect, she couldn't help being flat-out impressed.

Who wouldn't want to be with the guy so willing to make other people's dreams come true?

In his perfectly tailored dinner suit, he was also the best-looking man in the giant ballroom. She let herself fall into the fantasy as they danced after the auction to music slow enough to justify him holding her.

But the fantasy crashed and burned when a tap on his shoulder indicated another man wanted to break into the dance. That other man? Her father.

She gasped, anger filling her faster than the air refilling her lungs and then she jerked back in involuntary reaction to her father's nearness.

"No." She shook her head. "I am not dancing with you."

"You are making a scene," her father censured her. He gave his patented smile to the King. "Pardon my daughter, she has clearly spent too many years living like a commoner."

Panic tried to claim Nataliya, but she refused to let it take hold. Looking around them, she realized they were the center of attention among the nearest dancing couples. Soon it would be the whole room, but she *would not* dance with her father.

"You will have to excuse us, but I do not enjoy the opportunity of dancing with my intended often enough to relinquish her to another." Nikolai adroitly pulled her back into his arms and shifted so he stood between her and her father.

Shock coursed through her and she nearly stumbled.

No one had ever stood between her and her father. Not once. Not her mother. Not the security detail hired to protect her family, not her royal relatives.

The idea that Nikolai would risk making a scene to back up her refusal to dance with the Count was so astonishing, she had no frame of reference for it.

This was the man who had spent the beginning of their evening making it clear he expected her to dress the part of his Princess and yet when it came to actions, he was not allowing diplomacy to guide him.

But rather her expressed needs.

Her father tapped on the King's shoulder again, his smug smile still in place. "I really must insist. It has been too long since I have seen my daughter."

"No." That was all Nikolai said, but he did it with utter freezing civility and spun her away.

"Do you want me to have my security alert the authorities? Count Shevchenko is breaking the restraining order you and your mother have out against him, is he not?"

"You know about that?" Although when they'd first been

exiled, her father had gone to Monaco with his latest flame, he followed Nataliya and her mother to Seattle when he ran out of money.

One trip to the ER later and her mother filed for divorce and the restraining order in the same week.

Her father had settled in New York, unwilling to risk jail time returning to Washington State.

"But apparently no one in your Volyarussian family does."

"Mama doesn't want anyone in her family to know." Her father's violent nature was never to be spoken of to anyone else. Mama had drilled that into Nataliya from her earliest memories.

While Mama had taken the order out and done more to break away from her toxic marriage than she'd ever done in Volyarus, Nataliya's mother felt deep shame for what her husband had done to her and their daughter. Mama had never wanted to talk about it, though she had started seeing a therapist.

Nataliya had learned young to carry the shame of her father's sins as if they were her own.

"Why?" Nikolai asked her.

And it took a moment for Nataliya to order her chaotic thoughts enough to realize what he was asking. "Because she's afraid they'll tell her she's wrong to have filed for it and kept it current? Because she's ashamed we need one? Because one simply does not talk about things like infidelity, much less abuse? Because she was made to feel like she carried the blame as much as he did for his actions? Take your pick."

"As you have been made to feel that his failings are yours?" Nikolai asked far too astutely.

"Does it matter? I know I'm not responsible for his actions."

"Maybe coming to realize that made you less willing

to tolerate the claim the contract between our families had on you."

He could be right. Nataliya had grown less willing to play her part as future bride of Prince Konstantin from the time she'd realized she wasn't paying the price for her mother's happiness, but for her father's sins.

Remembering what else Nikolai had asked, she sighed. "No authorities. The order is filed in Washington, not New York. It would be a hassle and he'd talk himself out of it anyway."

"I will not let him near you."

"Why would you promise that?" How could he know that even her father's proximity sparked irrational panic in Nataliya?

"Did you know that he put his last mistress in the hospital?"

She shook her head, feeling guilt that was not hers to feel. Nataliya was not responsible for the actions of her father. Not now. Not in the past.

It had been a difficult lesson to learn, but she'd refused to spend her entire life feeling shame for her father's ugly choices.

"Neither you, nor your mother told your family what he was really like?"

"We were already so ashamed of his public behavior, we couldn't share what he was like at home."

"You were a child. She was the wife he did not honor." Nikolai's tone was certain. "Neither of you had any shame to carry."

"I know that in my head but getting my heart to believe has been a years' long process."

"I did not know he would be here."

"Me either. Do you think he knew I would be?"

Nikolai inclined his head austerely. "Our plans have been of utmost interest to the media."

"It's the fairy-tale story of the decade." Nataliya's mouth twisted cynically. "The King who's courting the lady who lives like a commoner."

"So you acknowledge I *am* courting you."

"I have never denied it."

"You simply refuse to confirm the outcome."

"Have you asked me to?" she asked, working not to roll her eyes.

"You're very much hung up on that issue."

"And you are very arrogant."

He shrugged. "It would be stranger if I was not."

"Haven't you heard? Humility is a trait to be admired."

"False humility has no appeal to me."

She huffed out a laugh, unable to stop herself. "Clearly."

"You think I should pretend not to know my own mind? Where is the integrity in that?"

"No, I don't think you should pretend. I think you should not be so sure you know best all the time."

"But I do."

"Hush. Just dance with me, all right? I've had an upsetting moment."

He pulled her just a little closer while remaining nothing but appropriate in how he held her. "Hushing."

"Do you always have to have the last word?" she asked, exasperated.

He just looked at her, as if saying, *No, see? Here I am not having the last word.*

In that moment, she wanted nothing more than to press her body into his and lay her head on his strong shoulder. Let him hold her and protect her, when she had never expected anyone else to protect her. When her entire life, all Nataliya could remember was doing her best to protect others.

She could still remember being no older than three or four and stepping between her mother and father, yelling at him to stop hitting her mama. He'd backhanded her so hard she'd hit the wall and she could remember nothing else from that night.

She didn't know if she'd been knocked out or it was just her spotty trauma memory at work again, leaving holes that often made little sense to her.

They were in the limousine on the way back to her hotel suite when she commented, "I think my father left early. It's not like him to give up so easily. I was sure he'd try to talk to me again."

"I had him escorted out."

"Aren't you worried he'll go to the press and accuse you of throwing your weight around?" That was exactly the kind of thing Count Danilo Shevchenko would do.

Nikolai did not look worried. "I think my reputation can withstand anything a disgraced count could attempt to throw at it."

There went his arrogance again, but she admitted she liked it, if only to herself. "I'm sorry."

"You have nothing to apologize for."

"Would you be saying that if I refused to honor the contract?" she couldn't help asking.

"But you are not going to refuse."

"You're so sure." When she still wasn't.

"You have more integrity than any woman I know."

"I know loads of women with integrity."

"As do I, but not one of them is more honorable than you."

"Even Queen Tiana?" She wished she could take the question back the moment it popped out.

He'd said he didn't want to talk about his first marriage. Besides, it made Nataliya sound insecure and she didn't like that.

He surprised her by answering though. "Yes." He looked

like he was thinking about what he wanted to say next. "Our marriage was not the perfect joining of two hearts the media painted it to be."

If the fact he'd answered was surprising, the answer itself shocked her. Nataliya remembered how in love he'd seemed when he'd married the daughter of one of the new Russian oligarchy. Nataliya had thought the other woman beautiful but spoiled.

And she'd felt bad for thinking that. She'd always assumed her impression of the other woman was skewed by Nataliya's own unrequited feelings for Nikolai. And she hadn't liked knowing that about herself.

"Thank you," she said now, not sure what else to say in the light of her own nosy question and his very unexpected, honest answer.

He shrugged, but his expression was forbidding. "I was not flattering you, merely speaking the truth."

"Still, it's a nice truth to hear. To be valued for something other than my womb and royal lineage is surprisingly satisfying." She wasn't going to mention the comparison with his dead wife where Queen Tiana came out second.

Or his admission his first marriage hadn't been perfect. That wasn't the important issue here anyway.

"I am glad you think so."

She bit back a sigh. It *was* nice to hear, but could his respect for her make for a strong marriage when he showed no actual desire for her despite having told her he thought she was attractive?

Biting her lip, she studied him and then finally asked. "Are you ever going to kiss me?"

There could be no doubt she'd surprised him. It showed on the handsome, strong features that rarely showed uncalculated reaction.

He gave her a repressing look. "I believe that should come after you have agreed to marry me."

"You don't think it might help me agree?" Or not. If they had no chemistry.

Which on her side she had no doubts of, but her doubts in his genuine attraction for her were growing with each date that ended without so much as a kiss on the cheek.

"I will not allow sex to influence my choices and would prefer you weren't under the influence of sexual need when you make yours."

"You do expect to have sex though? After we are married?" He didn't really anticipate using IVF to get her pregnant, did he?

She didn't realize she'd asked that last out loud until the look of shocked horror on his features told her she had.

"Yes, we will have sex. There will be no test-tube babies for us."

"Okay. Good."

"Your lifestyle to this point has not indicated a desire for sexual intimacy."

"I've already explained that to you." She made no effort to prevaricate.

For whatever reason, she didn't want Nikolai to believe she'd ever gone to bed with another man while she would have been perfectly happy for Konstantin to make that assumption.

"You have already told me you are attracted to me. Are you saying that is not true?" he asked her, like a man trying to figure out a very difficult puzzle.

It was all she could do not to give in to sarcasm. He could not be that dense. "It's not my attraction to you that I'm doubting."

"But I told you I wanted you," he said like that should be it.

The final word on the subject.

"I think with some things, actions speak with more assurance than words."

"We are not having sex before our wedding night." He laid down the law like the King he was. "Our first child will be conceived within the bounds of marriage. As heir to my throne it would be grossly unfair for us to risk anything else."

"There are such things as birth control."

"We can wait."

She sat back into the corner of her seat, her arms crossed over her chest, feeling very put out and knowing he would not understand why *at all*. "Of course we can. Far be it from the King of Mirrus to act with spontaneity."

"I had my fill of spontaneity a long time ago." His expression said his memories in that direction were not good ones.

When he'd been married? Before that? After? She wanted to ask. So badly but knew she wouldn't.

Because as much as he'd guessed about her life as a child, she had no plans to ever share the memories that still haunted her nightmares.

With an imprecation, he grabbed his phone and sent a text, then crossed the limousine to join her on the leather upholstery on her side.

She stared up at him. "What's going on?"

"I'm letting my past dictate my present and that's as stupid as reliving it."

"You're not making any sense."

But the expression in his eyes was saying plenty. His gray eyes were molten with desire, his body rigid with self-restraint. And that's when she knew he wanted her too.

"You *want* to kiss me," she said wonderingly.

"Yes," he ground out.

"So, do it!" Why did men always make things so complicated?

She gasped in shock when he took her up on her offer.

Nikolai's tongue was right there sliding between her parted lips. This was no polite peck of lips.

Nikolai took possession of her mouth with passionate domination and Nataliya fell into the kiss with every bit of desire coursing through her virginal body.

He pulled her close, one hand cupping her breast through the lace of her gown and she moaned. She'd never been touched like this. She'd never even been kissed with tongue.

And she liked it all. Every new sensation building something inside her so that unfamiliar tension coiled within her.

She put her hands on his chest, squeezing his pecs, then feeling down his stomach, wishing his shirt were not in the way.

He made a sexy growling sound deep in his chest and yanked her into his lap, deepening the kiss. Everything went hazy, passion burning all rational thought from Nataliya's brain as the kiss went on and on and on.

He carefully peeled the fabric away from her body, slid his hand into the bodice of her dress and cupped her breast, pinching her aching nipple between his thumb and forefinger.

She let out a little cry against his lips, overwhelmed by the amazing sensation, and the pleasure in her core spiraled tighter.

He rolled her nipple back and forth, sending pleasure zinging directly from there to between her legs and unfamiliar feelings built inside her until she felt like she would scream with them.

It was too much and not enough and she did not know how to ask for what she needed. But then he pulled her closer and she felt his hardness against her hip, through their clothes, and something about that intimacy just sent her pleasure skyrocketing. The most amazing sensations washed over her until her body went rigid with her climax.

She ripped her lips from his to let the pleasure out in a scream and he kissed down her neck and back up to her mouth.

"So perfect, so passionate," he said in a tone that only added to the pleasure floating over her.

She collapsed against him, awash with sensation but so lethargic she could not have moved for anything.

"Sexually compatible." This time his tone was pure smug arrogance.

And even that didn't turn her off.

"Last word again?"

"I deserve it, don't you think?"

"Maybe this time."

He rapped his knuckles on the window and that must have been some kind of signal because minutes later, the limousine slid to a stop.

The door did not open however and she was grateful. He helped her get herself back together and off his lap.

"I will see you tomorrow," he reminded her.

They had plans to go on a tour of Central Park, because she'd said she wanted to. Later, they were going to have dinner together again.

Another perfect date.

Maybe it would end with another perfect kiss.

CHAPTER FIVE

KISSING NATALIYA HAD BEEN a good decision.

No way was she still worried that he did not desire her. As if.

If anything, his sexual feelings for her were so strong, he had almost dismissed his idea of fulfilling the contract in his brother's stead out of hand. Nikolai refused to be at the mercy of his libido. Again.

Only he'd realized that wanting her was not a bad thing. Having her would be a better thing. All he had to do was keep his emotional distance and never allow her to use his desire for her to control him.

Knowing that she wanted him, had always wanted him, even when she'd tried her best to hide it? That gave him the certainty that she would not withhold herself from him as Tiana had done. Would not use his desire as a weapon against him.

Nataliya was too honest and forthright to play those kinds of games, regardless.

He ignored the small voice telling him that all women were capable. He would not put himself in a position for sex to become a bargaining chip.

Never again.

But that did not mean he could not allay her fears on that score.

Nikolai was proud of both his superior decision making skills in sharing that intimacy with her. When she had climaxed in his arms, he'd wanted to shout in triumph. Nataliya had proven she could not withhold her reactions from him and that was something he needed to know after the pain of his first marriage, where sex had been a bargaining chip, a battleground, but never just pleasure.

And though her response to him had shot his libido into the stratosphere, he'd maintained the control he'd fought to hone.

He'd wanted to take her right there in the limousine, but he hadn't even undressed her. Nataliya's uninhibited passionate response had been deliciously surprising and nearly obliterating to his self-control.

But he *had* controlled himself and that was what mattered.

As he'd told Nataliya, his heir would not be conceived outside the legal bonds of matrimony.

A marriage he had no doubts *would* take place regardless of her posturing.

So, she wanted a proposal. He was a king, but he was also a man with superior intellect. He would give her the proposal of her dreams and she would finally agree verbally to what they both knew was a foregone conclusion.

Their marriage.

Nataliya was relieved that Jenna and her boyfriend were not back yet when she entered the hotel suite.

She needed some time. To parse what that kiss meant.

No way could she legitimately wonder if he wanted her. He'd been hard and she'd felt it. The fact he hadn't taken it farther than a kiss was a tick in the plus column. Nikolai could and would control his own sexual desires when necessary.

That boded well for the concept of fidelity.

Even so, she needed time to deal with the emotional aftermath of her first orgasm with another person and how vulnerable it made her feel.

Because as much as she respected that he hadn't pushed for more, the fact she was the only one who had come was a little disconcerting. She'd never seen herself as very sexual. Yes, she'd always wanted him, but in a vague, undefined way.

She'd experimented with toys, but her pleasure had taken longer to achieve and not been as devastating.

Far from having the slow fuse she'd always thought, with him, it was short and explosive.

Oh, man. So explosive.

It was time to do some research.

Research she should have done weeks ago, but she'd been putting off.

She didn't want to do a deep dive into Nikolai's life, but she wasn't marrying a man who had a long-term mistress like her uncle or a string of them like his own brother and her father.

She needed to know just how he lived his life now and if he was currently involved with another woman.

You could just ask, her conscience reminded her.

But Nataliya needed cold hard facts and as much as she knew Nikolai expected every word he uttered to be taken as gospel, her past made that kind of blind trust impossible.

She ordered a pot of coffee and pulled out the laptop that beat her desktop for speed and memory. It was a pretty cool betrothal gift. Sort of fitting she was using it to check out how smart betrothal to the King would be then.

Several hours later, Nataliya had some answers. And they were all good ones.

She'd hacked into his financial records, run his name and face through her personalized media and social media search engine. She'd checked out every single instance of travel for him in the past year, every expenditure in and out of country and done a less thorough but adequate search for the years since his wife's death.

Everything had come back empty. No apartments paid for by him but occupied by a woman. He'd had companions at some of the more prominent social functions, but he'd usually brought a cousin who was now married to one of his top aides. Nothing that would indicate he had liaisons, mistresses or even the occasional lover since his Queen's passing.

In short, on paper anyway, he was her dream guy.

For a woman, who had never thought to marry for love, that was a pretty big deal.

Nataliya woke after about four hours' sleep, still tired but feeling more solid about this royal courtship she was experiencing. She'd known Nikolai was not a carbon copy of his brother, but she'd needed to be sure.

About the fidelity thing. About the fact that there were no other personal contenders for the position of his Princess.

There would always be plenty of women with the right breeding and the desire for the role, but he had not been courting any of them.

Which meant what?

That he *wanted* her in that role? That the timing had been right, and he'd decided to remarry just when his brother was deciding to renege on the contract?

She couldn't dismiss the honor thing, because she'd come to accept that for Nikolai, maintaining family honor and fulfilling his house's terms in the contract were very important to him. Like obsession-level importance.

Whether he'd been raised with an overweening sense of integrity, or it was something innate in Nikolai. Either way, she no longer disregarded it as a very real motivation for him.

And that gave her hope for their future if they were to have one. A man that focused on maintaining family and personal integrity would not look at his marriage vows as multiple-choice options.

And he wanted her. He'd proven that.

Regardless of what others in her position might think, that mattered. As his Princess, Nataliya would lose all the trappings of a *normal* life she'd worked so hard to attain, but she would insist on having a stable and normal marriage, or as normal as possible married to a king who was also a billionaire business mogul.

That meant sharing a bed and a life. She was not Queen Oxana, and Nataliya would not spend her life finding satisfaction in her duty and her position.

There had to be more.

She'd seen that more in Maks's and Demyan's marriages, knew that even if her husband did not love her, he could give Nataliya more than what she'd seen between her aunt and uncle or her own parents, much less the other royals of that generation in Volyarus.

She would have more, or she would not marry.

No matter what she'd signed when she was eighteen.

Later, Nataliya was not at all surprised that they were going to have a horse-drawn carriage for their tour of Central Park.

Nikolai had a canny knack for knowing what she might enjoy most.

She was surprised, however, that the carriage looked so elegant and that it was drawn by two perfectly matched horses of the kind of quality she recognized as beyond the means of the average tourist company.

"Are these your horses?" she asked him in shock.

"They are now." He flashed her a slashing, arrogant smile. "I bought them from stables with an excellent reputation in Upstate New York."

"And the carriage?"

"Purchased for this occasion."

"You don't think that's a little over the top?"

"I am a king, Nataliya. I do not ride in conveyances that cater to the masses."

But to *buy* a carriage? "You sound really snobby right now."

"Not simply intelligent about my own safety?"

He was talking about assassination attempts. In his father's lifetime, the former King had survived one and she had no idea if Nikolai had ever been the target of such an attempt. She had no doubt that if he had, he would have kept it very quiet.

"I stand corrected," she acknowledged. "But I still think you have no clue how the average person lives."

"And you do." He said it with satisfaction.

Nataliya gave him a surprised look. "You like that?"

"Very much. Mirrusians live all over the globe in all walks of life. The royal family should understand them if we are expected to serve their needs."

"That's a very progressive view."

"I am a progressive man."

A man who was getting married based on a contract his father had signed? She did not think so. "Maybe in some things."

"I am no throwback."

"No, I'd say you are the inevitable product of growing up royal in the twenty-first century in a country that is still a full monarchy."

"Volyarus is also a monarchy."

"I am aware." She settled back into the comfortable leather squabs of the carriage. "What happens to this carriage after today?"

"It will be sold and the proceeds donated to the charity we've been supporting with our courtship."

"Konstantin didn't like my online auction."

"You hit at his pride."

"It was intentional," she admitted. "But you provide gifts *for* the auction."

"It is a worthy cause." He took her hand, in an unexpected public display of affection that should be entirely innocent.

Only she felt that touch go right through her and had to take a deep breath and let it out slowly not to give herself away.

His knowing look said she hadn't been all that successful. "So, going back to our earlier words, are you a proponent of constitutional monarchy?" he asked, but didn't sound worried or even shocked by the idea she might be.

"Power should always be checked."

"And those checks, do they always work?" He brushed his thumb over her palm, sending electric sparks along that nerve-rich center and up her arm.

She curled her fingers around his thumb to stop him so she could think clearly enough to focus on answering him. "No, but having them gives the people that power is supposed to protect more of a chance of actually enjoying that protection."

"Does your uncle know you have these prorepublic leanings?" Amusement laced Nikolai's tone.

"Technically, he is my second cousin."

"But he sees himself in a closer role. You call him uncle."

"Not anymore, I don't." It had taken her long enough, but she'd come to realize that family was more than a word. It was a relationship, and her "uncle" had removed himself from their relationship a long time ago.

Now that seemed to startle Nikolai, when her beliefs that *his* power should be checked by a parliament didn't. "Why not?"

"Fifteen years ago, he sacrificed me and my mother to protect his good name when the whole time he has been the biggest risk to scandal in the royal family." Mama had always known too.

Nataliya had only learned of her King's infidelity as an adult and quite by accident, but then she'd spoken to her mother about it, hurt and angered by the monarch's hypocrisy. She'd learned then that Mama had known since the beginning.

It had sparked one of their rare arguments.

"Because of his long-term mistress."

"Exactly." The woman he'd refused to marry because of her divorce but had never been willing to give up. "You know about their long-term affair. She's not the secret he believes she is. If the media starts digging, they won't have to go very deep to reach a royal scandal of epic proportions."

"You do not think King Fedir has things in place to protect the monarchy in such an event?"

"He may think he does, but his relationship is too long-standing for him to deny it with any chance at being believed. Too many people know about it. Too many bills have been paid for her through the palace accounts."

"I'm sure King Fedir has taken precautions so that those bills cannot be traced back to him."

"I traced them. And as we both saw at the hackathon, I'm good, but I'm by no means the only good hacker out there."

"You hacked into your uncle's financial records?"

"I hacked into the palace financial records."

"You didn't know about the mistress," he said in wonder.

"Before we left Volyarus, no I did not. In fact, I did not discover her existence until a few years ago."

"And realizing he maintained that relationship put a different complexion on his actions with you and your mother fifteen years ago."

"Yes. I realized that he expects everyone but himself to sacrifice for the sake of *his* throne."

"Isn't that a bit harsh? He has a whole country's well-being he must take into account."

"Not if it means giving up the woman he loves, but not enough to marry. If you can call the sort of selfishness that drives him love at all."

"You judge him harshly."

"I paid a high price for his pride, but Mama, who had already paid a terrible price for being married to my father, was forced to give up even more." And Nataliya wasn't sure she would ever forgive her King for making her mother pay that price.

"The Countess seems to have built a good life for herself in her exile."

"Mama has, but she should not have had to learn to live without her family and friends. It wasn't fair."

"Do you feel that way about the contract? That it is not fair?"

Nataliya thought about that for a minute, never having put the contract in those terms.

"I think me being pressured to sign it and accept the terms when I was eighteen was not fair. I would fight tooth and nail to stop my own child from doing the same."

He nodded but said nothing. Still waiting it seemed for her to answer the core of his question.

Did she think it fair that she was contracted to marry him?

Instead of answering that, she offered some truth of her own. "I did a deep dive into your life last night."

"I thought you looked tired." He took both her hands in his and smiled down at her, obviously not worried about her investigation. "Did you get any sleep?"

"A few hours." She licked her lips, her gaze caught on his mouth, wanting to taste.

His gray gaze darkened with desire. "A nap might be in order this afternoon."

Was he offering to take it with her? She shook her head. No, of course not.

"Is that all you're going to say?" Nataliya asked, stunned he wasn't offended.

"What do you want me to say? I cannot claim I did not expect you to use your skills to discover if I have any skeletons in my closet. Your main concern about marrying Konstantin was his tendency to have uncommitted sex with women."

"He wasn't in a relationship, not like my father."

"But it still gave you pause."

"You know it did."

"You would not have found anything similar in my background."

"Not even a discreet long-term mistress."

"I am not King Fedir either."

"No. You are kind of an anomaly among powerful men. I'd wonder if you had a repressed libido, but I felt the evidence of your arousal in the car last night."

Far from being insulted by her remark, he laughed. "I can assure you, my libido is everything you will want it to be."

"I don't doubt it." She looked to their tour guide-slash-carriage driver and only now realized he had earbuds in.

She probably should have noticed he wasn't giving a running commentary, but Nataliya had been so caught up in Nikolai, for once in her adult life, she hadn't paid the utmost attention to the situation around her.

His smile said he knew. "Just noticed he's in hear-no-evil, or rather *private discussion* mode?"

"Yes."

"That's not like you."

"I thought we were doing a tour."

"The commentary will start when I give him a signal."

"Your guards are in the pedicabs ahead of and behind us, aren't they?" She'd just noticed that too.

"They wanted to be riding their own horses, but you would not believe the regulations governing any and all activity in Central Park."

"Even a king has to submit to red tape."

He nodded, his expression rueful. "If I'd had more time…"

He'd had time enough to buy gorgeous matching horses and a carriage.

He did some more of that thumb brushing, this time on both of her palms and she shivered.

"You wouldn't have been sure of me, if I hadn't kissed you last night." He sounded very pleased with himself.

"Maybe. I'm not sure," she admitted. "I kind of see you as this larger than life man. Yes, you are a king, but you're not a despot."

"You don't think so?" he asked, like her opinion actually mattered.

"You're the kind of king that makes me not worry about you not having a parliament, unless I'm worried about you taking too much on and not having anyone else to help carry the burden." Why was she being *so* honest? She'd never have been this open with anyone else.

Nikolai's expression could be seen as nothing less than satisfaction. "King Fedir?"

"Would benefit a lot by having some checks of power in his life."

"So, you think I am a good king?"

"Yes."

"And a good man?" he asked.

"Yes." She'd always thought so, but she'd had to be sure.

"You have no questions about things you may have discovered last night?"

"I didn't discover anything. That's the point, isn't it? Were there things to discover?"

"About me? No."

"Then about who?"

"Does it matter?"

If his father, or brother, or someone else had done something she might have questions about? "No. I don't think it does, but you would tell me, wouldn't you, if there was something that would affect me?"

"Yes." Nikolai looked so stern when he said that, but not shifty.

So, she believed.

"I think if I were a different woman, raised in a different way, I might think the contract was unfair," she said, finally answering his initial question. "If *you* were a different man, you wouldn't feel the need to fulfill its terms on behalf of your house."

"Perhaps."

"But I am who I am. And honestly, I wasn't raised to believe in fairy tales and happy endings. I don't remember Mama ever suggesting she hoped I found true love." More like Solomia had hoped her daughter would not end up married to a man who would physically hurt her.

But even with that hope, Mama had still encouraged her daughter to sign that contract ten years ago, with no idea about what kind of man Konstantin was.

"I don't think the contract itself is unfair." Nataliya acknowledged as much to herself as to him. "I *did* sign it. I did agree to the terms. I never expected to marry a man I loved, but I won't marry a man I cannot trust."

"My brother is trustworthy."

"Maybe, but his double standard about dating and sex make it hard for me to see him that way." She didn't want to talk about his brother. "Regardless, if we marry and are blessed with children, then believe their well-being will be more important to me than that of Mirrus."

"But that is not how a royal thinks."

"Then I guess you'd better make sure I never have to choose between duty and my children."

"That's a heavy promise you want me to make."

"No. My promise to you is that if you don't succeed at that, I will not be browbeaten into doing something that could hurt those I love. Period."

"That is the perspective of the common man."

"A perspective you said the royal family needs."

"Yes."

"So, that implies you are going to take my opinions into consideration when making decisions for Mirrus."

"It does, yes."

"But you hardly know me."

"You are not the only hacker available to dive deep into someone's life."

"Plus your family has had me under surveillance for ten years." Someone paying attention could know a great deal about her.

"That is true."

"You've read the reports?" she couldn't help asking.

"All of them."

All of them? "That's a lot of reading."

"Deciding to enforce the contract and fulfill its terms was not a spur-of-the-moment decision. I do not make those." He said the last like his own warning.

"I believe it." Though at first that was exactly what she'd thought he'd done. "You came to Volyarus intending to put yourself forward as the Prince of your house referred to in the contract."

"I did."

"Did Konstantin know?"

"No. It is not my habit to take others into my confidence."

"I think I'll expect you to take me into your confidence, if I marry you."

"We are separate people. Our duties will live in harmony but not always overlap."

"Are you trying to warn me that I won't see much of you if I marry you?" That might actually turn out to be the deal breaker nothing else had.

His jaw went taut. "That will be up to you."

"What do you mean?" she asked, her brows drawn together in confusion.

"Though I travel some for diplomatic reasons, all business travel is Konstantin's purview. I spend most of my time in Mirrus."

"Wouldn't your wife do the same?"

"Tiana did not. She found life in Mirrus stifling and preferred traveling with friends in warmer climates."

That made no sense. No more sense that he would tolerate it. "But she was the Queen. Surely her duties precluded long vacations in Jamaica."

"Monaco was her favorite haunt, but as to her duties, she found those stifling, as well."

Nataliya didn't know what he thought about that. His expression revealed nothing.

"I am used to working long hours," she offered.

"Will you expect to continue with a career after marriage?" Something about that question made him so tense, she couldn't miss it, despite how he was so careful to maintain an expressionless mask.

"If I were to marry a king, I think the job of being his Princess would keep me sufficiently busy."

"Not all women would agree."

"Really? I can't imagine a single woman of my acquaintance who would attempt to maintain a full-time career as well as the full-time job of Princess."

"So you do see it as a job."

"Being a wife is a role, but being a princess? That's definitely a job."

"I'm very glad to hear you say that."

What else didn't she know about his marriage to Tiana? Nataliya had not known that Tiana spent so much time away from Mirrus, but she'd been careful in her research to respect Nikolai's personal privacy. Other than confirming that Tiana had not had a bunch of visits from the Palace Physician for unexplained injuries, Nataliya had purposefully not looked too deeply into his marriage.

Just because she *could* find out just about anything about a person's life, didn't mean she *would* do that. It was a matter of her own personal integrity.

They spent the rest of their tour talking about their families, getting to know each other on a level that no amount of reading investigative reports could achieve. Nikolai never did indicate their tour guide start his commentary.

And she didn't mind at all.

She wasn't surprised she enjoyed the King's company.

Nataliya always had.

He was the guy she'd had her first crush on and being older and wiser only made those feelings seem deeper. But she didn't love him.

Would not let herself.

She felt something for him though, that would make refusing marriage to him impossible.

Not that she was sharing that revelation with the arrogant King.

CHAPTER SIX

NATALIYA DID END UP taking a long nap that afternoon because their dinner reservations weren't until eight.

Nataliya expected to be taken to an exclusive five-star restaurant with a month-long waiting list for dinner.

Because so far Nikolai had pulled out all the stops for this courtship.

So, she was a little surprised to find herself at Central Park for the second time that day. An eight-person security team surrounded them as they exited the limousine.

"What are we doing back here?"

"Having dinner."

"I thought we had reservations."

"I said dinner was at eight. And it will be." He sounded so complacent, almost smug, like he knew what he'd planned was going to please her.

She couldn't help wanting to push his buttons a little. Laughing, she said, "I'm not exactly dressed for a picnic with hot dogs from a local vendor," she teased.

The look of horror on his face was worth the tease. "Trust me—that is not what we are having for dinner."

"You're such a snob." She found herself reaching for his hand and having to pull hers back before the telling movement gave her away.

He made it so easy to forget they weren't really dating. That this courtship was the result of a contract signed a long time ago.

"I am a king. I would and have eaten grubs in order not to offend my hosts in both Africa and Australia, but if the choice of venue is up to me? We are never eating from a food truck." He spoke with the conviction he usually reserved for matters of real import.

It made her smile. "I'm not sure hot dog carts are considered food trucks, but I get your point. Thousands of foodies would tell you that you don't know what you are missing though."

"I will live with the loss," he said dryly.

She shook her head, her smile undimmed. "You just watch. One day I'll convince you."

"Watch yourself, *kiska*. You are sounding dangerously like you are considering a future with me."

"Perhaps you should be the one watching out. Maybe I am," she admitted, some things having solidified inside her while she'd slept and rejuvenated that afternoon.

"I am very glad to hear that." He was the one who reached for her hand, bringing it to his mouth to kiss the inside of her palm.

She gasped, that small salute sending tingles of pleasure right to the core of her. It was not a carnal act, but her body's reaction was as basic as it got. Nataliya craved Nikolai like she'd never desired another man, and the more time they spent together the stronger that craving got.

It scared her and excited her at the same time.

Knowing that she was developing a need for him that only he would ever be able to fill frightened her, but the knowledge he wanted to marry her mitigated that fear.

If he were a man like her father, she'd run fast and far from both her feelings and him, but Nikolai would never betray her as the Count had betrayed Nataliya's mother over and over again.

They came into a clearing and unexpected tears pricked her eyes at what she saw.

It was so over-the-top, but even at first glance the amount of thought that went into setting it up was obvious.

Standing lanterns surrounded a table set with the official linens she'd only seen in the Mirrus palace. Eggshell white, they were embroidered in gold and navy blue with the coat of arms for the House of Merikov. Fine white bone china with the same design sat atop gold chargers she had no doubt were pure precious metal and the crystal on the table sparkled elegantly.

The eight-person security detail, rather than his usual four, suddenly made sense. The table settings alone were worth thousands, if not tens of thousands and the centerpiece looked like a vase Oxana had in her sitting room. Mama had told her as a child not to touch it because it was priceless.

When royalty used that term, they meant it.

But beyond the opulence of the setting was how much care had been taken to bring a taste of Mirrus to New York. A small, ornate, gold-leafed trinket box sat next to one of the place settings.

It didn't take a computer genius to know what was in that box. The official betrothal ring of the House of Merikov.

"It's beautiful," Nataliya said in a hushed voice, that trinket box taking her breath away.

Nikolai led her to the table, relinquishing her hand to pull Nataliya's chair out himself. "I have pleased you. I am glad."

"You've been pleasing me this whole courtship, and you know it." She made the mistake of looking up and found herself frozen by the molten depths of his gaze.

"I have tried."

Oh, man. She needed to get a hold of herself. Forcing herself to look away, she settled into her chair. "Enough with the false humility, Nikolai," she mocked, though she felt like doing anything but mocking. "You are a king. You do not consider failure as an option."

That ornate trinket box to the left of her plate affirmed that truth as much as it stole the very breath from her body.

He moved around the table and took his own seat, his attention fixed firmly on her. "And yet, to succeed, ultimately I need your cooperation."

"It's nice to hear you finally admit that."

His left brow rose in sardonic question. "I have never denied that your agreement is necessary."

"But you *have* acted like you assume you already had it." And why it should strike her that that kind of arrogance could be sexy, she did not know.

"You signed the contract, but only you can decide if you are going to fulfill its terms." He flicked his hand to signal someone.

A waiter came out of the darkness around them to shake out Nataliya's napkin and lay it smoothly across her lap before doing the same for Nikolai. Moments later, water and wine were poured in their crystal goblets and a starter of fresh prawns was served over a bed of arugula.

She savored a prawn before smiling at him, because she wanted to. "My favorite."

"I know."

"How?" she asked curiously, pretty sure she hadn't mentioned this weakness to him.

"A man reading your comings, goings and habits for the past ten years can learn a great deal if he wants to." And would be a fool not to, his tone implied.

After all the deep dives into someone else's life she'd done for Demyan, as well as the one she'd done on Nikolai, it felt strange to know that a *king* had spent so much time not only reading up on her but interpreting the very mundane details recorded by those who had watched *her* over the past decade. "And you wanted to?"

"Can you doubt it?"

"It just seems like overkill for you to pay such close attention."

"Does it? Didn't you do the same?"

"Not really, no. I only looked at certain areas of your life for the past couple of years." She'd been interested in patterns that would reveal behaviors she could not live with.

Nataliya had been content to learn his likes, dislikes and views through the more regular method of simply getting to know him.

"Believe me, after my first marriage, I had no desire to be surprised by any aspect of your life or nature." He made it sound like his first marriage had offered up some unpleasant surprises.

Remembering the way he'd been with his Queen, Nataliya found that difficult to believe.

But then, who looking at her family would ever have guessed her father was the violent man he had been with her and Mama?

"Doesn't that take some of the mystique out of it?" As she asked the question, Nataliya realized how foolish it was.

That kind of mystique belonged in romance, but their relationship was not based on anything so emotive.

His look said he was surprised by the question. "I do not think a marriage for a sovereign needs to have mystique."

"I would say you do not have a romantic bone in your body," she teased, covering her own embarrassment at the knowledge that very thing wasn't what they were about. "But this whole scenario says otherwise."

Which was no less than the truth, so maybe, he could take a little bit of the blame for how hard she found it to remember this courtship wasn't about romance.

"You deserve to be treated as the special woman you are, but that does not make me romantic," he said decisively.

Warmth unfurled inside her at his words, despite how surprised she was by his claim.

"You don't consider yourself romantic?" she asked, startled.

The man had been nothing but romantic in his courtship of her, despite the fact it was based on all sorts of things *besides* romance.

"Romance is based on illusion and I have no illusions left."

Okay. No question. His marriage had *not* been the perfect union she had always assumed, unless he'd had a relationship she didn't know about since Tiana's death.

"You sound so cynical, but that is not how you treat me." And she was glad.

"There is nothing about you which to be cynical about," he said with some satisfaction.

"I'm not perfect." Not even a paragon. She was after all the woman who had embarked on the first dates article in order to get Konstantin to back out of the contract when her King refused to renegotiate its terms to leave her out of it.

"No, but your integrity is bone-deep and your understanding of duty uncommon in the current age."

She found it interesting he believed so strongly in her honesty, knowing how she'd sought to manipulate his brother. But then she hadn't done anything *wrong* in her efforts to get out of the contract. Maybe more than anything, that revealed how much this King did not believe in the double standard of fidelity so many men in positions of power seemed hampered by.

Nevertheless, she reminded him, "We've had this discussion."

"Yes. You have promised that if it came between our children's happiness and duty, you would choose their happiness. That is not a deterrent to me."

"Apparently it's not." But she didn't understand how it wasn't. Did he think she'd give in when it came down to it?

He would learn differently if the situation ever arose.

"We share the knowledge that more than our own happiness rests on our shoulders, but the well-being of an entire country. That does not mean we will both not make every effort to see our children happy that we can."

That was good to hear, but too practically put to justify the squishy warmth inside her right now.

Doing her best to ignore those feelings, she acknowledged, "I was raised to understand my place in the world and that it was not the same place as Jenna's, or the other *normal* people like her."

Nataliya had done her best to have a normal life, but she belonged to the royal family of Volyarus and always would do.

He nodded. "Jenna, while a good friend, does not have the welfare of a country to consider when she decides how she spends her time."

"You're saying I do." Despite her ever-present knowledge of her place in the world, Nataliya had never really thought that she took that into account in *everything* she did, but she wasn't sure she could deny it either.

"You always have."

When she'd been little, Nataliya had known she could not talk about what happened in her home, not only because of the shame she and her mom felt, but because *a lady did not tell tales.* And she had known she was Lady Nataliya since she knew her own name.

As she'd grown older, that knowledge of who she was *had* continued to influence her. When she'd been tempted to test her hacking skills at the university in ways others did, she'd stopped herself, knowing if she got caught it could bring embarrassment to the royal family.

One of the reasons she was so good was that she'd had to be positive she could not be traced or trapped when she tried a hack. Her absolute need not to be caught had made her better.

Nataliya hadn't been born a princess, but she had been born into the royal family.

Because her father had been such an embarrassment to the throne, she and Mama had been forced to make choices for the good of Volyarus even other nobility of their country would not be required to make.

While those choices had hurt, Nataliya had never denied they were necessary.

The way the exile had been handled by King and Queen? That had not been okay.

The way she and Mama had been made into pariahs right along with her father? That had not been okay.

The fact that her mother's exile had never been lifted? That had not been okay either.

But Nataliya did not resent her place in the world or what it required of her to fill it.

"If it had been up to you, would you have left my mother living in exile for all these years?" she asked him as their soup course was laid.

"You mean, if I had been in your uncle's position? I should hope that I would show more concern for one of my subjects, much less a woman as close to me as a sister. It is true that in life we are sometimes called to pay the price for another's sin, but it is not my habit to dismiss that cost to others."

"Have you ever been faced with a similar situation?"

"Yes, I have." But he did not elaborate and then Nikolai frowned. "However, in a very real way, it was up to me. I did not pressure my brother into fulfilling the terms of the contract."

"Why not?"

"I was allowed to choose my wife."

"And you felt guilty that he had not."

"Yes." He paused, considered, like he was deciding how much he wanted to say. "That was part of it certainly."

"What was the other part?"

He approved the wine for the soup course and then met her gaze, his mysterious and dark. "When you were a teen-ager, you used to watch me like I was a football star."

"You knew about my crush?" She should have been em-barrassed, but somehow she wasn't.

She wasn't ashamed of the feelings she'd once had for him, even if she never wanted to be that emotionally vul-nerable again.

That crush had turned into unrequited love that she had not managed to stifle despite her best efforts until he'd lost his wife and his grief acted as a barrier to her heart she'd never been able to erect on her own.

"I did and I felt it was unfair on you both to press for-ward a marriage that would cause you both discomfort if not pain under those circumstances."

She'd never thought he'd noticed her obsession with him. Nataliya gave Nikolai a self-deprecating smile. "I thought I was so good at hiding it."

"Who of us as teenagers is that good at hiding any-thing?" he asked with some amusement.

"I'm pretty sure that even as a teenager, you were an expert at hiding any feelings you did not want to share."

"I had posters of…" He named a popular American film star. "All over my side of the room at boarding school."

"But she would have been old enough to be your mother!" Nataliya exclaimed, laughing.

"I thought she was everything sexy."

"And now?" Nataliya asked, wondering if he had an-other secret celebrity crush.

Nikolai gave her a sultry look. "My tastes have refined. I'm turned on by sexy computer hackers who forget dates."

"I didn't forget—I was late."

"Because you forgot."

How did a woman forget a date with a king? She didn't,

but the first week of his courtship, Nataliya had gotten caught up in her work to the extent that Jenna's frantic phone call wondering where she was had been necessary.

"You weren't angry you had to wait."

"Naturally not. I find it admirable that you take your work so seriously."

"The duty thing again?" She sighed and knew she owed him the truth. "It's not about focusing so seriously on my job—it's that I really get lost in it and have no awareness of time passing or even people coming in and out of the room with me."

"I find that charming." His heated look said he found it something else too. Hot.

How? She didn't know, but she was glad. "Here's hoping that doesn't change because I'm unlikely to. It's a personality trait."

"You're very blunt."

Her mouth twisted in consternation. "Not a great trait for a diplomat, I know."

"For a princess who is a diplomat by role rather than career, I do not agree. I believe that your ability to be forthright will be a benefit to our House."

She laughed. Couldn't help doing so. "You're the only one who has ever considered that flaw a strength." Even her beloved mother found Nataliya's blunt manner something to censure.

"Honesty is not a flaw."

"Even when I say truths I shouldn't?"

"I have never heard you say anything you shouldn't," he claimed.

"Um, are you practicing selective memory, or lying?" she asked.

"Neither."

"But I offended your father and your brother during that little tribunal at the Volyarussian palace."

"And their attitude to you offended me."

"It did?" She thought about how Nikolai had responded in that confrontation. "It did."

"Yes. Nothing you said that day should not have been said," he repeated with an approving smile. "So, you too saw it as a tribunal?"

"What else? My so-called *uncle* and your father, not to mention your brother, were determined to put me on trial."

"And instead they found themselves on the wrong side of having to defend their own actions and attitudes."

Looking back, she realized that was true. No one had expected her to take them to task, but she had. And Nikolai, without condemning his own brother, had backed her up.

So had Oxana and Mama, in their own ways.

They ate in companionable silence for a few minutes before she said, "I've been thinking about what I would like to do careerwise if I were to become The Princess of Mirrus."

Subtle tension filled his body, like he had gone on alert. "Yes?"

"I would like to continue what I do for Demyan…" she trailed off when that subtle tension went overt.

His jaw went hard, his body going ramrod straight, but all he said was, "Yes?"

"I like what I do, but I wasn't sure there was a place for me at Mirrus Global."

The tension drained out of Nikolai and his smile was blinding. "You want to use your powers for my company rather than Yurkovich-Tanner?" His delight at the idea was unmistakable.

She grinned. "Yes, but only part-time."

"Because you understand that to be my Princess is in itself a job that requires time and attention? I could not have chosen a better lady to stand at my side if I had searched the world over."

The compliment was over-the-top, but she got the distinct impression he meant every word and that did things to her heart she didn't want to examine too closely. "You really are something special, you know that?"

"Because I like the idea of headhunting my own wife from my rival?" he asked, in full arrogant-guy mode.

She rolled her eyes at him. "Yurkovich-Tanner is not your rival. You are business partners."

"But I have been jealous of Demyan's hacker for years."

"You didn't know it was me." She didn't make it a question.

Nataliya and Demyan had done an excellent job of hiding her true role at Yurkovich-Tanner since she'd been hired on and he discovered her abilities as a hacker.

She was the one who had discovered the Crown Princess's pregnancy after Gillian and Maks broke up. Demyan had used Nataliya on the most delicate matters. Only now did she realize that was because he had always seen her as family, and he trusted her implicitly.

"I did not." Nikolai winked. "Once we found out at the *tribunal* I was worried you would want to continue working for your cousin."

That's why Nikolai had gone all tense just now? He'd been thinking about it even then?

"When I marry, my loyalty will belong first and foremost to my husband." She was still talking in couched terms, but it needed to be said.

"That is a great boon coming from a woman with such a formidable sense of loyalty."

She shrugged, a little embarrassed. "You're always so complimentary."

"I think very highly of you. I would have thought you would have realized that by now."

Coming from the man she admired above all others, that was kind of an amazing thing to hear. More than amazing, it touched Nataliya's heart in that uncomfortable way all over again and even filled it.

Everything around her went into sharp focus as something she had simply not allowed herself to see became glaringly obvious. This one man touched her emotions in a way no one else did, and with a simple compliment, because he lived in her heart.

She still loved him.

She'd never stopped, though she'd done a good job of pretending to herself for the sake of her own sense of honor.

She'd felt bad for loving a married man, and like a monster when he'd lost the wife *he'd* loved. Nataliya had also realized it was not fair to love one brother and marry another.

So, she'd convinced herself that her *crush* was over, that her feelings for Nikolai were nothing more than teenage hormones.

But this feeling inside her was so big, she could barely contain it. She adored the man who had always been her hero.

At first, she'd just had an almighty crush on the man, but she'd learned to respect so much about him from early on. Yes, he'd taken over as King for the sake of his father's health, but Nikolai had done so with a fully developed agenda that put the people of Mirrus first. He was a staunch conservationist and environmentalist which wasn't easy to manage with the economic needs of his country, but he did it.

He was respectful to others, didn't lose his temper or throw around his weight just because he could and he was loyal to his family. Loyal like her own uncle only pretended to be.

Had *he* been the reason she'd been so determined to end that contract? Had her subconscious finally realized that she simply could *not* marry his brother?

She couldn't be sure that it played no part and she wasn't sure how that made her feel.

Because her integrity was important to her.

"I think I still have a crush on you," she blurted. And while that was blunt it wasn't the whole truth, but telling the man who had made it clear he did not and never would love her that he owned her heart was not on.

He smiled at her, the expression unguarded for just a moment so she saw the difference between his normal smiles and this one. "I *really* like your honesty, *kiska*."

Everything inside her seized with the need to claim this man. "I'll marry you."

His smile fell away, but he didn't look unhappy, just really serious.

Silently, he stood up from his seat, and then he moved around the table to take one of her hands to pull her to feet, as well. "Will you marry me, Lady Nataliya?"

She stared at him in confusion. She'd just said she would. Then she realized what he was doing. Giving her the proposal.

And something else clicked. He'd *always* planned to propose tonight. That little trinket box had been a hint, but he had *not* intended for it to be the question.

She liked knowing that. A lot. She'd told him she wanted a proposal and because it was something he could give her, he had done. "Yes, Your Highness, I would be honored to be your Princess."

Then he kissed her, despite there being bodyguards all around. It wasn't a chaste kiss either.

His mouth claimed hers, his tongue sliding between her parted lips to tangle with hers. It was like the other night, but not.

She felt absolutely connected to this man and his arms around her in this very public place proclaimed she was his, as he was hers.

The kiss went on for long moments until flashes behind her eyelids made her open her eyes and she realized they'd drawn the attention of some enterprising paparazzi as well as park visitors using their camera phones.

"We're going to be viral by tomorrow," she husked.

"You were agreeing to be my wife—I do not mind the entire world knowing that."

"Me either." She sighed. "But I think we've given them enough fodder for gossip."

"Do you think so?" He lowered his head and kissed her once more.

Because he wanted to show he wasn't ashamed of claiming her? Because he was too arrogant to let her call things to a halt? Just because he wanted to?

She didn't know and didn't care as she responded with a passion-filled joy she'd never thought to experience.

CHAPTER SEVEN

WHEN NATALIYA RETURNED to her hotel later that night, she called Mama to warn her about the formal announcement going out the next day.

Nikolai had never doubted Nataliya's answer even if he had been willing to ask the question.

"Are you sure this is what you want?" Mama asked, sounding worried.

"Why are you asking me that now? You didn't ask me ten years ago when I signed that contract if I was doing what *I* wanted." Nataliya didn't know where the words came from.

She sounded bitter, but she wasn't bitter. Was she? She'd never thought she was.

Her mother had done the best she could, but she hadn't been raised to stand up to family pressure, or even to stand against an abusive bully that called himself a husband.

Only it did feel like it was ten years too late to be asking Nataliya if she wanted to be a princess.

"Ten years ago, I was still desperate to go home, desperate to return to life as I knew it." Went unsaid was the truth that Solomia had been prepared to allow her daughter to pay the price to make that happen.

"And I was the conduit for that happening," Nataliya spelled out.

"You were born into a royal family—your life was never going to be entirely your own. No more than mine has been."

So, why ask if marriage to Nikolai was what Nataliya wanted now? "Did you ever want something different for me?"

LUCY MONROE   103

"Why, when I believed that was the way life should be?"
Her mother's sigh was clear across the phone. "I'm not the
same woman I was ten years ago."

"So you don't still believe that?"

"If I could go back ten years, I would insist you *not* sign
that contract," her mother said fiercely.

"Why?"

"Because at the time I didn't realize it could mean you
would end up married to the King." And her mom's tone
made that sound like the worst imaginable fate.

Nataliya didn't understand why. "Not because you didn't
think an arranged marriage was a bad thing."

"No, actually. I didn't want you to love your husband like
I loved your father. It made our relationship too inequal."

"You believe I love Nikolai like that," she said with
dawning understanding.

Her mother was worried about Nataliya being hurt the
way she had been.

"Don't you?"

"Nikolai is not anything like my father," she said instead
of answering. Nataliya had never lied to Mother and she
wasn't going to start now.

"You look at him with such fascination," her mother said,
like that was a tragedy. "You always have done. Even before
that contract. When the idea of you marrying Konstantin
came along I thought I saw a way of protecting you from
the pain of living with a one-sided love."

"Because you didn't think Nikolai could ever love me."

Her mother's scoffing sound was answer enough. And
surprisingly hurtful. "He was infatuated with Tiana from
the time he first laid eyes on her. They were of an age. She
sexually enthralled him. I knew because I recognized the
signs. I was enthralled with your father and I ended up
badly hurt because of it."

"So you didn't want me to love my husband?" Nataliya asked with disbelief. "I think that's a little extreme."

"Not in the world I have always lived in. How many of our family's marriages are based on love, or even include romantic love, do you think?"

"Maks and Demyan both love their wives deeply."

"Your cousins have been very lucky and so have the women they married because incredibly, they share an abiding, reciprocal love."

"But you don't think any man would love me that way?" Nataliya asked painfully.

"My dear daughter, you are more comfortable with computers than people. You are no femme fatale, or even sexually aware socialite like Queen Tiana was. I love you with my whole heart—"

"But you don't think Nikolai ever will," Nataliya interrupted. "Well, that's fine. He wants me." She did not doubt that at all now. "And I want him. I don't need him to fall in love with me."

The secret hopes in the deepest recesses of her heart said otherwise, but no one else ever had to know about those.

"I sincerely hope for your sake, that is true. Just promise me…" She paused as if searching for words.

"Promise you what?"

"If he ever hurts you, with his fists or his infidelity, you will leave. The first time. Not the fiftieth."

As much as her mother's earlier words had hurt her, these showed just how deeply the Countess loved her daughter. Mama dove into the wedding preparations after that, insisting on flying to Mirrus and liaising with the official wedding planner in situ and Solomia planned to still be there when Nataliya arrived for her visit.

Home in Seattle, Nataliya was happy to discover that Nikolai continued to text and call as often as his schedule allowed.

He also continued to send what he now called betrothal gifts for her online auction. And that touched her in ways she wouldn't have admitted to anyone else. Even Jenna.

They made plans for Nataliya to travel to Mirrus so that she could spend time with him and his family before the wedding.

"You are aware that I have known your family for a long time now," she said one evening on the phone as they discussed her upcoming trip.

"But not as my future bride. Both my father and brother need to come to terms with treating you like *The* Princess of Mirrus."

Nataliya wasn't surprised that neither the former King nor his second-eldest son, Prince Konstantin, were keen on her in the role. She'd offended them both and didn't regret that. So how could she regret that they *had to come to terms* with her as the future Princess of Mirrus?

"I notice you don't mention your younger brother," she teased, knowing full well that Dima liked her just fine.

"He thinks you're a goddess since you convinced me to allow him a gap year between the university and graduate school."

She laughed. "Does he know how easy that was?"

"And let him believe I'm *easy*? No chance."

"You'd prefer he think I have undue influence."

"Influence yes. Excessive amounts?" he asked with dismissive candor, no teasing in *his* voice. "Not likely."

He said stuff like that sometimes that made her think she needed to ask about his first marriage, but Nikolai clammed up whenever Tiana was mentioned in passing, much less asked about directly.

"Don't worry. I'm not in this for my influence over the King."

"Why are you in this?" he asked. Then sighed. "Forget I asked that. I know why you said yes to my proposal."

"You think so?"

"You would not go back on your word."

"So you think I said yes because I signed that contract?" she asked, wondering how he could be so blind to her feelings.

Of course she'd never voiced them, but he'd noticed her teenage crush when she'd thought she'd done a much better job hiding it than the love that she could no longer deny she felt for him.

"Why else?" he asked, as if there really couldn't be another reason.

And she had to smile, though he could not see it. "Because I want to be *your* wife."

"You are good for my ego." His voice was rich with satisfaction, but more than that, Nikolai really sounded pleased.

And she thought that was definitely worth admitting that much of the truth. "I don't think your ego needs inflating," she teased.

"You might be surprised."

"Nikolai?"

"Yes?"

"Were you happy with Tiana?"

Silence pulsed across the phones for long moments. Then he sighed. "At first, I was deliriously happy. Later, I regretted ever meeting Tiana much less marrying her."

Nataliya had to stifle a gasp of shock. "Your marriage looked so perfect from the outside. You grieved her death. I know you did."

"I did, but relief was mixed with the grief. And I lamented the loss of my unborn child as much, or more than, my wife."

"I'm sorry."

"I was too, but that time in my life is over. You and I will start a new chapter."

"We already have." It was no less than the truth. For both of them.

Despite the shortness of their engagement, Nikolai found himself unexpectedly impatient for the event in the weeks leading up to his wedding.

Far from assuaging his desire for his intended bride, the knowledge that she *would* be his soon only made him want her more.

He'd been surprised by how much he craved sex with Nataliya. Though lovely, she had none of the overt sensuality of Tiana, and the women shared almost nothing in common physically. Tiana had been a petite, curvy, blonde socialite. He'd *thought* she was his idea of sexual perfection.

Then he'd started looking at Nataliya as a potential bride and discovered that statuesque five-foot-nine innocence really did it for him. He could not wait to touch and taste her modest curves, to see how sensitive the nipples tipping her small breasts were. He wanted to touch the silky mass of her dark hair, to feel her body pressed all along his length.

She was going to fit him perfectly.

He had a purely atavistic anticipation of becoming Nataliya's first lover and spent more time fantasizing about their wedding night than he wanted to admit. He would certainly never allow Nataliya to know how much he wanted her.

He'd learned his lesson.

But that didn't mean he didn't crave her. He did. Nikolai had never had a virgin in his bed. Though he'd believed his first wife to be untouched until their wedding night.

She'd laughed at his surprise, telling him not to be such a throwback.

And he had taken her criticism to heart, realizing that it

would be wrong to expect something from her he had not himself practiced.

Because although he had never found uncommitted sex the tension relief that Konstantin did, Nikolai *had* had a few partners when he was at the university.

In fact, he'd thought he was sexually sophisticated until he had married.

Tiana had been an expert at using her sensuality to tie him into knots. Nikolai had made several decisions under the influence of his desire for her brand of sexuality.

He would never be so weak again.

His virgin fiancée was not going to play those kinds of games, he thought with a great deal of satisfaction. Even if Nataliya had enough sexual experience to know *how* to play the *tease and withhold* game, she would not do it.

It was not only in physical appearance that his future wife differed so strongly from the woman he had once made his Queen.

Nataliya had all the honor that Tiana had lacked.

Nataliya would *never* take bribes in exchange for influencing her husband's political or business decisions. She had even made it clear that their marriage would harbinger a shift in her loyalties from the Volyarussian royal family to *his* family and people.

Knowing how willing she had always been to sacrifice for the good of the Volyarussian monarchy, he found a great comfort in that truth.

Yes, Nikolai had made a very good decision when he determined to make Nataliya his Princess.

CHAPTER EIGHT

NIKOLAI SENT HIS personal jet to fly Nataliya to Mirrus for her visit.

That didn't surprise her. The social secretary and public relations consultant waiting on board for her did. Jenna had agreed to travel with her as her stylist.

The magazine was happy because Jenna was also doing a new series of articles on the personal fashions for *The Princess of Mirrus*, including an exclusive on her wedding dress and those of her attendants.

"We've both been hired on a trial basis, Lady Nataliya," the social secretary explained. "His Highness wants you to have final decision about the people who make up your team."

"Of course he does," Jenna said. She thought Nikolai pretty much walked on water.

Nataliya rolled her eyes at her friend. "Do you think I would tolerate anything else?"

"Well, you are fulfilling a draconian contract that most modern women would reject outright. Even if it is to marry King Yummy." Jenna waggled her eyebrows.

The PR consultant looked pained. "If we could refrain from mentioning the contract." She gave Jenna a stern look. "And from using terms such as *King Yummy*."

Unperturbed, Jenna just grinned. "Things like that contract don't stay secrets."

"The contract has never been a secret," Nataliya said with some exasperation. "And this modern woman is not naive enough to believe that everyone gets married for nothing but *true love*."

"That is true, but we would prefer the international

media pick up on the romantic element to your relationship with His Highness," the public relations consultant said repressively.

"What romantic element?" she asked.

It was Jenna's turn to look pained. "Please, Nataliya. Even I can see the sparks that arc between you two when you are in the same room."

"That's chemistry, not romance," Nataliya maintained. She might love her fiancé, but she was under no illusion the feeling was mutual.

The PR consultant looked like maybe she was regretting taking this job. Even temporarily. "His Highness has engaged in a very romantic courtship, my lady."

"Nataliya, please."

The consultant gave Nataliya a slightly superior look. "It might be a good idea to get used to being addressed by your title, before you become The Princess of Mirrus."

Nataliya's mouth twisted with distaste, but she nodded. The other woman was right, but that didn't mean Nataliya had to like it.

However, she did have experience with formal protocol as part of the royal family of Volyarus. And she was not unfamiliar with being addressed as *lady*, simply not enamored of it. But she'd have to get over that and she knew it.

By the time they reached Mirrus, Nataliya's new social secretary had briefed her on how her visit to the small Russian country would go. As the future Princess of their King, she would be greeted on landing with a formal procession and would be attending not one, but three royal receptions in the five days of her visit.

Nikolai had been right. It would be very different from the times she had spent in Mirrus before.

If Nataliya had been hoping for more time getting to know the man she planned to marry, she realized that wasn't going to happen.

He was there, with the officials, when her plane landed however.

Her social secretary sighed, the sound someone makes after watching a really sweet movie. "His Highness is smiling."

Her gaze locked on Nikolai's handsome countenance, Nataliya could do nothing but nod. He *was* smiling.

Which she realized wasn't something he used to do. Like at all.

But during their courtship, he'd graced her with that slashing brilliance often. And she'd basked in the warmth of it. Even as she was not consciously aware of how uncommon it was.

"Oh, that will make good copy," the PR consultant said.

And Nataliya's answering smile slid from her face.

Nikolai's brows drew together, and he took what looked like an involuntary step forward.

"Good grief. Lay off with the PR perspective, would you?" Jenna demanded of the PR consultant as she shouldered past the other woman to stand right behind Nataliya. "He wasn't smiling at you for public relations. He's happy you're here, friend."

"This is not proper protocol," the PR consultant reminded them. "Your stylist should not be in position to have photos with you."

Nataliya turned her head to look at the PR consultant. "Jenna is my friend before anything else and as such she is always welcome in the frame with me."

The other woman shook her head, actually taking hold of Jenna's arm to pull her back. "She can be your *friend* but not in optics. She's not from Mirrus. She's not from the nobility. Miss Beals isn't the right sort of person for you to favor in the PR angle."

"Please, take your hand off of Jenna." Nataliya waited until the other woman complied. "We can discuss this later.

I'm not sure your views and mine are on the same wavelength."

The look the other woman gave her said she agreed, but it wasn't the PR consultant who had it wrong. That was going to be a problem, but right now Nataliya needed to greet Nikolai.

She smiled and went down the stairs to the tarmac.

The King stepped away from the rest of the dignitaries and reached for her hand. "Welcome to Mirrus, Nataliya."

He didn't use her title and Nataliya's smile returned. "I'm very glad to be here. Nikolai."

Then he did something entirely unexpected. Nikolai leaned down and it seemed like he was about to kiss her.

Mesmerized by his nearness, she did not move. And then he *was* kissing her. In front of the dignitaries, the press and the special guests given permission to greet her plane.

All of those people faded from her consciousness as his lips played over hers. She leaned toward him and he let her, making no move to keep protocol-worthy distance between them.

Nikolai lifted his head, an expression of satisfaction stamped clearly on his features, but she did not understand its source.

"I think I'm going to have to let the PR lady go," she blurted. "We don't see the world through the same lens at all."

He nodded. "Okay."

"You don't mind?"

"Both she and the social secretary, Frosana Iksa, know they were hired on a provisional basis."

"The provision being that I approved them?"

"Exactly."

"I like Frosana. I think she'll make a good social secretary, but the public relations consultant called Jenna out for standing next to me."

"Jenna is your friend. Where else would she stand?" he asked, showing that he understood life was about more than strict protocol.

"Exactly."

And maybe the PR consultant could change her perspective to more reflect Nataliya's, but somehow she doubted it.

That was the last moment they had for anything resembling private conversation as she was introduced to cabinet ministers and the C-level management from Mirrus Global.

She noticed that neither Prince Evengi nor Prince Konstantin were present.

But Nataliya did not allow that to bother her. If they were making a statement, that was not her problem. If they were too busy, again, not her problem.

She wasn't marrying either of them and if they had anything to say about her becoming The Princess of Mirrus, that was between them and Nikolai.

Since he'd made it clear he wanted her to marry him, she trusted the savvy, modern King to know his own mind. And how to handle opposition from within his own family when it came.

There were even dignitaries in the car with them on the way back to the palace, but Nataliya was pleased to see that Nikolai had arranged for Jenna to ride with them as well, cementing in the minds of those present her friend's role and the respect the royal family expected to be accorded to the best friend of the future Princess.

Nataliya's mother was with Prince Evengi at the palace when they arrived, the pair looking thick as thieves as they went over wedding preparations in the drawing room.

Mama gave Nataliya a warm hug and kisses on both cheeks before doing the same for Jenna. "I'm so pleased you could be here to support Nataliya, Jenna. You're a good friend to my daughter."

Jenna hugged the Countess back. "Are you kidding? I'm living the fairy tale without any of the angst."

Mama laughed, but Prince Evengi looked inquiringly at Jenna. "You believe Lady Nataliya is living a fairy tale?"

"Well she is marrying a handsome king," Jenna said drolly, showing no discomfort at being addressed by a king, but dropping into a curtsy as Nataliya had taught her to do even as she answered so frankly. Then she tacked on, "Your Highness."

"Ah, the Countess has coached you in protocol. That will help both your and Nataliya's acceptance now and in the future."

"Actually, it was Nataliya. She's perfect princess material. But you knew that, or you never would have signed that contract ten years ago."

Nataliya had to hold back her laughter at the look of consternation on the King's face.

"So I have reminded my father more than once in the last weeks."

Nataliya was a lot more shocked by Nikolai's willingness to air discordance with his father in front of others than by his championship of her. He was too strong willed to ever tolerate even the former King's second-guessing his choice of wife.

"I believe you were the author of the articles on Lady Nataliya's foray into dating," Prince Evengi observed to Jenna.

"I was. It turned out to be a nifty bit of PR for your son's courtship of my friend."

"It did at that." He frowned. "But that was not the intention of that article, was it?"

"No. The intention of the article was to highlight first-date styles for each season."

"And here I thought it was to embarrass my younger son into withdrawing from the contract," Prince Evengi said wryly.

"But how could that be when his older brother was not in the least embarrassed by the fact the woman he chose to court was attractive to other men?" Jenna asked innocently.

"You are quick on your feet," Prince Evengi said without a shade of irritation. "That will do you well if you choose to attend the receptions introducing Lady Nataliya."

"I'm invited?" Jenna asked, for once not sardonic, but surprised.

"Of course you are, dear," Mama inserted. "You are my daughter's best friend."

"I'm her stylist."

"Because she trusts you more than anyone else, or we would have a different stylist here for the week, but you still would have been invited to join her."

This was news to Nataliya, but she didn't doubt her mother's words. Mama was no longer the eager-to-please woman she had been when Nataliya was a child.

Prince Evengi took the news that Nataliya wasn't convinced the PR consultant would be a good fit with her with a frown, but one look from Nikolai and even the arrogant former monarch did not voice his evident displeasure.

"She came with the best of recommendations and had a great deal of experience working with royalty," Mama said musingly.

"I do not want a consultant who thinks every aspect of my life is a PR opportunity." Nataliya understood that her life had changed irrevocably when she agreed to marry Nikolai, but she was still a person in her own right with a life she intended to live happily.

"You have agreed to marry a king. Your life is no longer your own," Prince Evengi said but without reproach.

So, Nataliya did not take offence. Particularly since he only voiced her own thoughts. "No. It now belongs in a very real way to the people of Mirrus, but it will never belong to a PR consultant," Nataliya answered with spirit.

"And here I thought at least part of it belonged to me," Nikolai teased.

The varying looks of shock at his facetious comment made Nataliya smile. "Yes, just as yours belongs to me."

"But neither of us is willing to be bossed around by petty dictators masquerading as our personal staff." This time Nikolai's tone was nothing but serious and the look he gave his father and then the various staff members standing around left no one doubting he meant exactly what he said.

"Perhaps Gillian has someone she might recommend," Mama suggested. "I think you and she have similar viewpoints on the matter of public relations balanced with family and life."

Nataliya nodded to her mother's comment, her gaze caught by the look in Nikolai's gray eyes.

And for just a second, it was like they were alone in the room. Then Prince Evengi said something. Nikolai's expression veiled and a discussion of the finer details of the wedding ensued.

Nataliya and Nikolai did not have a private moment until after the formal dinner and reception that evening.

Nataliya had been introduced to a good portion of the Mirrus nobility, Prince Evengi doing the honors and exhibiting none of his reticence about her becoming the next Princess of Mirrus. Nataliya had met some of these people before when attending Nikolai's coronation and later Tiana's funeral, but of course they responded entirely differently to her in her new role.

There was a great deal of curiosity in the looks directed at her, though no one was gauche enough to give it voice.

But she *had* been intended for the second son and now she was marrying the King.

Despite the curiosity and the fact that formal functions had never been Nataliya's favorite thing, she managed to enjoy her evening. Mostly because while his father had taken on the role introducing her, Nikolai still contrived to be by her side for almost the entire evening, making it clear the wedding was not something he was being pressed into.

Nataliya and Nikolai were now walking in the private courtyard gardens. Nataliya found herself enchanted by them, lit beautifully to highlight the evening-blooming flowers and fountains.

"It's gorgeous out here." She had not seen this garden on her previous visits.

"My mother loved exotic flowers, not just orchids. She designed this garden as a private retreat for our family." Nikolai looked around as if remembering happy times. "There are both day-and night-blooming flowers."

"Don't they die in winter?" Nataliya asked while wondering what the gardens looked like during the day.

They were so magical now, she was almost afraid to see them and be disappointed.

"There is a retractable glass ceiling that is closed when temperatures drop."

"Amazing."

"And decadent, yes, but it made my mother happy and I find having a place in the palace that is reserved for family and only the closest of friends beneficial, as well."

"So, no using it to impress VIPs?" she asked, only half joking.

"No. Though my father argued doing just that many times with my mother, but she stood firm." Nikolai's smile was reminiscent.

"And he loved her enough not to gainsay her?" Nataliya asked, finding it difficult to imagine the arrogant former ruler in the role of adoring spouse.

"He respected her. I do not know if he loved her. That element of their relationship was not my business."

"He must have respected her a great deal not to start using it the way he wanted to once she was gone."

"Yes." Nikolai gave Nataliya a knowing look. "My mother was also formidable of nature. Much like someone else I know, she refused to be budged on matters that were important to her. I would not have put it past her to demand a deathbed promise from my father not to *desecrate* her garden."

Nataliya wished she'd had the chance to get to know his royal mother. She sounded like an amazing and strong woman. "Are you calling me stubborn?"

"Are you trying to imply you aren't?" he countered.

She shrugged. "You don't get far giving in." She'd learned that early.

"No, you do not."

"You're pretty stubborn yourself."

"And arrogant, or so you've said."

She couldn't deny it. "Was it all for PR?" Nataliya found herself asking, when in fact she'd had no intention of doing so.

Her mind had actually been on the promise she needed him to make her.

Nikolai led her to an upholstered bench with a back, its design in keeping with the Ancient Roman theme throughout the garden. He pulled her to sit beside him, the large central fountain in front of them, giving a sense of privacy that was probably false. But still, it was nice.

"Was what all for PR?" he asked her, genuine confusion lacing his voice. "I thought we'd just established this garden is not for public consumption, relations or otherwise."

Oops. "The PR lady said your courtship was a perfect romantic public relations coup."

"You are asking if my attempts at showing you how well suited we are were in some way motivated by a desire to look good for the public?" he asked, still sounding more confused than offended.

"Konstantin breaking the contract wasn't going to look good in the media." Nataliya sighed. "If I'd broken it, it wouldn't have looked any better. The press would have gone looking for the why and they might have found the same thing I did."

Nikolai looked surprisingly unworried by that prospect. "He might have been labeled the Playboy Prince, but I'm not as concerned about things like that as my father."

"You aren't?"

"No. I would be furious with either of my brothers if they married and then continued to play the field, but prior to marriage? I expect them only to behave with honor. And in answer to your question, no, my courtship of you was not a PR stunt."

"Courtship is a very old-fashioned word."

Nikolai's powerful shoulders moved in an elegant shrug. "In some ways, I'm a very old-world man."

She thought about his subtle change to her wording and smiled. "Yes, I think you are."

"In your own way, you are also very old-world."

She could not deny it. Perhaps it had been spending her formative years living with the volatile and pain-filled marriage of her parents, or simply being raised to respect duty and responsibility as paramount in her life, but Nataliya approached the world very differently than the friends she'd made in the States.

Even though she'd lived there more years than she had in Volyarus.

Nataliya's mouth twisted wryly. "Jenna calls the contract draconian."

"Haven't you thought the same thing?" he asked.

"Yes."

"But still, you honored it."

"My agreement to marry you had more to do with you than the contract," she told him with more honesty than might have been wise.

Nataliya had no intention of admitting her love for a man who didn't want it, but she wasn't going to have him believe she was more motivated by duty than she was.

Looking back, she wondered if she would have still backed out of the contract even if Konstantin hadn't proven himself to be a man she would never trust.

She could not imagine a wedding night with any other man than Nikolai.

"You do me a great honor saying so." The words were formal, but the look he gave her was heated.

Her body responded to that look in an instant, her nipples going hard and sensitive as they pressed against the silk of her bra. Nataliya pressed her legs together, the feelings in her core ones she'd only ever experienced with him.

The air around them was suddenly sultry.

"You have offered me the same assurance." Her voice came out husky and quiet, revealing the effect his intense regard was having on her. And there was nothing she could do about that.

They weren't kissing. Or talking about intimacy, but sexual desire was roaring through her body like a flash flood, drowning every other thought and emotion in its wake.

"You want me." His tone was filled with satisfaction laced by something like wonder.

Which made no sense. Considering what he knew of their history, he could not be surprised she wanted him.

Although the level of passion he drew out of her shocked even Nataliya.

She literally shook with the need to touch and to be touched by this man.

Nataliya leaned forward and tipped her head up so their lips were only a breath apart. "Of course I want you." And his unhidden desire for her only fed that craving until she had no choice but to act.

Pressing her hands flat against his chest, inside his suit jacket, so she could feel the heat of his body through the fine fabric of his shirt, she let her lips touch his.

He growled deep in his chest but made no move to take over the kiss.

Nataliya's fingers curled into the fabric of his shirt while she moved her lips against his, teasing the seam of his mouth with her tongue as he had done to her.

His lips parted and his tongue came out to slide along hers, but it was not enough. She needed more.

More touch.

More of his mouth against hers.

More of his body and her body together.

More.

More.

More.

She climbed onto his lap, her legs straddling his hard thighs, the soft silky fabric of her cocktail dress cascading around them in a rustle of silk.

She pressed down against the hard ridge in his trousers, the layers of cloth between her most sensitive flesh and his no barrier to sensation. Without conscious thought, she rocked against him, increasing that sensation, driving her own pleasure higher.

He groaned, hard hands clamping on her hips.

For one terrible moment, she thought he was going to stop her, but he pulled her even closer, guiding her to a more frenzied rocking and suddenly she wasn't in control of the kiss anymore.

And she didn't care.

He knew exactly what she needed.

More of him.

And he gave it to her until the spiraling tension inside her made it almost impossible to breathe.

She broke her mouth from his. "Please, oh, please, Nik."

"Please what, *kiska*? Please this?" And one of his hands slid up her torso to her nape and then the hidden hooks holding the halter of her bodice together were undone and silk was sliding down bare and heated flesh.

Nipples already aching with arousal went so hard she hissed in borderline pain.

But he knew and he touched and squeezed and rolled and played before dipping his head to take one turgid nub into his mouth.

Nataliya cried out as ecstasy exploded in sparks through her.

Nikolai's mouth demanded nothing less than everything she had to give. And she gloried in the giving.

They rocked together, one of his hands on her hip and the other playing with her breasts. She kneaded his chest like the kitten he called her and gloried in the rising sensations.

Suddenly his hand on her hip moved to press against her bottom, increasing the pressure between their cloth-covered intimate flesh. His body went rigid and he groaned into their kiss like he was dying.

But he wasn't. He was experiencing the ultimate pleasure with her.

And knowing that was all her body needed to explode in the kind of ecstasy she hadn't known she could feel. Even after what she had already experienced with him.

These intense sensations were in a class all their own.

Her womb clenched and she knew that if he'd been inside her when this had happened, she would have gotten pregnant. It was too powerful not to have borne fruit.

She bit her lip and met his molten gaze. "And I can't wait for our wedding night. I used to think sex wasn't all that."

"You've never had it—how would you know?" he asked with an intimate smile.

"I never cared that I didn't have it," she told him. "And just because I never had sex with another person doesn't mean I didn't learn my own body's reactions."

"Hmm, I'd like to learn some more of your body's reactions." He frowned. "But not tonight." He looked around the garden. "I cannot believe we did that here."

"Do you regret it?" she asked.

"No." He helped her straighten her clothes. "But we are lucky we were not discovered. Although only family is allowed in these gardens, any one of them could have walked up on us."

"That would have been terribly embarrassing," she acknowledged, but she was still glad she had the effect on him that she did. "Sometimes I get the feeling you don't *want* to want me."

"Of course I do. Believe it, or not, but if I had not found you attractive, I would have found an honorable way around that contract."

"I believe it." But that didn't answer the truth that sometimes he said or did things that implied he refused to allow himself to desire her *too* much.

And maybe that was the key. The too much. Because Nataliya remembered how he used to look at Tiana. And there had been no tempering in the desire Nikolai had felt for his first wife.

Whatever had happened between the two, it had taught this proud King that sexual desire that went too deep was dangerous.

Putting those thoughts aside because she could not change his past, or her own for that matter, Nataliya focused on their future. "I need a promise from you before we marry."

"Yes?" Nikolai shifted Nataliya so she was sitting sideways on his lap, but still so close to him their body heat mingled.

"I need your word that you will be faithful." Nataliya loved both her mother and her Aunt Oxana, but she had no desire to live their lives.

"Haven't I already given it?" His patrician brows drew together. "I asked you to marry me. And a promise of fidelity will be included in our marriage vows."

"Yes, but I need you to promise me personally. To say the words and mean them."

"You know I keep my promises." There was no little satisfaction in his tone at that truth.

"I do."

"And you want this one?" Nikolai confirmed.

"Among others."

"Very well," he said without asking what the other promises were. "I promise never to have sex with another woman while I am married to you."

"I promise never to have sex with another man," Nataliya offered, feeling something profound and right settle inside her.

His gray gaze flared with emotion and she knew she'd done the right thing.

Swallowing, Nataliya forced herself to continue. "I need you to promise that you would never physically hurt me, or the children we will have together."

She waited for Nikolai to get angry, but he didn't. He simply nodded.

"I promise to always use my strength to protect you and our children. I promise never to strike you. I promise you will always be safe with me." He was so serious and she could hear the sincerity lacing his deep, masculine voice.

"I promise you will always be safe with me, too." A person didn't have to be stronger, or bigger to hurt someone else. Only willing to do harm. And she wasn't.

CHAPTER NINE

THE REMAINDER OF Nataliya's visit to Mirrus went without
incident, but there was also no repeat of the explosive passion in the garden.

She enjoyed meeting people at the receptions and was
really happy with the plans in place for her wedding to the
King. Her mom was over the moon about everything and
that just added to Nataliya's sense of rightness about it all.

Yes, she had to live her life for herself, but knowing her
choices were fulfilling some of her mother's dreams for
her only child was nice.

Despite not being aware of Nikolai and Nataliya's time
together in the garden, Prince Evengi and Mama contrived
to make sure that Nikolai and Nataliya were not alone together for the remaining days of her trip.

Something Nataliya was seriously regretting as he escorted her to the airfield for her return to Seattle.

They were alone now; even Jenna was riding in another
car, but the trip to the airport was not long enough.

"Are you sure you have to return to the States?" Nikolai asked.

His question startled Nataliya, because though he'd
made it clear he was looking forward to their marriage,
he'd never intimated he wanted her to move to Mirrus
sooner than planned.

Nataliya frowned, her own disappointment in the answer she had to give riding her. "Yes. I've barely started
packing up my things."

"We could hire movers."

She smiled, liking his enthusiasm, but shook her head.
"No. I need to sort through stuff and decide what to do with

my furniture." It would be silly to move all of her things only to discard half once they reached Mirrus.

"Donate it."

She laughed. "I think I'll post pics to social media first and make sure none of my friends want anything."

"Your friends would want secondhand furniture?" he asked, sounding just a little shocked.

And Nataliya had to laugh. "Yes, Nikolai. Plenty of people are happy not to have to buy a new kitchen table, or sofa."

"Surely it will not take three weeks to dispose of your furniture." His handsome features were cast in frustrated lines.

And she wanted to smile again, but she held back, thinking he might take her attitude the wrong way. But he was a king and this near petulance was charming. "It will take me two weeks to work out my notice and get together with my friends to say goodbye. I'm actually coming back the week before the wedding. I thought you knew that."

He made a dismissive gesture with his hand. "I am glad of that, but I do not understand why you have to return to Seattle at all."

"I told you—"

"You have to work out your notice," he interrupted in a very unroyal-like way. "But Demyan will have to learn to do without you sooner, or later."

"In two weeks to be exact," she pointed out. "And there are still my friends."

"You're moving to Mirrus, not falling off the face of the earth. You do not have to say goodbye when surely it will be a see-you-again-sometime moment."

"For some, it may be. Like Jenna. But others I probably won't ever see again. Their lives and mine won't cross."

"Are you upset about that?" he asked.

"I'm a little sad naturally, but if I moved to another part

of the country for my job the same thing would happen. Life is full of change."

"Your mother isn't happy we're getting married so quickly."

"But she is *thrilled* we are getting married. Mama will adjust to the timing of it."

Nikolai grimaced. "She pulled me aside and asked if I realized that our expedient marriage would give rise to gossip."

"She's probably right." They'd been over this, or had they? They'd talked about so much.

"You're not worried about it?"

"No. I'm not." Nataliya had learned long ago that she could either live in fear of the scandal mongers or ignore them. She chose to do the latter. "If we *had* anticipated our wedding vows and I had gotten pregnant, it would not have been a tragedy."

Nikolai looked startled at that. "Because people are already speculating?"

"That's one reason."

"And the other?"

"I would not be embarrassed to walk down the aisle pregnant with your child."

"You're something of a rebel in the royal family, aren't you?"

Nataliya shrugged. "Maybe? My experiences have taught me what is important."

"And gossip doesn't make it on the list."

"No."

"I will miss you, Nataliya." Nikolai gave her one of his genuine smiles, the ones that melted her. "I enjoy your company very much."

"I'll miss you too," she admitted.

He kissed her then, a soft, tender kiss that said goodbye and see you soon and I'll miss you.

She was still in a daze of emotional wonder when she boarded the plane and strapped into a seat beside Jenna.

"I think I'm going to have to break up with Brian," Jenna mused in a light tone at odds with her words.

Nataliya jerked her head around so she was facing her friend. "What? Why?"

"Because his kisses don't affect me like that."

"What kiss?"

"Please. Why else would His Highness have wanted you to himself if it wasn't to kiss you goodbye without an audience?"

"He did kiss me."

"I figured. You came on the plane in trance."

"I wasn't in a trance."

"Close enough." Jenna searched Nataliya's features. "I understand you agreeing to marry him better now though."

"Because I get a little spacey after he kisses me?"

"Because you love him."

Nataliya went still. "It's not a fairy tale, Jenna."

"No, but you love the King and he's pretty darn into you."

"He doesn't love me."

"Does that bother you?" Jenna asked, curiosity but not judgement on her face.

"It should, shouldn't it?"

"I don't know. If you were someone who wanted to marry for *true love*, maybe. But you're not. Even though they had an arranged marriage, your mom fell hard for your dad and he claimed to love her back, but that wasn't a recipe for happiness for any of you."

"No, it wasn't."

"Look, I get it. I'm not sure about the love thing, but I know I'd rather be in a relationship with a man who could kiss me stupid than a man who I don't miss when I'm away from him for almost a week."

"You really are going to break up with Brian."

"Yep."

"I *do* love Nikolai and I think he needs to be loved."

"Whereas you need to be respected and appreciated and I don't think anyone after these past few days is in any question how highly your future husband esteems you."

That esteem was put severely to the test a week later when Count Shevchenko gave a "tell all" interview that barely sideswiped the truth.

Yes, he was her biological father and yes she had signed a contract that included marriage between the two royal houses ten years ago.

But from that point it was pretty much fabrication and fantasy, and nasty fantasy at that.

Furious that he had not been invited to the wedding and even more angry that his daughter's elevation to Princess would not mean a lift of his own personal exile from Volyarus, the Count gave chapter and verse on the personal aspect to the contract signed ten years ago. He implied that Nataliya had not been content to marry a mere prince and had set her sights on the widowed King.

He painted his daughter as a scheming manipulator whose only interest was in her social position and wealth.

Nataliya was still reading the four-page spread in one of the most notorious gossip rags with international circulation when her phone's ringtone for Nikolai sounded.

Demyan, who had provided the paper and voiced support for her before she started reading, asked, "Is it King Nikolai?"

She nodded, having made no effort to pick up the phone.

"Are you going to answer it?"

Nataliya shook her head.

"Why?"

"I'm afraid."

"He's not going to call off the wedding because your father is a cretin."

"Won't he?"

Demyan grabbed Nataliya's phone and swiped. "No." Then thrust the phone at her.

She pressed it to her ear.

"Nataliya, *kiska*, are you there?" It was Nikolai's voice.

Of course it was Nikolai's voice. He didn't sound angry, but then he was a king. He didn't go around yelling when he got mad.

"Nataliya?" he prompted in an almost gentle tone. "I can hear you breathing. Say something, *kiska*."

"I…" She had to clear her throat. "I'm here."

"Are you all right?"

"Have you read it?" she asked in turn, without answering a question she actually wasn't sure she had an answer to. Was she all right?

Her father was doing his best to upend her life. Again. The last time he got her exiled from her country and her family. This time? Would he destroy her chance at marrying Nikolai?

A heavy sigh. "Yes, I have read it. I want you to come to Mirrus. I can protect you from the paparazzi here."

"You want me to come there?" she asked, trying to understand that request in light of how ugly the publicity was likely to get.

"You are not a little girl, Nataliya. He cannot destroy your life again. No one will ever take your home or family from you again. I will not allow it."

"I don't have a home." She wasn't even sure where the words came from, except a tiny part of her heart that still held the wounds from her childhood.

Seattle had been her home for the last fifteen years, but her apartment was almost empty now, in preparation for her move to Mirrus. Only would Mirrus be her home now? After the article?

"He won't have only this up his sleeve," she warned Nikolai. "My father's probably planning to do a televised interview too."

"Your home is now the Palace in Mirrus and soon you will be my Princess. He can say what he likes, but nothing will change that."

"But he's always going to be a problem." She realized now how true that was.

Her father had no intention of staying quietly in the background. Apparently, he had no qualms about how he achieved the spotlight either.

"We will determine a plan of action for dealing with the Count, but I don't want *you* dealing with the intrusiveness of the media without my support."

Picturing just how intrusive things could get, Nataliya could feel the color draining from her face. Would the honorable thing to do be to withdraw entirely from her connection to Mirrus? And even her own royal family?

Her thoughts started spiraling and Nataliya felt dizzy with them.

"What's he saying?" Demyan demanded, putting his hand on her back and encouraging her to lean forward. "Breathe, Nataliya. Just concentrate on breathing."

"Hold on a second, please, Nikolai," she said into the phone as she attempted to take a couple of deep, calming breaths.

He cursed. "You are not all right."

Nataliya just took another breath as the world came back into focus. She sat up, all the while aware that Nikolai was barking out orders to someone on his end of the phone.

"You can call back later, if this is a bad time," she offered.

"Nyet. No. Do not hang up on me, *kiska*."

"Okay." She looked at Demyan and wondered what he was making of all this.

Her cousin's expression was grim, but he reached out to squeeze her shoulder. "It is going to be okay, Nataliya."

She just shrugged, not at all sure he was right.

"Put me on speaker, please, *kiska*."

"Why?" One of the protocols all the royals learned early was never to use the speaker function on their phones. Too easy to be overheard.

"I can hear Prince Demyan," Nikolai said. "I'd like to speak to him too."

She still thought it was odd, but Nataliya did as requested.

"What is going on?" Demyan demanded toward the phone.

But Nataliya answered. "Nikolai wants me to go to Mirrus, to avoid the media."

Something like relief flitted over her cousin's hard features. "That's a good idea."

"I'm not running away." Her father wasn't going to make her abandon her job or her plans.

She wouldn't let him.

"Coming home is not running away," Nikolai opined.

"Be reasonable, Nataliya," Demyan added. "The vultures aren't going to let you go to the grocery store without incident, much less anywhere else."

"I have commitments throughout next week." She took another deep breath and let it out slowly, reminding herself that she was not a little girl to be pushed around by her father's whims. "I'll be fine. I'll stay at Mama's." She'd been planning to do that anyway, for her last couple of days in Seattle, as the shelter she was donating her bed to was scheduled to pick it up then.

"But your mother is not there. She is here. And her home is not secure."

"Her condominium is in a gated community. They even have security that do rounds."

"A rent-a-cop in his golf cart?" Demyan snorted derisively.

Nikolai was worryingly silent.

"Nikolai?" she prompted when he had not replied several seconds later.

"Yes, *kiska*?"

"I'm going to be fine but thank you for worrying about me." She had a lot of thinking to do and she knew she wouldn't make an unbiased choice if she went to Mirrus.

She couldn't simply consider what she wanted, but what was best for Nikolai and the people of Mirrus.

"You will be fine, yes. Demyan, please keep Nataliya inside the building until I arrive."

"Arrive? What do you mean arrive? You can't just drop everything and come here."

"Are you coming to Mirrus?" he asked.

"In a week." Maybe. "Nikolai, we need to think about how best to handle this and it might not be me coming to Mirrus in the near future." Or at all.

Demyan made a sound of disagreement.

Nikolai cursed again and then said, "I will see you in a few hours."

"But, Nikolai, there's no need." How was she supposed to make her mind up to break things off if he was there, tempting her?

"I know what you are thinking, Nataliya *moy*, and it is not going to happen. We are not breaking the contract. You are not backing out of this marriage." There was not a bit of give in Nikolai's aristocratic tones. "Prince Demyan?"

"I'll keep her inside, Your Highness."

Nataliya gave her cousin a look, but he just shrugged. "It makes sense, Nataliya, and you know it."

"Nikolai, you must realize that my uncle will want me to cancel the wedding to avoid further scandal," Nataliya said.

Demyan's grimace said he agreed.

"I repeat, we are *not* canceling our wedding," Nikolai said forcefully. "Any attempt to make you pay for your father's actions will be met with not only my disapproval, but retaliation."

Instead of looking annoyed by Nikolai's threat, Demyan grinned. "Good."

Nataliya was still trying to process that her fiancé was *not* looking for the easy way out of the scandal. Would not even hear of Nataliya backing away from their betrothal.

He'd been pretty adamant all along, but she found it incomprehensible Nikolai wasn't even considering it in the face of her father's behavior and the potential ugliness to come.

"I will see you in a few hours, Nataliya."

Nikolai and his larger-than-normal security team stepped off the elevator on the top floor of the Yurkovich-Tanner building in Seattle.

Prince Demyan was waiting, no doubt having been apprised of Nikolai's arrival. "She's in her office. Working."

The other man's tone let Nikolai know what he thought of that state of affairs and it wasn't approval.

"That sounds like Nataliya."

The Prince grimaced, but nodded. "My cousin has a full ration of our family's stubbornness."

"I have noticed."

"She'll pretend she's fine, but she's taking this hard," Prince Demyan warned as he turned to go down a soft carpeted hall. "Follow me."

Nikolai's security team took up different positions in the hall until only one remained at his side.

"That is to be expected," Nikolai said to Prince Demyan as they walked. "It is her father after all."

"Trying to ruin her life. The bastard."

"Indeed."

The Prince stopped outside a door and turned to face Nikolai. "You won't let her down, will you? She's going to try to sacrifice her own future for the greater good. I know her."

Prince Demyan's expression didn't bode well for Nikolai if his answer was anything but no. It didn't worry Nikolai because he had no intention of letting the very special woman be hurt any more than she had already been by her father's reprehensible behavior.

And she was going to be his Princess.

"You mean like she did ten years ago when she signed that contract."

"Yes."

"She wants to marry me." Of that Nikolai was entirely convinced.

"I agree, but are you going to let her go?"

"Never," Nikolai assured the other man. "I will stand by her as her own family did not all those years ago."

Prince Demyan nodded, his expression grim, nothing to indicate he had taken offense at Nikolai's words. "Our King did not do well by her or the Countess."

"No, he did not."

The Prince's demeanor stiffened. "Fedir and Oxana have made decisions that were difficult for the good of our country." As their unofficially adopted son, Demyan had always had leave to use the familiar address for the King and Queen.

"Even so, it is not a decision you would have made." Prince Demyan could be entirely ruthless, hence his marriage to the one woman who could have destabilized the economy of Volyarus, but he was fiercely loyal.

And Nikolai had learned that the Prince had ensured his wife-to-be was more than adequately protected with their prenuptial agreement. He was not the type of man to allow someone else to suffer unfairly.

Prince Demyan inclined his head and offered more truth than Nikolai was expecting. "Or that my adopted brother would make as sovereign."

"I believe that." Nikolai had done his homework on the entire family when he became King and his brother's betrothal became his responsibility and not that of their father.

"But that does not mean our King acted out of anything but duty and the belief that he was doing what was best for Volyarus."

"It would seem loyalty is a family trait."

"Nataliya is very loyal," Prince Demyan said, proving he knew exactly what Nikolai had meant.

Nikolai nodded. "It is one of the many things I admire about her."

"Good." The Prince opened the door and stood back to allow Nikolai entry.

Nataliya looked up from her computer, her face pale, her eyes haunted. "Nikolai! You're here."

"I told you I would be." He could only hope that his stubborn fiancée would cooperate with Nikolai's plan for dealing with the problem of her father.

"But you must have gotten on a jet almost immediately."

"I did." He instructed his remaining guard to wait outside the door and then closed it on him and her cousin.

Nataliya looked at the closed door with a worried expression. "I think Demyan wanted to talk strategy."

"You and I will do so. After."

"After?"

He crossed the room and pulled Nataliya from her chair and right into his body. "After we have greeted properly, and I have assured myself that you are all right."

"I'm fine."

He just shook his head and then kissed her.

She melted into him, no resistance whatsoever, kissing him back, her arms coming up and around his neck. Passion flared between them as it always did when they were this close, but he could sense a fragility in her that was not usually there.

And it was that fragility that allowed Nikolai to lift his head. "You are such a temptation, but I do not think you are fine at all."

"He said horrible things about me. I never did anything to him, but he never loved me." Nataliya snuggled into Nikolai, seeking comfort in a way that was both surprising and welcome. "I thought he couldn't hurt me anymore, but he can, and I don't like it. Mama will be so hurt. She's moved on with her life, but he's going to dredge everything up again. All the old pain while heaping on a new dose. It's just not fair."

"You have not spoken to her?" Nikolai knew the Countess had planned to call her daughter.

Nataliya shook her head. "I couldn't. She'll be devastated and it's all my fault."

"None of this is your fault," Nikolai argued, fury filling him that his sweet and loyal fiancée could take the blame for her reprobate of a father's actions. "All culpability lies one hundred percent with the Count."

Nataliya didn't answer, just leaned more securely into Nikolai, as if seeking strength. "I can't believe you came."

He was more than happy to share his with her, but knew she had plenty of her own. "I cannot believe you would think I would do anything else."

"But your schedule." Her head tucked perfectly under his chin, like she was made to fit against him like this.

"Can be adjusted," he reminded her. Nikolai rubbed her

back, finding the action soothing and hoping she did too. "Just as yours must be."

Her head came up at that. "You're going to insist I return to Mirrus with you, aren't you?"

"I am hoping you have reconsidered that course of action on your own."

"And if I haven't?" she tested.

"I will leave it up to you to explain to my cabinet and my company why I am in Seattle when I am supposed to be in the palace for several important meetings prior to our wedding."

"You can't stay here!"

"I will not leave you alone to face the vultures of the press."

Nataliya sighed. "Demyan already told me that I didn't have a job to come to anymore."

"Did he?"

Her cousin went up a notch in Nikolai's estimation and he already respected the Prince.

"He said I was being recklessly stubborn."

"And what do you think?"

"I think you're both ignoring the most expedient course of action and I cannot figure out why. And in any case, I don't want to feel like a coward."

"There is nothing cowardly about coming home." He completely ignored her reference to expediency.

Their definition of that course of action wasn't going to match.

"And Mirrus is my home now?" she asked, her expression unreadable.

"You know it is."

She nodded and something in his chest loosened. "It is." She looked away from him. "I never thought I was weak, but I want to go back with you. I want to go through with the wedding."

Hearing the last loosened the remaining fear he had not wanted to acknowledge. She was not going to walk away from him. "No one could make the mistake of thinking you are weak," he promised her.

"You don't think so?" Nataliya was looking at him again, her lovely brown eyes shiny with emotion.

"No, but if they do, they are idiots."

"Why would a father be so cruel to his only child?" she asked, like she expected Nikolai to have the answer.

He didn't; he only had the truth he knew. "I am sorry, *kiska*, but your father is a cruel man all around. As to why the articles and why now, I do not think it is as simple as him wanting revenge for his continued exile."

That seemed to startle her. "What then?"

"Money."

"You think he hopes to extort money from us? But if that was the case, wouldn't he have threatened before going to the tabloids with his ugly allegations about my character?" Wasn't that how blackmail worked?

"He has done one interview in print, an interview that has forced everyone involved to sit up and take notice. As you said earlier, he could do much more, but right now he believes his bargaining position is strong."

"But blackmail? He couldn't think he'd get away with it. With King Fedir, that might even fly. After all, there's a reason my father has been able to draw his allowance from the family coffers annually, but with you? He must know you will never pay him a penny."

Nikolai liked very much that she knew him that well. "You do not think so?"

"No." She rolled her eyes. "He'd have better luck getting blackmail payments out of a nun who'd made a vow of poverty."

"Interesting analogy, but you are right." Nikolai had

plans where her father was concerned and not one of them included paying a single penny to the grasping Count.

"You're talking like you know the Count wants money."

"I do know. He made the demand while I was en route."

Nataliya's natural lovely tone went paste white. "What does he want?"

"Right now? A single large payment followed by a yearly stipend to ensure his silence in the future. He's getting none of that," Nikolai assured her.

Before Nataliya could respond, a knock sounded at the door.

"Come," Nikolai commanded.

It opened to reveal the Prince. "Your guests are waiting in the lobby."

CHAPTER TEN

NATALIYA TRIED TO step back from Nikolai, but he wasn't having it. His arms remained firm around her as she tried to make sense of what her cousin had said.

"You never react like I expect you to," she told Nikolai.

Her proper King, who was known for his dignified demeanor, winked at her. "Just think, you will never grow bored with me."

There was an underlying seriousness to his teasing that Nataliya wished she understood better.

She patted his muscular chest, feeling daring with her cousin standing right there. "No chance of that happening."

"If we could suspend this somewhat nauseating chitchat, everyone is waiting," Demyan said sardonically from his place in the doorway.

"Give us a minute," Nikolai instructed her cousin.

Demyan nodded and left.

"Are you ready?" Nikolai asked her.

"Ready for what exactly?"

"We're about to give a press conference."

"What? Why?"

"We're going to detooth the tiger."

"But my uncle." No way had King Fedir agreed to such a thing.

"Is not the sovereign in charge here."

But King Fedir could be impacted in a very detrimental way. There was a risk her uncle's own long-hidden scandal would come out if her father decided to exact revenge, though she wasn't sure Danilo would risk losing what income he still received from the Volyarussian royal coffers.

Either way, her former King's actions were no more her responsibility than her father's had been.

"What is that sound you made?" Nikolai asked her, as if they weren't in the middle of an intense discussion.

"Surprise," she answered, with no thought of hiding her thoughts from him. "I just thought of my uncle as my former King."

"I am your King now." Pure satisfaction laced Nikolai's tone.

She smiled, her heart beating fast for no reason. Or maybe for every reason. "Yes."

"It is my honor and my privilege to protect you and your mother as members of my family. And I will do a better job than your former King."

"Your arrogance is showing again."

"Perhaps. Will you do the press conference with me?"

"You're asking me?"

"I am."

"Yes, but I'm not sure what we are supposed to say?"

"In this one instance, I would consider it a personal favor if you would follow my lead."

"Okay."

"There's something else."

"What?"

"Beyond the press conference, we have two legal options open to us. We can file criminal charges against the Count for blackmail. Even if he has a good lawyer, he'll spend some time in prison. In addition, you can sue for libel and drag him through the courts for the foreseeable future. We don't have to win the case to bankrupt him with legal fees. He lives beyond his means as it is."

For the first time, Nataliya had hope her father would not prevail. Why hadn't she considered legal recourse?

Because to do so would cause scandal, and that was anathema to the Royal Family of Volyarus, but there was no way past scandal in this situation. Even paying the black-mail wouldn't guarantee her father's silence. He was vindictive and cruel and not always smart.

He could get angry and do something that would harm himself more than her or Mama in the end, but it would still harm them. Just as his actions had with their exile.

"He could go to prison?"

"All calls to the palace and to my personal cell phone are recorded."

Which meant that they had recorded evidence of the attempt to extort the King. "He should have gone to prison for what he did to my mom when they were married. He's broken the law again and I think he should pay the consequences of that, but I need to talk to my mother before I decide."

"I would expect no less from you. The charge doesn't become any less serious waiting a day or two to file." Nikolai cupped Nataliya's cheek. "You understand that in trying to blackmail *me*, that even if we do not file a complaint here in the US, he is already guilty of treason against the Mirrusian Crown. If he ever attempts to enter our country, he will be detained, tried and most likely end up incarcerated."

Nikolai could have no idea how good that news sounded to Natalia.

Detooth the tiger indeed. "And the press conference?" she asked.

"We will set the story straight."

Jenna arrived then, for moral support, but also to help Nataliya get ready to face the press.

Again, Nikolai had thought of everything.

When they reached the lobby, both Nikolai's security and that for Yurkovich-Tanner were in position. There was a table covered with a cloth and bunting in the colors of the

House of Merikov. The Mirrusian Royal Crest was displayed prominently on the front.

The cavernous lobby was packed. News crews from the major networks were there along with journalists for reputable entertainment shows, magazines and newspapers.

Demyan stood to one side, along with people Nataliya did not recognize.

One of those people stepped forward, introduced themself as the press liaison for King Nikolai of Mirrus, thanked everyone for coming, gave a few instructions for holding questions and the like and then introduced Nikolai and Nataliya.

"I want to thank you all for coming," Nikolai said in confident tones. "Understandably my fiancée, Lady Nataliya of Volyarus, has been deeply saddened and upset by the spurious interview given by her father, the disgraced Count Shevchenko."

Nikolai smiled reassuringly down at Nataliya and whether it was for show or because he cared about her feelings in that moment, she felt better.

"The one thing the Count got right was that there was in fact a contract. Neither my people, nor King Fedir has ever tried to hide that fact."

Murmurs erupted in the room, but soon died down as it became obvious Nikolai would not continue until there was silence.

"That contract was not between Lady Nataliya and my brother."

"But she was expected to marry him?" a bold reporter called out.

He was shushed, but Nikolai answered. "That contract was signed ten years ago. If they intended to marry, I think it would have happened by now, don't you?"

Laughter erupted into the room.

Nikolai waited until it calmed down before going on.

"The truth is that when I realized I'd mourned my deceased wife long enough, I looked around me and Lady Nataliya was the woman I saw."

Nataliya did her best to keep her smile and not show the shock she felt on her face. Did he mean that, or was it part of the damage control?

"My brother made his disinterest in fulfilling the contract official, leaving the way open for me to court the woman I wanted to stand beside me, but make no mistake, I had every intention of stealing Nataliya from my brother if he did not step aside."

Gasps sounded throughout the room, and the tap of furious typing on touch screens.

Even knowing how that all had come to pass, Nataliya almost believed Nikolai's version.

"So, the idea that Nataliya set her sights on me because I am a king when she was promised to my brother is a total fiction. The fact is, it was entirely the other way around. I set my sights on her and I courted her with every intention of success."

"How do you feel about that, Lady Nataliya?" a female reporter asked.

"Honored. And very pleased with the outcome. Anyone who thought Prince Konstantin and I would have a made a good couple doesn't know either of us very well."

"You don't like the Prince?" someone asked.

"I'll like him just fine as a brother-in-law," she promised.

Laughter erupted again.

The rest of the press conference was more of the same, and Nataliya's sense of unreality grew. How much of what Nikolai said was the truth and how much was *spin*? When the courtship had first started, it would not have mattered to her, but now?

Now that she realized she loved him, the answer to that question was of paramount importance.

More reporters and cameramen congregated on the walk outside the Yurkovich-Tanner building. These weren't the ones invited to the press conference. These were the ones who had read that sleazy interview with her father and wanted their pound of flesh.

Nataliya could see them from her seat beside Nikolai in the helicopter as it lifted off from the roof. They were traveling via helicopter rather than the jet he had arrived in because he had refused to allow her to be exposed to the clamoring press waiting like jackals.

She couldn't help feeling a certain satisfaction knowing the vultures had been deprived of their prey.

Not all journalists were bottom feeders. In fact, she was of the opinion *most* weren't. Her best friend being a prime example, and she'd been impressed by those who had shown up for the press conference.

But the ones hoping to get a word from, or a picture of, the scandal-tainted Lady Nataliya were the type who gave journos a bad name.

The rest of Nataliya's things were being packed up by movers and would be taken to Mirrus the following morning. Her social secretary, Frosana, was busy either canceling her final engagements with friends or rescheduling virtual get-togethers from the palace.

As they flew over the sea's choppy waters and Nikolai worked on his computer, dialing into meetings via a live feed from his laptop, Nataliya realized that her life had finally changed irrevocably.

The wedding was just a formality.

She no longer worked for Yurkovich-Tanner. Nataliya no longer lived in her own pretty condominium she had bought with her own money. She could no longer meet Jenna at their favorite coffee shop.

Nataliya would never again go shopping on her own, or go hiking by herself, or do anything alone again. Not really. Even when there was the illusion of privacy, it would only be that. An illusion.

From this point forward, she would always have a security detail. Though the wedding had not yet happened, she was already considered a part of the Royal House of Merikov.

Nataliya didn't have the title of princess yet, but this flight represented the end of her personal independence.

Maybe that was why she'd fought against going to Mirrus ahead of schedule.

Nataliya knew that this time, when she stepped foot on Mirrus soil, her entire life would change. Permanently.

Because of the man sitting beside her.

Her father had really picked the wrong victim when he'd tried to blackmail King Nikolai Merikov.

If there was a more stubborn person, as certain of his course, Nataliya had never met him.

Nikolai had decided that Nataliya would make a good wife and Princess to his people. And he had allowed no one to dissuade him, not his family, not his advisors, not even Nataliya herself.

Certainly, he wasn't going to allow a man like Count Danilo Shevchenko to undermine the King's plans.

Nataliya wasn't sure what Nikolai would make of her love for him, but she was sure it wasn't part of his plan.

Affection? Yes. She could see he wanted that, but a more consuming emotion? No.

Definitely not on his agenda to give or receive.

At first that had given Nataliya a sense of peace, but as her love grew she realized how difficult it would be to keep it to herself.

Especially when he acted like he had today, like her comfort and safety were *the* top priority. When he refused to give in to pressure and take the *easy* way to anything if it wasn't the *best* way.

He was such an honorable man.

Such a good man.

"What?" he mouthed to her.

"I'm fine," she assured him, knowing he would be able to read her lips, as well.

They weren't talking via the internal communication headsets because he was using his headset for the meeting he was dialed into via his laptop.

He clicked something and then his voice came through her headset. "You sighed."

"I did?" He noticed? While in a meeting?

"You did."

"Just realizing everything is different now."

"Everything became different the moment you agreed to marry me."

That was true. "But that difference wasn't real."

"And now it is?"

"Yes."

"Good."

She laughed. "No commiseration?"

"I am pleased you realize the weight of our choices. Your sense of honor and commitment are exemplary."

"You're such a sweet-talker," she said, tongue in cheek.

Unbelievably, color burnished his aristocratic cheeks. "I am not a romantic man." He said it like he was admitting a grave shortcoming.

Nataliya smiled, but shook her head. "I disagree. You put on a very romantic courtship, but even if you hadn't? Believe me, I could not imagine a more romantic gesture than for you to clear your schedule and come to Seattle to bring me home."

The press conference had been pretty amazing too. He'd done something she knew her uncle wouldn't have.

"You didn't sound like you thought I was being romantic this morning."

"I was still fighting the final change to my life, I think," she admitted.

His brows drew together, like the idea of fighting one's duty was incomprehensible. "You knew it was coming."

"In two weeks."

"You're a little set in your ways, aren't you?" he asked like he was just now realizing that fact. "Not fond of change."

Her smile was self-deprecating. "Yes, I can be. Change is inevitable but not always my friend."

"This change will be good."

"If I didn't believe that, I wouldn't have agreed to marry you." She gave him a reassuring smile. "And please don't think I need romantic dinners in the park to be happy. The way you stood up for me today? The way you wouldn't let anyone make me a scapegoat for my father, even when I thought I needed to, that's the kind of romance that secures affection for a lifetime."

It wasn't the declaration of love her heart longed to make, but it was more than she thought she'd admit before the day's events.

"I can hope situations like that do not arrive often, but be certain I will always take your part."

"I believe you." And that? Was kind of amazing.

She trusted him in a way she trusted no one else. Not even her mother, whom Nataliya adored.

"I am glad."

Nataliya noticed one of the men at the conference table on the laptop's screen waving like he was trying to get Nikolai's attention.

"I think they need you." She indicated his computer. "I'm fine on my own."

He nodded and clicked back to his meeting without another word, trusting her at her word and Nataliya realized she really liked that too.

CHAPTER ELEVEN

THE DAYS LEADING up to her wedding were much busier than Nataliya had expected. Since she hadn't planned to be in Mirrus for several days, the fact she magically had a full schedule was another reality check.

Nataliya had always been aware that being a princess, especially The Princess of Mirrus, was a job. What she was coming to see was how much someone in her position had been needed.

The fact she was on call to Mirrus Global for her specialized computer skills took up some of her time, but so far she hadn't been pulled into anything really tricky or time-consuming.

She saw almost nothing of her fiancé during the day, their schedules both full without overlap. They dined together every evening, but even the dinners that were not State business offered no opportunity for her and Nikolai to talk privately.

He insisted on them spending an hour together each evening in the palace's private garden, but they never repeated the passionate kisses they had shared before she'd returned to Seattle.

She wasn't sure why.

It wasn't because he didn't want her. The sexual tension between them only got higher and higher as their wedding approached.

Nataliya didn't have enough experience with this sort of thing to know exactly what to do with that, but one thing she was not? Was a shrinking violet.

So, one evening a couple of days before the wedding, while they sat in the garden talking, like they had every evening for the past week, she reached over and laid her hand on his thigh.

Nikolai's reaction was electric. Her soon-to-be husband jumped up and moved several feet away before spinning around to face her. "What are you doing?"

Since she thought the answer to that question was more than obvious, Nataliya frowned and tried to make sense of his overblown response. "What's going on, Nikolai? I thought we agreed there was nothing wrong with sharing our passion?"

"We did." He looked like he was in physical pain.

She let her gaze slide over him and couldn't miss the erection pressing against his slacks. Did it hurt?

"Stop that!" he admonished.

"Stop what? Looking at you?" she asked with disbelief. "Yes!"

This was just getting stranger and stranger. "Why?"

"I promised your mother," he gritted out.

"Promised Mama? That I wouldn't look at you?" That didn't make any sense.

"That I would not touch you again before our wedding night," he ground out.

Irritation filled Nataliya, both at her mother for asking for such a thing and at Nikolai for agreeing to it. "At all?" she clarified.

He shrugged.

"What does that mean?" She made no effort to hide the annoyance in her tone.

He winced. "It means that I'm on a hair trigger here. If I touch you or allow you to touch me, if I kiss you…" He visibly shuddered at the thought. "This thing between us is going to explode and I will break my promise."

"That you made to *my mother*?" Nataliya's voice held a wealth of censure. "*Why* did you make that promise?"

He was too smart not to have known what a challenge it would be to keep.

For both of them.

"Because she asked me to."

"And that was enough?" Nataliya's voice rose on the last word.

The look he gave her from his steely gray eyes implied she should understand. "She's your mother."

"And *I'm* the one you are going to marry."

"Yes."

"So, why promise my mother something you had to know I would not like? Something that would be so difficult for us both?"

"At the time, I did not think you would be here on Mirrus until a couple of days before the wedding. It did not seem like a hardship."

"And now?"

He scowled, the look close to petulant.

"Not as easy as you thought, huh?"

"I would not make such a promise now."

"You thought, easy way to win some points with the future mother-in-law," she teased, her irritation evaporating, if not her sexual frustration.

"Something like that."

Even kings worried if their mothers-in-law approved. Who knew?

Even so. "You're usually better at foreseeing the potentially bad outcome. You didn't think, hey, this could backfire on me?"

"First, I do not think *hey* anything. Second, no, I did not foresee the potential for backfiring."

"You'd better have a pretty spectacular wedding night planned," she warned him.

His smile was devastating. "You are very demanding for a virgin."

"Maybe I wouldn't be so demanding if I had any choice about that status changing before our wedding," she grumbled.

"You could always seduce me," he offered.

She tilted her head to one side, studying him. "And that would not make you feel like you broke your promise?"

His expression said it all.

"That's what I thought." She nodded and then promised, "I will never knowingly undermine your integrity."

An arrested expression came over his aristocratic features. "That means a great deal to me."

"Why?" She shook her head. "I don't mean it shouldn't." She paused. "I think it just surprises me that you would not have taken it as given."

"There was a time when I did, but I learned I could not."

"With Queen Tiana?" Nataliya asked, bewildered by the possibility.

They had seemed so in love, but maybe she needed to rethink her belief on that.

"Da."

"You so rarely mention your first marriage." In the beginning, Nataliya had believed that was because he still grieved the loss of his wife.

Now, she wasn't so sure.

"Tiana was not above using her position as my wife and confidant for her own gains." Nikolai's voice was devoid of emotion.

But that confidence had to have cost him, in terms of pride, if nothing else. Nataliya could not wrap her head around his deceased wife using him, much less her position, in that way.

"That shocks you," he opined.

"Yes."

"Because you could not imagine doing such a thing."

"No." There was no point Nataliya trying to prevaricate. If it made her sound provincial rather than royal, that could not be helped.

"I believe you. And that makes me very happy." His tone wasn't lacking in inflection now. It positively rang with satisfaction.

Nataliya smiled, pleased that in this way at least he saw her as superior to the beauty he had married. "I'm glad."

"We are going to have a good marriage." He sounded very sure of that.

But that was nothing new. He'd been certain from the beginning. It was Nataliya who had taken some convincing.

"With a really special wedding night."

His sexy laughter followed her into her dreams that night and she woke with a sense of hope and happiness that only increased as Nikolai played out the humorous role of paying the bride ransom the day before their official ceremony. Because of the security necessary and the guests who would be attending their wedding, some traditions were more royal than orthodox.

Nataliya wore a vintage gown for the wedding. Despite its short lead-up time, the affair had dozens of the world's elites as guests.

The other couple of hundred guests were by no means to be dismissed. Nearly the entire nobilities of both Volyarus and Mirrus were in attendance, along with billionaire business associates.

Jenna was there, and although she would cover the wedding in an article she would write later, her only role at present was that of maid of honor or *witness* according to the traditions of the church.

Nikolai's *witness* would be his brother Konstantin, which had been suggested by the fixer to show the younger man's support of the proceedings despite being the one Nataliya had first been intended to marry according the contract. Nataliya didn't really care who stood up with Nikolai.

She was simply happy Jenna would be by *her* side at the wedding. Mama still insisted on calling it a *crowning* according to church tradition, because of the religious crowns placed on both her and Nikolai's heads during the ceremony. Not to be confused with the Princess Coronation ceremony, where Nataliya would receive an official royal tiara.

That would happen *after* the wedding.

Jenna's fashion magazine's photographer represented the favored press presence and would be the only press allowed to photograph the official coronation, while having access to areas the other media guests did not, as well.

Nikolai had made known his displeasure with news outlets that had run stories based on her father's spurious allegations of Nataliya's avarice and scheming. Excluding them from the official coronation was only part of it.

Which was why Jenna's photographer was in the room with Nataliya now as the stylist Jenna had recommended put the finishing touches on Nataliya's *look*.

"You definitely look regal enough to be The Princess of Mirrus, *Lady Nataliya*," Jenna teased, using the title she never did when they were alone.

Nataliya had been pleasantly surprised when no one suggested she choose someone with a higher rung on the social ladder than Jenna to be her maid of honor and said so now. "I'm so glad you're here with me. I'm pretty sure I'd be a bundle of nerves otherwise."

"I think the fact you are marrying the man of your dreams has more to do with why happiness is overriding nerves, but who am I to say?" Jenna responded with a laugh. "And there never was any chance someone might argue your choice to have me as your only attendant. Your mom and King Hotty put the kibosh on any dissent before you even floated my name to the wedding planner."

"How do you know that?" Nataliya demanded.

"Because unlike you, my dear friend, *I* listen to gossip."

Nataliya just laughed and got ready to promise the rest of her life to serving the people of Mirrus, as their King's Princess.

The Russian Orthodox church that hosted the wedding had been built the first decade of Mirrus' settlement.

The gorgeous structure had been the setting for every wedding in the House of Merikov since. Like Saint Basil's in Moscow, Mirrus' cathedral had multicolored rather than gold conical-topped spires, but inside the gold-leafed icons were lavish works of art from another century, and the intricately designed floor tiles breathtaking.

Her gown a replica of the one worn by the first and most beloved Queen of Mirrus in the country's history trailed behind Nataliya down the center aisle in thirty feet of rustling satin train. The guests filling the church were in a hazy glow, but Nikolai, waiting at the front for her, was in sharp focus.

He looked unutterably handsome in his Head of State military regalia, but even wearing an off-the-rack suit, she knew this man would leave her breathless.

The expression in his steely gray gaze when she joined him at the front of the church was so intense, it sent goose bumps along her arms and made her breath catch.

This man had a plan and she was part of it.

During the *procession* Nataliya was glad she had practiced negotiating her train or this moment could have been an unmitigated disaster. She was even more relieved that she would be changing into a more modern gown created by a high-end Russian designer before attempting to circulate at the reception later.

She wasn't thinking about her dress, or her need to stay very still not to mess up the train, when the priest began to speak the words of the age-old ceremony in Russian. He repeated each vow in Ukrainian before Nikolai and Nataliya made their promises.

Her heart pounding in her chest, Nataliya was surprised at how profound the moment felt.

She knew she loved the man she was marrying. Accepted that he did not love her, but she had not considered how bound to him the vows she spoke would make her feel.

She had anticipated the weight of her role as his Princess settling on her, but not this feeling that her heart and her life were irrevocably tied to this man. To a king.

The look in Nikolai's eyes said he felt a similar level of profundity.

Which perhaps should not have surprised her, but it did.

He kept his promises. Knew she kept hers.

It was a moment of total connection between them.

They were both making commitments they intended to keep. Absolutely.

As much as Nataliya was not a fan of big gatherings, she put on her game face, smiling until her cheeks ached as she was introduced or reacquainted with the upper echelon of society.

She accepted every good wish on her future happiness with a king with equal warmth, refusing to allow the hundredth thank you be any less sincere than the first.

However, when Jenna sidled up next to her and asked if she was ready to go, Nataliya wanted to shout, *Yes*!

She couldn't though. "We've got hours yet," she informed her best friend in an apologetic whisper.

"Not according to your husband, you don't."

Nataliya startled and looked around for Nikolai. "What do you mean?"

They'd spent more of the reception together than she had expected, but it would have been impossible to remain at one another's side throughout the evening.

And now, she couldn't see him anywhere.

"His Highness sent me to get you."

"Get me?" Nataliya felt like she wasn't tracking.

"He said something about a promise he made about your wedding night?" Jenna prompted.

Heat washed into Nataliya's cheeks. No way was she going to explain that particular promise to even her best friend.

"Where is he?" she asked.

Jenna nodded her head toward the south doors to the palace ballroom. "Come with me."

Somehow, Jenna, who had not been born to nobility, was negotiating the room like a seasoned campaigner. She had Nataliya in the corridor outside mere minutes later, explaining to anyone who impeded their progress that His Highness needed Princess Nataliya for something.

Unsurprisingly, a security detail waited, but neither of the men said anything as Jenna continued to lead the way to one of the hidden hallways used by the royal family to navigate the palace. Then they were going through a set of thick doors that led to the outside behind the palace where a sleek black limousine waited.

One of the security detail stepped forward to open the door and help Nataliya inside, still silent.

The interior of the limousine was empty but for her cell phone on the seat. She picked it up and settled onto the soft leather. It rang in her hand as she was reaching for the seat belt.

Nikolai's face flashed on the screen.

She answered. "Really? You changed my ringtone for your calls?"

"I thought it was appropriate." Amusement warmed his voice.

"Somehow I don't think of you when I think of modern hip-hop."

"And yet the song is very appropriate."

It was a modern ballad by a popular female artist about desire and fidelity. Not a song she would have thought he even knew. "Not exactly subtle." As all things royal should be.

In a hip-hop song. Who knew?

"You may want to change it later," he conceded.

And she smiled. He'd made the change as part of this special night.

"Where are you?" Should that have been her first question? Maybe.

"In the SUV in front of you."

She remembered there being an SUV in front of the limousine and one behind. A quiet cavalcade without the flags of station waving.

"Why there and not here?" she asked.

"You deserve a very special wedding night. Not for our first time together to be in the back of a limousine." The promise in his voice sent shivers of desire through her.

Nataliya's hand tightened on the phone. "And if you were here, it would be?" she goaded.

"Of a certainty."

How was it possible for the sexual intensity between them to be so hot? "Is it always like this?" she wondered aloud.

"No," he assured her in a growl. "It is not. What we have is uncommon."

But not love. Not on his side anyway. "Was it like this with your first wife?"

He inhaled, like the question shocked him, but he answered. "At first, something like it, but looking back I realize that it was never this intense. Maybe because Tiana and I didn't wait." He paused, like he was thinking. "I don't know, but as much as I desired her, there was never a time I thought I wouldn't be able to control myself if I was with her."

And he felt that way with Nataliya? She couldn't help liking that, but she didn't doubt that if *she* told him no, ever, he would control himself just fine. He meant he didn't think they could control themselves together.

"Like that first kiss in the garden." Neither of them had been showing any sort of control then.

"Yes."

"At first?" she asked. "Will it get less intense?"

"No," he said without hesitation.

"But you said that with Queen Tiana…" Nataliya allowed her voice to trail off.

He knew what she was talking about.

"What I had with my first wife was different," he said with certainty. "I was enthralled by her. She used sex to control, to manipulate, but I didn't realize it until we'd been married more than a year."

No question he was alone in the back of the SUV with the privacy window up. Just as she was. Or they would not be having such an intimate and revealing conversation.

Nataliya shifted, trying to alleviate the feeling of need that even talking about his dead wife was in no way diminishing. "Even if that's true, I cannot imagine she wasn't just as enthralled by you."

"Because you are." Nikolai sounded very satisfied by that fact.

"You know I am."

"We are well matched."

"Yes." She could not deny it. Nor could she deny that she wished he was with her, the setting of their first time sharing full intimacy be damned.

"Where are we going?"

"Somewhere we can have that spectacular wedding night you demanded."

"How long until we get there?"

"Only about forty-five minutes."

"Did you just say *only*?" she demanded.

"Relax, *kiska*, we will be there before you know it. I will keep you entertained." And he did, telling her his plans for the night ahead.

By the time the limousine stopped, Nataliya was so hot and bothered she couldn't fumble her seat belt open. When she finally got it, she surged toward the door with no sense of aplomb and even less reticence.

Nikolai was there to take her hand. He practically yanked her from the car and right into his embrace.

"Lost your cool, Your Highness?" she asked him breathlessly as her body pressed against his hardness, her own cool nowhere in evidence.

"*Da*," he growled out, reverting to Russian. He told her he wanted her, that she was too beautiful to resist, in the same language. Then he swept her high against his chest.

She gulped in air and tried to regain a little of her equilibrium. "I thought carrying the bride over the threshold was a western tradition."

He didn't reply. Didn't look at her, just focused on covering the distance to the door of the mountain chalet in long, impatient strides.

Something in the corner of her vision caught her eye and Nataliya gasped. "You brought me to a glacier?"

The chalet sat high on a craggy hill overlooking a pristine blue glacier.

"Tomorrow," he gritted out as the door swung open in front to them.

"Tomorrow, what?"

"Talking." He acknowledged the woman who had opened to the door with a nod, but no words.

Nataliya gave the older woman a little wave and received a warm, very amused, smile in return.

Nataliya nuzzled into the curve of where his shoulder and neck met. "You're in kind of a hurry, huh?"

His big body gave a shudder, but he didn't slow down as he carried her determinedly up the stairs. And then they were in a huge master bedroom, the solid door slamming when he kicked it closed.

She would have teased him about slamming doors, but suddenly *that* moment was upon her. They were going to make love…have sex. Whatever they called it, Nataliya knew it would change her forever.

Her King made no move to let her go.

Inhaling his delicious masculine scent, she pressed a kiss to his neck, letting her tongue flick out to taste.

Everything inside her tightened, the pleasant throb between her legs she'd had for the last thirty minutes of the drive up the mountain becoming a sensual ache.

With a groan, Nikolai released her and then quickly stepped back, putting distance between them that she did not want.

She moved to follow him, but he put his hands up as if warding her off.

"What?" she demanded.

"You are a virgin."

"So? Tomorrow, I won't be."

"Precisely." He turned toward the door.

She stood in stunned silence until his hand landed on the handle. "Where are you going?" she demanded.

"You need gentle."

That was debatable. Nataliya wasn't feeling *gentle* right now. She was *hot and bothered*.

"So?"

"So, I need some time."

"Why?"

"So I can give you gentle."

"I don't want gentle," she informed him.

He spun to face her. "You think that, but—"

"Stop, right there," she interrupted. "Be very careful before you try to claim you know more about what I want and need than I do. I am a twenty-eight-year-old woman. I am a virgin by choice, not because the men in my life knew what was best for me and protected poor little old me."

And being a virgin did not mean she was ignorant about sex, or her own body's needs.

"You will be a passionate advocate for the rights of women in Mirrus."

"Right now, I'm not thinking of anyone but us." She stepped out of her shoes. "Either you respect me enough to let me make my own choices, or you don't."

She waited, wondering if she could have misjudged this man and his intentions so badly.

Air filled her lungs in a breath of relief as his hand dropped from the doorknob. "It is a matter of physical necessity, not believing I know your body better than you do."

It so was, but she could forgive him because he wasn't in possession of all the facts.

"I have toys," she told him baldly.

"What?" He stumbled back, like her words profoundly shocked him.

"I am a twenty-eight-year-old woman. If you have a fantasy of a naive virgin in your bed, we can play that scenario out sometime, but right now I just want *you*."

"What kind of toys?"

She rolled her eyes. "I'll show them to you sometime. Maybe you'll want to use them with me, but not tonight."

His already dark eyes flared with heated desire. "No. Not tonight."

Done with the waiting. Done with *any* delays, Nataliya reached behind her back and pulled the zip down on the designer dress she'd changed into for the reception.

He didn't ask what she was doing, or make any more sweet but inane comments about how she needed gentleness when Nataliya was so hot she thought she might combust if he didn't get inside her soon.

Nikolai stripped with more speed than finesse, baring his gorgeous body to Nataliya's eyes.

He was beyond fit. Muscles bulged on his biceps and chest, usually hidden by the formal attire of a king, his sculpted thighs showing why he'd found carrying her up the stairs so easy.

She let out a pent-up breath, her own dress a pool around her feet. "You are beautiful."

"I believe those are my words to you."

Her throat had gone dry and she couldn't reply with a witticism, just shook her head. He was everything she could have imagined wanting in an intimate partner.

She didn't need physical perfection, but it was standing right in front of her and she had no more words to tell him how turned on he made her.

The sight of his masculine body finished what his words on the phone had started and she *wanted*. She *needed*.

She went to shove her panties down her legs, but he was there just that quickly. His hands over hers. "Let me."

She nodded, her own hands sliding out from under his to press against his sculpted chest. She circled the eraser-hard nubs of his nipples, brushed her fingertips over them just as he undid the catch on her bra, releasing her breasts. Her already turgid nipples tightened as they were exposed to the air.

They both gasped.

He cupped her breasts, swiping his thumb over the hardened peaks. "You fit my hands too perfectly."

She moaned at the sensation coursing through her, but passivity was not on her agenda. Nataliya leaned forward and took one of his small male nipples delicately between her teeth, gratified by the groan of pleasure that came from her royal husband.

She'd read that some men loved having their nipples played with, some didn't like it, and some didn't care either way, but it did nothing for them. She was glad he was of the first type. She liked getting the kind of reaction she was getting from him.

His impressive erection jutted out insistently from his body, the head brushing against her skin and exciting her even more.

The years she'd fantasized about this man were nothing compared to the reality of having the freedom to touch as she pleased and the knowledge he wanted to do the same to her.

She kissed a trail upward until their mouths met again; all the while his hands were busy pulling sensual pleasure from her body with knowing touches to her breasts.

Without breaking the kiss, he pushed her panties down her thighs. He waited for her to step out of them and then dropped to his knees to brush her thigh-high stockings down with caresses along her inner thighs, then pulled them from her feet with sensual mastery.

This man understood a woman's body and how to give intense pleasure.

Nikolai shifted back just a little and then looked his fill at her now naked body. "*Krasiva.*"

"I thought that was my word for you," she said breathlessly, her knees threatening to buckle.

"You said it in English."

She would have laughed, but he ran a probing finger between the folds of her most intimate flesh. A strangled sound came out of Nataliya as she was touched so very intimately.

Nikolai surged back to his feet, pulling her into his body, rubbing against her with no evidence of reluctance. His hands cupped both her breasts and squeezed. The air in her lungs left her in a whoosh and though she gulped in air, Nataliya couldn't catch her breath.

Not with the way he touched her.

No hesitation, no excessive gentleness. He played with her breasts while she mapped his body with her hands.

She tilted her head and then they were kissing again, the hunger between them voracious and unabated. They kept kissing and touching until they fell together on the bed, their bodies pressed so tightly together she could feel every nuance of the ridge of his erection against her stomach.

He rolled them and she spread her legs, encouraging him to shift so his steel hardness rubbed against her clitoris.

She tilted up, seeking more stimulation, but it wasn't enough.

He reached down and pressed a finger inside her.

Pleasure rolled over her, her womb contracting in a moment of ecstasy unlike any she'd ever felt on her own. He pushed upward with his finger, hitting that spot inside so rich with nerve endings. Her climax crested again and she screamed, the sound swallowed by his mouth.

He caressed her through the ecstasy, but even though she'd just had the most intense orgasm of her life, her body was craving more.

And he gave it to her.

Nikolai pushed her thighs just a little wider and pressed inside, stretching swollen and slick flesh with his rigid erection.

"Yes!" she cried out, the sensation of him inside her absolutely perfect.

The pain of him pushing through her virginal barrier was masked by the incredible sensual pleasure racking her body. Clearly trusting her to know what she wanted, he set a hard and fast rhythm. She tilted her pelvis upward, matching his movements, demanding more with her body.

Their bodies grew slick with sweat, their breaths mingling in panted pleasure and the ecstasy built again.

"Come for me," he demanded as he pistoned into her body with unfettered passion.

"You come for me," she gasped back.

Everything inside her contracted in a rictus of pleasure so strong she could not even scream. His body went rigid and Nikolai tossed his head back, a primal shout coming from deep in his chest.

Every little move of his body triggered aftershocks of pleasure in hers. His groans said he was experiencing the same.

"That was amazing," she said with panting breaths.

He didn't reply with words, but kissed her, his lips soft and perfect against hers in the aftermath of such a primal loving.

She didn't know how long they remained connected like that.

But eventually Nikolai rolled off her, his arm going around her waist. "I suppose you want to take a shower."

"I do?" she asked, having no thought of doing so.

"We are all sweaty."

"So?" Sex was supposed to be messy, wasn't it?

"You don't mind?"

"Do you?" she asked, really not wanting to move, even for a shower.

"No." He nuzzled into her shoulder. "I love that you smell like both of us together."

"How primitive of you," she teased.

He went to shift away from her but she followed, leaning forward to kiss his muscular chest. "I like it too. Let's be throwbacks together."

The rigidity that had come over his body relaxed. "You do?"

"Hmm mmm." She snuggled into her new husband. "Thank you."

"For?" he asked, like he didn't want to misunderstand.

"Listening to me. For treating me like a woman and not just a princess."

"I will always try to listen to you."

Even his promises were perfect. He knew he couldn't promise to always get it right. Only to try.

"And I will always try to listen to you."

CHAPTER TWELVE

NIKOLAI AND NATALIYA lay together for a while, pressed together from chest to hip and Nataliya reveled in the intimacy of it.

But they had been on sexual edge for too long and the desire between them inevitably built again.

This time, he was gentle and teasing, showing her just how much pleasure he could bring to her body with a slow buildup. She returned his touches, learning what made him moan, what made him give that contented growl that said she was connecting to him more than sensually.

She wanted to be on top during their coupling this time and he let her without hesitation. Nataliya brought them both to another culmination of pleasure and collapsed onto him after.

Eventually, they did make it to the bath, where she learned the slide of naked bodies in the water could be terribly arousing.

The sun was rising over the glacier out the huge wall of windows when she and Nikolai finally settled into sleep, their bodies entwined.

They slept away the morning, but rose to have lunch together. The entire side of the chalet facing the glacier seemed to be made of windows, so the dining room overlooked the incredible view just as the master bedroom did.

"This place is amazing."

"It is our personal getaway."

"You mean the family doesn't use it?" she asked in surprise before dishing some more fruit onto her plate.

She was ravenous.

"Not without my permission and with rare exception,

I do not give it. The people of Mirrus can visit the glacier from the other side of the chasm."

"Aren't tourists allowed?"

"No. The park is owned by the royal family and only open to the people of Mirrus."

Conservation was a big thing on the island, so she wasn't surprised. "But the chalet is *yours*, not the royal family's?"

"Yes." He placed another fluffy pancake on her plate, seeming to enjoy watching her eat so enthusiastically. "It is a retreat for the King."

Nataliya looked around herself with satisfaction. "It's the perfect honeymoon destination." It afforded the privacy that would be lacking in their daily life and she was really happy to know they had this retreat to come to when they needed it.

"I'm so glad you think so."

Something about the way he said it gave Nataliya pause. "Didn't Queen Tiana like it?"

"She never came. Nature was not her thing."

"But it's so beautiful."

"Tiana had no interest in seeing the glacier. She refused to go anywhere she could not be entertained."

"You two weren't very well suited." Nataliya sucked in her breath and nearly bit her tongue in her chagrin saying something like that. "I'm sorry. It's not my place to judge your past relationship."

But he wasn't offended. Nikolai's smile was approving and warm. "If not you, then who?" He sipped his coffee. Black, no sugar or cream. So not how Nataliya enjoyed the bitter elixir. "You are right. Once we were married, I realized how little in common I had with my wife."

"That must have been hard, but still, you loved each other." And Nataliya was just realizing how very much she wanted that emotion from him.

"Love?" he mused. "I thought I did, but now I'm not so

sure. She had me sexually enthralled. *She* was enthralled by the idea of being a queen."

"I'm sure she loved you." How could Queen Tiana have felt anything else for this amazing man?

"Are you? I am not." He didn't sound like he was bothered by that fact.

But she knew he had to be. She remembered how he'd been with Queen Tiana. Whatever he thought now, Nikolai had loved the other woman. And while that hurt Nataliya a little, she recognized that their marriage would probably be a much happier one.

Nikolai asked, remembered pain reflected in his steely gray eyes, "If she loved me, would she have gone skiing on that dangerous slope, knowing she was pregnant with my child?"

"She was very athletic," Nataliya offered. "Her sports acumen was renowned."

Queen Tiana had been known for her skiing prowess as well as her skydiving feats. She was very good at any sport she tried and she always did the most challenging aspect of those sports. The former Queen had been lucky right up until the end too, never having broken so much as a pinky in all her exploits.

"I'm sure Queen Tiana never even considered it might not go well for her to take that slope."

"I've never been sure. Yes, she enjoyed the adrenaline rush of high-risk sports, but she was a queen, pregnant with the heir to the throne." He looked at Nataliya with an expression she could not read. "Tiana did not want to be pregnant. She had wanted to wait to have children, but her birth control failed."

"All this time, I thought she didn't know," Nataliya admitted.

Everything in the media, every statement given by the palace, it had all said at the time that the tragedy was made worse by her taking a chance she hadn't realized she was taking.

"That she was pregnant? Oh, she knew. As I said, she wasn't happy about it. She refused to allow her pregnancy to curtail any of her pleasures."

Nataliya didn't know what to say. She couldn't imagine making the same choices as Queen Tiana, but those choices had been the other woman's to make. Even if they felt incredibly selfish to Nataliya.

"I could tell my brother absolutely no when he wanted to participate in extreme sports," Nikolai said, frustration lacing his tone. "He recognizes my role as his King. My dead wife? With her, I had no authority."

Nataliya got what Nikolai was saying. Konstantin had given up any hopes of participating in extreme sports because of his role as his brother's heir. Queen Tiana had disregarded not only her role as Queen, but the risk to her unborn child who would become the heir to the throne.

Even so. "Um... I don't really want you bossing me around like my sovereign either."

"What about as your husband? Do I have any sway over your actions in that regard?"

"Of course you do, just I expect you to listen to my counsel when something is important to me in regard to your actions. But ultimately, though we will listen to each other, we are still self-governing."

"You live in a monarchy now, you do realize this?"

"Yes. But you aren't the type of monarch to dictate the actions of your people."

"You think not?"

"I wouldn't have married you otherwise."

"Then I hope you will not be too disappointed to realize that I will not allow you to take the kind of risks Tiana did. Not with your own safety and definitely not with the safety of any of our future unborn children."

"You sound really stern right now."

"You do not sound intimidated, but I promise you. I learned my lesson."

"And I promise *you* that while I intend to make my own decisions, you never have to worry about me putting my own safety at risk or that of our children, born, or otherwise."

The only high risk she'd taken was the one to her heart by marrying him.

They went hiking that afternoon, the lush forest awash with summer plants and flowers. They didn't see as much wildlife as they might have done but for the security detail ahead of them and the one that came behind.

Too many people. Too much noise.

Nataliya didn't mind because nothing could detract from the beauty of Mirrus. And as much as she might enjoy seeing moose or even a wildcat, she wasn't keen to see a bear. Even a small brown one.

"I'm glad you haven't encouraged tourism to the detriment of this beauty," she told Nikolai as they walked.

"We have been fortunate that Mirrus Global and the other industries on the island have never been reliant on the tourist season."

"I know about the mining." Which posed its own challenges for conservation. "And the high-tech arm of Mirrus Global."

"Mirrus Global isn't the only high-tech company we have based here. One of the world's most advanced AI developers is a citizen and his company employs many others."

"I'd like to meet him."

"Of course you would." Nikolai smiled down at her with indulgence.

Since the barely banked desire was there as well, Nataliya didn't take offense.

"Nevertheless, a certain amount of tourism is beneficial." He took her hand and kissed the back as if unaware of doing so. "If for no other reason, than offering an opportunity for our people to meet potential partners from a new gene pool."

She laughed, thinking he was joking but realized he wasn't. "You're serious. That happens? A lot?"

"Enough to make the management of our tourism industry worth the headache it brings to environmental and resource management."

"Although the education system through high school is top-notch on Volyarus, Uncle Fedir has fought against building a university every time the issue comes up. Maybe that's why." She'd spent so many years living in the greater Seattle area that some of these nuances to a small, island country were new to her, despite having been born in Volyarus and being a member of its royal family.

Nikolai nodded. "We do not have a university for the same reason."

"But aren't you afraid young people won't return to the island?" she asked, thinking that had to be a real detriment.

But Nikolai shook his head. "We are both small countries, only able to support a finite population. Attrition is not always a bad thing. Voluntary attrition is preferred over involuntary."

Like her and her mother's exile?

But thinking about it, Nikolai's attitude about natural attrition made sense. If everyone stayed, both small countries would be very different places. They would be crowded. And the problems that came with higher populations would plague them. Higher crime. Unemployment. Poverty. etc.

"I never even considered that. Both countries have a lot of citizens working in other countries while maintaining their citizenship."

"Yes. And sometimes their children return to live."

"Do you allow immigration?"

"Our numbers are by necessity extremely low, but we have few requests for permanent residence. Living in a country that lacks the amenities of big cities because we do not have them and has months in the winter with only a few hours of sunlight isn't for everyone."

She considered that. "It is very isolated, but it's so beautiful."

"I am glad you think so. It is my hope you will find life here as fulfilling as I do."

They continued to hold hands as they walked, and Nataliya made no effort to overcome the illusion of intimacy and romance the small physical connection provided.

Their honeymoon lasted only a week, but Nikolai was a reigning monarch with duties even his father and brother could not perform in his place. And yet, during their honeymoon, he never once allowed state business to take precedence over their time together.

It was a heady feeling for Nataliya to be the center of her royal husband's attention.

And the sex?

Was off the charts. She learned he had no compunction about dragging her off to bed in the middle of the day. He learned that she was no retiring maiden, unwilling to initiate lovemaking.

They made love often and by the end of the week, Nataliya felt more connected to Nikolai than she ever had to another person.

Their first official state event as a married couple was the night after their return to the palace.

Nataliya did her best to maintain a cordial demeanor, but she spent most of the evening managing her response to subtle and even some overt bids to get her to speak to her husband on one matter or another.

She complained to Nikolai later as they were going to

bed. "I don't understand what they hope to gain having me bring a topic up to you rather than them." Nataliya let the disgust she felt by the grasping behavior show in her tone.

"Perhaps they believe you will attempt to use my obvious affection for you to sway my opinion."

"Is your affection for me obvious?" She hadn't noticed him being all that affectionate since returning from their honeymoon.

In fact, his very dignified manner was taking some getting used to after such an intensely sensual week where they touched constantly, whether they were having sex, or not. He had been more overtly affectionate with her *before* their wedding than since their return to the palace.

Nataliya wished she knew what caused the difference. Because she'd look for a way to change it.

He looked chagrined whether by her question or his own thoughts, she couldn't tell.

"We have been home for thirty-six hours," he informed her like she didn't know. "In that time, I have texted you several times, eaten every meal in your company and called you for no other apparent reason than to check on your welfare."

"Um…you kept track?" She hadn't. Maybe she should have. Apparently that kind of communication indicated a *deep* affection on his part. Who knew?

His gorgeous lips twisted in grimace. "My aides have. And you can be sure that the gossip of my *besotted* state has spread like wildfire through the palace."

She crossed the huge bedroom they shared until she stood only a few inches away from him, but for some reason couldn't make herself reach out and touch him.

Perhaps them sharing a room was another indication of his regard? She knew her aunt and uncle did not, but she'd never considered their marriage all that healthy. At least not since becoming an adult and realizing her uncle had a "secret" lover.

"Did you share a room with Queen Tiana?" she asked out of curiosity.

"Naturally. This is not the nineteenth century."

She smiled. "No, it isn't. So, what do the gossips say about the *deep affection* I hold for you?"

He stilled, his hands on his unbuttoned shirt, his head swiveling so their gazes caught. "You hold me in *deep affection*?"

"Yes." It wasn't as if Nikolai didn't already know she had had feelings for him for a long time. She wasn't using the L word, might never use it, but he had to know her feelings ran deeply. "Didn't your aides point out my behavior?"

After all, she'd texted him just as often, answering any communication from him immediately, regardless what else she might be doing.

"No. They did not remark on it."

And it clicked. "They're worried about you."

"I believe so, yes." He went back to removing his clothes, his body shifting so he was turned more away from her than toward her.

"They know Queen Tiana influenced your decisions." And that must lacerate pride as deeply rooted as the King's.

He jerked his head in acknowledgment and then looked away, pushing his slacks down his thighs.

Refusing to be sidetracked by the sexy vision before her, Nataliya reached out and laid her hand on his arm. "You know I won't ever do that."

"I do." But he still wasn't looking at her.

"They don't."

"No."

"That is their problem," she pronounced.

He jerked back around to face her. "No, it is also my problem."

"No, it is not. You know I won't try to manipulate you.

That's all that matters. Eventually, they will see that I'm not like her, but it is not on you to convince them."

"They have a right to be worried." And he hated admitting that.

That much was obvious.

"Sure," she acknowledged. "Just as my mom is going to worry about how you treat me until she sees for herself you aren't going to change into a monster."

His brows furrowed, offense coming over his features. "I promised you."

"You don't think my father ever promised never to hit her again, never to hurt me again?"

"I am not him." This time his tone left no doubt he was offended. Deeply.

"No, you are nothing like him," Nataliya agreed. "You are everything I could have ever hoped for in a husband."

"Unlike my brother."

"Even if your brother was as wonderful as you are, he has the singular disadvantage of not being you. It wasn't fair of me to sign that contract when I knew I cared for you."

"You were a child."

"I was legally an adult and the feelings I had for you were very adult." Nataliya no longer felt guilty for those feelings.

She knew the difference between having feelings and acting on them. She never had because he had been married and then she had been promised to his brother.

But now? She could do as she liked.

"You are my wife. You get to act on those adult feelings," he said, as if reading her mind.

The kiss they shared was incendiary and the lovemaking after had an emotional quality Nataliya couldn't define. And really? She was too tired and sated to even try.

She just snuggled into her husband's muscular body feeling safe and held in very deep affection.

* * *

A couple of weeks later, Nataliya was in the study in their suite, looking for some research she needed for a meeting she was supposed to attend with the labor council.

She had some ideas for employment-driven voluntary expatriate living she hoped they would be willing to listen to, but she was prepared for skepticism. Because so far, that was all she'd met with when she attended meetings in her official capacity as The Princess of Mirrus and a member of Nikolai's cabinet.

She'd been shocked when he'd given her an official title and list of duties that showed he regarded her as equal to his brothers and father. Even so, his cabinet ministers, business associates and other politicos treated her ideas with indulgence rather than attention.

Her mother reminded Nataliya that she had to build relationships before she would get the trust and sometimes even the respect Nataliya knew she would need to do her job as The Princess of Mirrus effectively.

It had not gone unnoticed that Nikolai made no indication he would be bestowing the title of Queen on her as he had his first wife.

Some took that to mean he had married Nataliya for mainly breeding purposes. She found such assumptions offensive. Yes, she would be giving birth to the heir to the throne, but that didn't make her a brood mare.

She didn't need to be Queen to hold an opinion or have a brain and use it.

Not that her job as The Princess of Mirrus was something she'd ever aspired to, but she would do it to the best of her abilities. It was how she was made. How her mother had raised her to be.

Nataliya could admit to herself, if no one else, that she enjoyed her couple of hours each day on the computer working in the elite tech department of Mirrus Global more than all the luncheons and meetings where she was treated like a nominal figure.

But she couldn't make changes if she didn't stay the course. And she'd noticed some changes that needed to be made.

For instance, as forward thinking as she considered Nikolai, she had done some deep digging and discovered a discrepancy in pay to female and male staff in senior positions both in the Mirrus Global and the palace staffs. She planned to address those with him in their meeting the following day.

She grabbed her papers and knocked a folder to the floor. Nataliya picked it up and recognized the logo for Yurkovich-Tanner.

Feeling no compunction about reading it, she flipped the folder open and started thumbing through the pages. It was a joint business proposal for the high-tech divisions of Mirrus Global and Yurkovich-Tanner, written by her cousin Demyan. So, it had been created with serious intention.

Demyan didn't put his name on anything he didn't believe in fully.

She would ask her husband what he thought of the proposal at their meeting the next day, as well.

Nikolai's administrative assistant showed Nataliya and her own personal assistant into the King's spacious office.

Nikolai stood on her entrance and indicated a set of sofas and chairs on the far side of the office. "Let's sit over here."

The dark paneling and nineteenth-century-style furniture gave off a decidedly royal vibe, but the hints at high-level technology were there to see if you recognized them.

Now that she was The Princess of Mirrus, Nataliya had an entire staff and her own set of offices, but all meetings with her husband were held in his.

Protocol.

It would be daunting if she hadn't been prepared for the changes coming into her life. At least that's what she told herself.

Nikolai took a seat kitty-corner to her, but far enough away to maintain professional distance. Again…protocol.

Someone came in with a coffee tray, but Nataliya didn't need more caffeine, so she ignored it. So did Nikolai.

He pulled out his tablet, looked down for a minute and then back up at her. "I've looked over the report you sent over. I agree we need to hire an equity auditor."

That had been easier than she expected, but she didn't make the mistake of saying so in front of their staff. She'd thought they'd have to take the report to the appropriate HR people. It was good to be King.

She smiled. "Thank you. Would you like me to take care of that, or did you have someone else in mind?"

"My staff will contact the firms you suggest in the addendum to your report."

She nodded. "That's wonderful." She was careful to monitor her enthusiasm, but Nataliya was thrilled and tried to let him know with her eyes.

His own eyes crinkled at the corners in a smile that did not reach his mouth. "We cannot allow such wage inequalities to continue."

"I agree."

They talked over some other things and he asked her opinion on taking Mirrus Global into a certain technology area. Offering her opinion also gave the opportunity to segue into asking what he was going to do about the combined venture proposal she had seen the day before.

"How did you know about that?" he asked, sounding wary.

She tilted her head, studying him and wondering where the wariness was coming from. "You left the prospectus on the desk in our study."

"I see." Rather than looking upset she had read it as she might have expected from his cautious reaction, tension leached from Nikolai's stance and expression. "And you thought, what?"

"On the face of it, it seems to be a win-win for both Mirrus Global and Yurkovich-Tanner, not to mention the two countries."

"Provided you trust Yurkovich-Tanner in their dealings with some of our most proprietary software."

"Well, yes." She frowned. "Don't you?"

"I make it a policy never to trust anyone outside my inner circle that completely."

That was not surprising. She'd be a lot more shocked if he was any other way. "That is understandable, but if you look at their track record, Demyan's office has never been responsible for a data leak." She smiled. "And he is your family now."

"Family are not always trustworthy," Nikolai said repressively.

Like Nataliya needed that reminder. "I am aware."

He nodded. "Good."

Not thrilled by his apparent lack of sensitivity where her dealings with her father were concerned, Nataliya nevertheless was ready to tackle the subject. "You said you had an update on the situation with the Count."

Nikolai jolted, like he was surprised by something. But she could not imagine what. Surely he expected her to ask?

After speaking with her mother, Nataliya had decided to press criminal charges against her father as well as filing a civil lawsuit against him.

"The first update is that he is no longer a count. While he has maintained his citizenship in Volyarus, he is no longer recognized as a member of its nobility and his exile has been formally extended to lifetime status."

"My uncle did all that?"

"You are calling him uncle again."

After a quick look at the staff and the security in the room, Nataliya nodded. "I have realized that life, not to mention our personal motivations, is complicated."

Nikolai inclined his head.

But Nataliya wasn't going to get any more private with her thoughts in front of an audience. "Is that all?"

"No. Danilo has been arrested and charged with attempted blackmail. He will be tried in Washington State. Both Mirrus and Volyarus have levied charges against him for crimes against the monarchy."

Chills ran down Nataliya's spine. "You insisted on that, didn't you?"

"Yes."

"Thank you." Her father would not be allowed to hurt her mother again and that was the most important thing to Nataliya. "I'm surprised my uncle went along."

"I am not. He had more to lose refusing than to risk by doing what he should have so many years ago."

"Do you think the civil suit is still necessary?" she asked, thinking pretty strict measures had already been taken.

But Nikolai nodded. "The charges against him do not carry a life sentence. Although he will never be allowed on either Mirrusian or Volyarussian soil again unless he wants to face a trial for those charges, he could still do you and your mother damage from America."

"And you think a civil suit will prevent that?"

"Winning a civil suit against him will go a long way in preventing him filing charges against either of you."

"For what?"

"You need to ask? Danilo will manufacture whatever tale he needs to in order to pursue his own ends."

Nataliya frowned and nodded. It was nothing less than the truth. "You're right."

Nikolai smiled a politician's smile, not a lover's and asked, "Did you want to discuss anything else?"

"No, but I would like to make sure we have time to walk in the garden tonight."

He looked startled.

"I miss you," she admitted baldly.

Also, she *liked* him texting her throughout the day and calling her when he had the chance. She didn't want that to stop because his staff thought she was less invested than he was in their time together.

"I will make sure my schedule permits."

Though she was tired, their walk in the garden was everything Nataliya needed it to be.

Nikolai held her hand and reverted to the more openly affectionate man she found so hard to resist.

Not that she needed to resist him.

He might not trust her cousin implicitly, but Nataliya trusted Nikolai. She loved him. So much.

Her unusual exhaustion was explained later when she realized she'd started her monthly.

Her first couple of days always left her nearly comatose with tiredness. She took vitamins to combat the symptoms, but the supplements only helped so much.

She was practically falling asleep as she slid into bed late that evening. There had been another State dinner and they'd come up to their suite later than they usually did.

He reached for her and she snuggled into his body, but when he started to touch her intimately, she stayed his hand with her own. "Not tonight."

His reaction was electric. He sat up and the light went on. "So, this is it? This is how you react to me telling you no about something that benefits your family?"

"What are you talking about?" she asked, even his uncharacteristic response unable to wash the tiredness from her brain. "I just want to sleep."

"Last night, you did not want to sleep."

"Last night I wasn't having my period," she informed him with more honesty than finesse.

"You're having your monthly?" he asked, like the idea was a foreign concept.

"Yes. Sorry, no royal babies just yet."

He waved his hand like that wasn't important when in fact it was incredibly important. Especially to everyone else. Even her mom wanted to know if Nataliya was pregnant yet.

She'd only been married three weeks!

"I thought…"

"What did you think?" she asked, not sure she even wanted an answer.

"That you were angry I said no to Demyan's proposal."

"Did you say no to it?" She didn't remember Nikolai saying that.

"Well, not yet, but my plans are to turn it down."

"Okay."

"Okay?"

"Only I'm really tired. Can you hold me and let me sleep?" she spelled out for him.

He settled back down beside her, pulling her upper body onto his chest, his arms wrapped securely around her.

She went boneless against him, making a soft sound of approval.

"You don't care about the joint venture?" he asked into the darkened bedroom, something strange in his tone.

"Not enough to talk about it now. Can we talk in the morning?"

He kissed the top of her head. "Yes."

Nataliya woke with a sense that something wasn't right.

Nikolai's arms were still around her, though they were

spooning now. Which was definitely *right*. It was the light coming in through the windows.

"What time is it?" She tried to move his arm so she could get up. "We overslept!"

How was that possible? Nikolai *never* overslept and frankly, neither did she.

His hold on her tightened. She wasn't going anywhere. "Do not stress yourself. I arranged for our morning meetings to be moved."

"How?" Both their schedules were set in stone as far as the staff was concerned. "When?"

"How? I called my administrative assistant and had her call *your* personal assistant and social secretary. When? Last night after you fell asleep. I don't think a foghorn would have woken you, much less my voice talking on the phone."

"I was pretty tired." She felt a lot better that morning, her supplements and the extra sleep having done wonders. "It's always like that the first couple of days of my period. I'm sorry."

He grunted. It was not a kingly sound. At all.

But it carried a wealth of masculine meaning. "*You* have nothing to apologize for."

"But you do?" she asked as she turned in the band of his arms to face him.

His gorgeous cheekbones were scored with color. "I do."

"What?"

"I doubted you."

"What did you doubt?" She did her best to remember the night before and tried to figure out what he was talking about. He'd been weird all right, but she'd been too tired to worry on it then.

"Last night when you turned me down, I thought you were withholding sex to get your way." He looked and sounded as embarrassed as a king could be.

Good. He should be.

Withhold sex? From him? Chance would be a fine thing!

"My way about what?" she asked in confusion.

"The business venture with your cousin."

"I have a *way* about that?" she asked, still not sure she got where the disconnect was coming from.

"I thought you wanted me to say yes and were making sure I did so."

Nataliya sat up, giving him a look so he would loosen his arms. "We talked about that. I promised I would never do it. You said you believed me."

"I did believe you. I do believe you."

"Then what was last night about?" The things he'd said made a lot more sense now.

"It was about bad memories."

Nataliya got that. She really did. "I am not her."

It was his turn to sit up. They faced each other in the big bed. "No, you are not. You could hurt me so much more than Tiana ever did."

"What are you saying?" How could that be possible?

He was implying Nataliya had some emotional hold on him.

"I have come to realize that while I was sexually besotted with Tiana, I never really loved her. My grief on her death had more to do with what could have been than anything that was."

"Okay."

"I realized on our honeymoon that *I do love you* and knowing the depth of my feelings for you when you do not feel the same has made me…" He paused, took a deep breath and then offered. "Insecure."

"You love me?" she asked, the shock of such a possibility making her heart race and her face go all hot.

"With everything in me. My staff and cabinet are right to worry. I would move heaven and earth for you."

"But Nikolai, I do love you. I have since I was a teenager."

"That was not love. You felt attracted to me like I was attracted to Tiana. Love is a much deeper emotion."

"Do you remember what we learned on our wedding night?" she asked.

"That we are insanely sexually compatible?"

"That I know myself better than you do. After all, I am living in my skin."

"Yes, of course."

"So, when I say I love you, I mean it."

"You mean it?" The smile that came over his features was so vibrant it almost hurt to see. "You mean it! You love me."

"I do."

The intimacy that followed was shocking. She didn't know they could have sex this time of month, but showers were an amazing thing.

Later, they shared a leisurely breakfast on the balcony to their palace suite.

"Did you love me when you accepted my proposal?" he asked.

She refrained from rolling her eyes. Barely. He'd been asking questions like this since they sat down. "Yes."

"Did you *know* you loved me?"

"Yes."

"And when you made your vows…"

"I meant every one. Nikolai, I love you."

"Enough to forgive me for doubting you?"

"I was never actually angry."

"But—"

"Nikolai, we both brought damage into this marriage."

"Your damage doesn't have you accusing me of things I would never do."

She was glad he recognized she would never use him the

way Tiana had. "My damage made it impossible for me to admit my love before you acknowledged yours."

And that shamed her. They'd both suffered pain because of her inability to offer emotional honesty.

"I did not tell you right away either."

"You realized you loved me on our honeymoon. Your timing has mine beat by a mile."

He grinned. "I do not care. You love me. That is all that matters to me."

"I've loved you half my life, it feels like. It's a permanent condition."

"Nothing could make me happier."

He named her Queen of Mirrus on their first anniversary and she wore a dress and robes that had to be accommodated for her tiny baby bump. They made it into the media spotlight often because the love between the King and Queen of Mirrus had the world enthralled.

It was the romance of the century.

Nataliya never cared about stuff like that, but waking every morning with the knowledge she was loved so completely made each day better. Her very dignified husband showed an affectionate side no one thought he had.

A side he had never shown another.

Nataliya was honored to be his Queen, but she adored being his wife.

And Nikolai made it clear every single day, in small and big ways that he adored being her husband.

* * * * * ✿

MILLS & BOON

Coming next month

SECRETS OF CINDERELLA'S AWAKENING
Sharon Kendrick

Almost as if he'd read her mind, Leon caught hold of her and turned her round, his hands on either side of her waist. She held her breath because his touch felt *electric* and he studied her upturned face for what felt like a long time, before lowering his head to kiss her.

It was…dynamite.

It was…life-changing.

Marnie swayed in disbelief, her limbs growing instantly boneless. How was it possible for a kiss to feel this *good*? How could *anything* feel this good? At first there was barely any contact between them – just the intoxicating graze of his mouth over hers.

He deepened the kiss and began to stroke one of her breasts. Her nipple was pushing against her baggy T-shirt dress towards the enticing circling of his thumb. Was it that which made her writhe her hips against his with instinctive hunger, causing him to utter something in Greek which sounded almost *despairing*?

The sound broke the spell and she drew back – though in the faint light all she could see was the hectic glitter of his eyes. 'What…what did you just say?'

'I said that you set my blood on fire, *agape mou*. And that I want you very much. But you already know that.'

Well, she knew he wanted her, yes. She wasn't actually sure about the blood-on-fire bit because nobody had ever said anything like that to her before. And although she liked it her instinct was not to believe him because even if they were true, she knew compliments always came with a price.

Yet what was the *point* of all this if she was just going to pepper the experience with her usual doubts, and spoil it? Couldn't she have a holiday from her normal self and shake off all the worries which had been weighing her down for so long? Couldn't she be a different Marnie tonight – one who was seeking nothing but uncomplicated pleasure? She had always been the responsible one. The one who looked out for other people – with one eye on the distance, preparing for the shadows which inevitably hovered there. Wasn't it time to articulate what *she* wanted for a change?

She cleared her throat. 'Would you mind speaking in English so I can understand what you're saying?'

She could hear the amusement which deepened his voice.

'Are we planning to do a lot of talking then, Marnie? Is that what turns you on?'

Something warned her she'd be straying into dangerous territory if she told him she didn't *know* what turned her on because she'd never given herself the chance to find out. But while she didn't want to lie to him, that didn't mean she couldn't tell a different kind of truth.

'*You* turn me on,' she said boldly and something about the breathless rush of her words made his powerful body tense.

'Oh, *do* I?' he questioned, tilting her chin with his fingers so that their darkened gazes clashed. 'So what are we going to do about that, I wonder?'

Continue reading
SECRETS OF CINDERELLA'S AWAKENING
Sharon Kendrick

Available next month
www.millsandboon.co.uk

COMING SOON!

We really hope you enjoyed reading this book.
If you're looking for more romance, be sure to
head to the shops when new books are
available on

Thursday 24th
June

To see which titles are coming soon, please visit
millsandboon.co.uk/nextmonth

MILLS & BOON

LET'S TALK
Romance

For exclusive extracts, competitions
and special offers, find us online:

 facebook.com/millsandboon

@MillsandBoon

@MillsandBoonUK

Get in touch on 01413 063232

For all the latest titles coming soon, visit
millsandboon.co.uk/nextmonth

MILLS & BOON

THE HEART OF ROMANCE

A ROMANCE FOR EVERY READER

MODERN

Prepare to be swept off your feet by sophisticated, sexy and seductive heroes, in some of the world's most glamourous and romantic locations, where power and passion collide.

ISTORICAL

Escape with historical heroes from time gone by. Whether your passion is for wicked Regency Rakes, muscled Vikings or rugged Highlanders, awaken the romance of the past.

MEDICAL

Set your pulse racing with dedicated, delectable doctors in the high-pressure world of medicine, where emotions run high and passion, comfort and love are the best medicine.

rue Love

Celebrate true love with tender stories of heartfelt romance, from the rush of falling in love to the joy a new baby can bring, and a focus on the emotional heart of a relationship.

Desire

Indulge in secrets and scandal, intense drama and plenty of sizzling hot action with powerful and passionate heroes who have it all: wealth, status, good looks…everything but the right woman.

EROES

Experience all the excitement of a gripping thriller, with an intense romance at its heart. Resourceful, true-to-life women and strong, fearless men face danger and desire - a killer combination!

To see which titles are coming soon, please visit

millsandboon.co.uk/nextmonth

JOIN US ON SOCIAL MEDIA!

Stay up to date with our latest releases, author news and gossip, special offers and discounts, and all the behind-the-scenes action from Mills & Boon...

 millsandboon

 millsandboonuk

 millsandboon

It might just be true love...